Contents

150 LEADING CASES

Law of International Trade

EDITORS: PAMELA SELLMAN
LLM, MA (Business Law), Barrister, Attorney (New York)
AND JUDITH EVANS
LLB, Cert Ed

OLD BAILEY PRESS

OLD BAILEY PRESS
at Holborn College, Woolwich Road,
Charlton, London, SE7 8LN

First edition 2002

ISBN 1 85836 364 0

British Library Cataloguing-in-Publication

A catalogue record for this book is available from the British
Library.

Printed and bound in Great Britain

Acknowledgements

The publishers and author would like to thank the Incorporated Council of Law Reporting for England and Wales for kind permission to reproduce extracts from the Weekly Law Reports, and Butterworths for their kind permission to reproduce extracts from the All England Law Reports.

Particular thanks are extended to Lloyd's Law Reports, published by Informa Professional, a trading division of Informa UK Limited, Informa House, 30–32 Mortimer Street, London, W1W 7RE (Tel: +44 (0)20 7017 5198; Fax: +44 (0)20 7017 5090; Web: www.informalaw.com) for their kind permission to reproduce extracts from the Lloyd's Law Reports.

Lloyd's Law Reports is the most authoritative and comprehensive collection of maritime and commercial case decisions available, reporting on cases since 1919 and with an archive of over 16,000 cases, Lloyd's Law Reports is the recognised citation in this area.

As the principal report in this area, you may wish to subscribe to Lloyd's Law Reports, which includes: a fortnightly journal; a fortnightly email alert service; two free bound volumes; and a free annual citator.

Today you can choose all this for just £500 (normally £590) – a small price to pay for the latest cases and the peace of mind that comes from having a world-cited primary source at your fingertips.

Please contact Helen Richardson on Tel: +44 (0)20 7017 5220; Fax +44 (0)20 7017 5274 or email: Helen.Richardson@informa.com quoting reference PLR0111A if you would like to order a subscription.

Preface

Old Bailey Press casebooks are intended as companion volumes to the textbooks but they also comprise invaluable reference tools in themselves. Their aim is to supplement and enhance a student's understanding and interpretation of a particular area of law and provide essential background reading. Companion Revision WorkBooks and Statutes are also published.

The *Law of International Trade: 150 Leading Cases* is designed primarily for undergraduate students who are studying Law of International Trade as part of the LLB programme.

In order to comply with the series limitation of 150 cases, as a general rule authorities more recent in date and higher in terms of status have been chosen. An attempt has been made to include cases, and extracts from judgments, which most helpfully and memorably establish, illustrate or explain the underlying principles.

Of course, many more than 150 cases are covered in the sense that reference is made to them in judgments and commentary.

The casebook includes decisions which affect various aspects of international trade, namely international sales contracts, marine insurance, carriage of goods, documentary credits and, of course, the increasingly important areas of multimodal and container transport.

The law is stated on the basis of cases fully reported on or before 1 February 2002. No account has been taken of cases where leave has been given for a further appeal.

Table of Cases

Cases in bold type are the leading cases. Page numbers in bold indicate the main references to them.

1   International Sale Contracts

Agricultores Federados Argentinos Sociedad Cooperative **v** *Ampro SA Commerciale, Industrielle et Financière* [1965] 2 Lloyd's Rep 757 High Court (Widgery J)

* *Nomination of substitute vessel*

Facts
There was an fob contract for the sale of maize to be shipped between 20 September and 29 September 1960. The maize was not delivered because the sellers purported to cancel the contract before the contractual time limit expired as the buyer had not in the sellers' opinion nominated a vessel that could take delivery within the contract period.

The buyers said the sellers had wrongfully repudiated the contract and claimed damages for the sellers' alleged breach of contract.

Held
Judgment for the buyers.

Widgery J:

'There is nothing expressly in this contract to provide the circumstances in which a particular vessel shall be nominated, and the rights of the parties are to be regulated by the general law as it applies to an fob contract. As I understand it, the general law applying in such a contract merely is that the buyers shall provide a vessel which is capable of loading within the stipulated time, and if, as a matter of courtesy or convenience, the buyers inform the sellers that they propose to provide vessel A, I can see no reason in principle why they should not change their minds and provide vessel B at a later stage, always assuming that vessel B is provided within such a time as to make it possible for her to fulfil the buyers' obligations under the contract.

If the buyer fails in his duty to nominate an effective ship then the seller equally is under a duty to mitigate his loss by selling the goods elsewhere, his only claim against the buyer is in that of damages.'

Comment
This case should be compared with *Cargill UK Ltd* v *Continental Ltd* [1989] 2 Lloyd's Rep 290, where the contract contained a clause providing for the buyer to give a provision notice followed by a definite notice of the nominated vessel. On the facts of the case the substitution was not allowed.

Arnold Karberg **v** *Blythe Green Jourdain* [1916] 1 KB 495 Court of Appeal (Banks, Swinfen Eady and Warrington LJJ)

* *Contracts cif are for the sale of goods to be performed by delivery of documents*

Facts
Two cif contracts existed for the shipment of beans from Chinese ports to Naples and Rotterdam. Payment was to be made cash against bills of lading on arrival. The bills were not tendered within three months from their date as agreed, because the carrying vessels had entered ports of refuge following the outbreak of war. When the documents were tendered the buyers refused to accept them and pay the price.

Held

The buyers were entitled to refuse the tender which as a result of the outbreak of war had become void and unenforceable. Carrying out such an obligation would amount to trading with the King's enemies.

Swinfen Eady LJ:

'... in contracts cif, all that the seller has to do is ship goods in accordance with the contract, obtain proper bills of lading, effect proper insurances pursuant to the contract, and, having done that, having once acquired documents that are proper and in order, thenceforward those documents are at the risk of the buyer and the buyers must pay against tender of those documents; and if before tender on the happening of any event, those shipping documents become inoperative in any way, that is at buyer's risk ... that is the ordinary consequence of a cif contract quite apart from the particular terms of (the individual contract).'

Banks LJ:

'Scrutton J in his judgment has used one expression with which I do not agree. The expression is the one in which he says that "the key to many of the difficulties arising in cif contracts is to keep firmly in mind the cardinal distinction that a cif sale is not a sale of goods, but a sale of documents relating to goods". I am not able to agree with that view of the contract, that it is a sale of documents relating to goods. I prefer to look upon it as a contract for the sale of goods to be performed by the delivery of documents, and what those documents are must depend upon the terms of the contract itself.'

Comment

The opinion of Banks LJ emphasises the seller's requirement under a cif contract to deliver correct documents but also the requirement to ship correct goods. If correct documents are tendered to, and accepted by, the buyer to a cif contract, the buyer will still have the right to reject the goods if on arrival they do not conform to the contract: see *Kwei Tek Chao* v *British Traders and Shippers Ltd* [1954] 2 QB 459 (below).

Bergerco USA v *Vegoil Ltd* [1984] 1 Lloyd's Rep 440 High Court (Hobhouse J)

• *Definition of 'direct' shipment*

Facts

In September 1978 Vegoil purchased a quantity of Alaska green peas, shipment New Orleans, cif Bombay, payment by documentary credit. The contract of sale required direct shipment to Bombay.

Bergerco tendered the documents to the bank and received payment under the credit. The vessel did not arrive at Bombay until January 1979 and Vegoil discovered that instead of sailing to Bombay direct, the vessel had called at several ports in the United States and at a port in Sicily. Vegoil rejected the goods for late delivery and sought return of the price on the grounds that Bergerco had breached the term of the contract of sale requiring direct shipment. Bergerco sought to claim that Vegoil had waived the term requiring the vessel to sail direct to Bombay.

Held

Judgment for the buyers.

The sellers were bound by the term in the contract of sale to carry the goods by direct transit to the port of destination and there was no evidence that their duty to perform this obligation had been waived by the buyers.

Hobhouse J:

'The requirement of a "direct" ship was one which was not going to call in at any port between the port of shipment and the port of arrival, in order to load or unload cargo.

This was not a direct ship.

The buyers had not waived the requirement of directness and could rightly reject the goods on arrival.'

Comment

It was held in *Petrograde Inc* v *Stinnes Handel GmbH* (1994) The Times 27 July that the place specified for delivery in an fob contract was a condition of the contract. The fob contract had specified that the port of delivery was to be Antwerp but the cargo was delivered at Flushing and the defendants were entitled to reject the goods. The court took the view that the need for certainty was a relevant consideration in determining the status of such a term and that disputes would frequently arise if the place of shipment were to be regarded as an innominate term.

Deviation may be permitted by the terms of the contract of sale. Where there is stipulation as to route in the contract of sale, the carriage must comply with such stipulation: *Colin and Shields* v *Weddell & Co Ltd* [1952] 2 Lloyd's Rep 1021. For the position under a charterparty: see *Whistler International Ltd* v *Kawasaki Kisen Kaisha Ltd* [2000] 3 WLR 1954 (in Chapter 5).

Biddell Brothers v *E Clemens Horst Company* [1912] AC 18 House of Lords (Earl Loreburn LC, Lords Atkinson, Gorell and Shaw of Dunfermline); affirming [1911] 1 KB 215 and reversing [1911] 1 KB 934 Court of Appeal

• *Time for payment for goods under cif contracts*

Facts
A contract was entered into for the purchase and sale of 100 bales of choice brewing Pacific coast hops in each of the years 1905 to 1912, to be shipped to Sunderland. The payment terms in the contract were stated to be 'Terms net cash' and the contract contained a provision that they buyer shall pay 90 shillings sterling per 112 lbs, cif London, Liverpool or Hull.

The plaintiff buyer was offered a bill of lading but refused to pay on it, arguing that he was not required to pay for the hops until they had arrived and a reasonable opportunity had been provided for their examination.

Held
The expression 'net cash' meant net cash against documents. The seller was entitled to payment following shipment and the tender of shipping documents. The buyer was not entitled to withhold payment until the goods had arrived at their destination, and a reasonable opportunity had been allowed to him for examination to see if they were in conformity with the contract. The expression cif was not, as the buyer's had sought to submit, 'merely a means of calculating the price to be paid for the goods by adding together the various items of which the price is composed' and it was not correct to say that the 'letters cif have nothing to say to delivery'. However, the buyer's right to reject remained unimpaired if upon arrival the hops were found not in conformity with the contract.

The judgment of the trial judge, Hamilton J, was approved in the House of Lords. He gave what may be regarded as the standard definition of the cif contract:

> 'The meaning of a contract of sale upon cost, freight, and insurance terms is so well settled that it is unnecessary to refer to authorities upon the subject. A seller under a contract of sale containing such terms has firstly to ship at the port of shipment goods of the description contained in the contract; secondly to procure a contract of affreightment, under which the goods will be delivered at the destination contemplated by the contract; thirdly to arrange for an insurance upon the terms current in the trade which will be available for the benefit of the buyer; fourthly to make out an invoice as described by Blackburn J in *Ireland* v *Livingston* (1872) LR 5 HL 395 at p406 or in some similar form; and finally to tender these documents to the buyer so that he may know what freight he has to pay and obtain delivery of the goods, if they arrive, or recover for their loss if they are lost on the voyage.'

Hamilton J also recognised that there was no doubt that the seller can perform his obligations cif merely by the tender of conforming documents to the seller and that the buyer is then obliged to pay. He said that cif terms:

' ... constitute an agreement that the delivery of the goods ... shall be delivery on board ship at the port of shipment. It follows that against tender of these documents, the bill of lading, invoice and policy of insurance, which completes delivery in accordance with that agreement, the buyer must be ready and willing to pay the price.'

Kennedy LJ in the Court of Appeal:

' ... the goods are at the risk of the purchaser, against which he has protected himself by the stipulation in his cif contract that the vendor shall, at his own cost, provide him with a proper policy of marine insurance intended to protect the buyer's interest, and available for his use if the goods should be lost in transit. ...

... the property in the goods has passed to the purchaser, either conditionally or unconditionally. It passes conditionally where the bill of lading is made out in favour of the vendor or his agent or representative ... It passes conditionally where the bill of lading is made out in favour of the purchaser or his agent or representative as consignee. ...

The vendor tenders the bill of lading, with the insurance policy and the other shipping documents ... to the purchaser, to whom from the moment of shipment the property has passed and at whose risk, covered by insurance, the goods were at the time of the loss.'

Comment

This is a rather straightforward case, frequently cited, relating to the respective rights and obligations of the parties to a cif contract. It places emphasis on the constructive nature of delivery which goes to the heart of a cif contract.

Bowes v Shand (1877) 2 App Cas 455 House of Lords (Lord Cairns LC, Lords Hasterley, O'Hagan, Blackburn and Gordon)

• *Date of shipment is part of description*

Facts

Two contracts for the sale of rice were made in London. The rice was to be shipped at Madras for London, during the months of March and/or April. Some of the bags of rice were shipped in February when the vessel arrived at Madras.

Held

Judgment for the defendants.

Blackburn LJ:

'...it was argued, or tried to be argued, on one point, that it was enough that it was rice, and that it was immaterial when it was shipped. As far as the subject matter of the contract went, its being shipped at another and different time being (it was said) only a breach of stipulation which could be compensated for in damages. But I think that is quite untenable. I think, to adopt an illustration which was used a long time ago by Lord Abinger, and which always struck me as being a right one, that it is an utter fallacy, when an article is described, to say that it is anything but a warranty or condition precedent that it should be an article of that kind, and that another article might be substituted for it. As he said, if you contract to sell pears you cannot oblige a party to take beans. If the description of the article tendered is different in any respect, it is not the article bargained for and the other party is not bound to take it ... In this case, what the parties bargained for was rice, shipped at Madras. The parties have chosen for reasons best known to themselves to say: We bargain to take rice, shipped in this particular region, at that particular time, on board that particular ship, and before the defendants can be compelled to take anything in fulfilment of that contract, it must be shown not merely that it is equally good, but that it is the same article as they have bargained for otherwise they are not bound to take it ...'

Comment

Bowes v Shand is still good law for the principle that the time of shipment is part of the description of the goods despite cases such as

Ashington Piggeries Ltd v *Christopher Hill Ltd* [1972] AC 441 and *Reardon Smith Line* v *Hansen-Tangen* [1976] 3 All ER 570 where courts have stressed that descriptive words go to the identity of the goods. Time is usually of the essence in a commercial contract and early or late shipment would be a breach of s13 Sale of Goods Act 1979 as well as being a breach of an express term.

Brandt (H O) v *H N Morris and Co Ltd* [1917] 2 KB 784 Court of Appeal (Viscount Reading CJ, Scrutton LJ and Neville J)

• *Buyer (with English representative) under duty to obtain fob licence*

Facts
The plaintiffs were a Manchester-based company. They purchased a quantity of aniline oil from the defendants. This purchase was on fob terms and made on behalf of an American company. During the five-month period over which shipment was to take place there was a prohibition on the export of aniline oil. The plaintiffs sued for non-delivery.

Held
The duty to obtain the export licence lay on the buyer and not the seller.

Viscount Reading CJ:

'I am unable to agree with the learned judge that the duty of applying for the licence was upon the defendants. They had contracted to sell fob. They had therefore contracted to put the oil on board a vessel selected ... by the plaintiffs. It was the duty of the plaintiffs to find the ship and the facts which it was necessary to state when a licence had to be applied for were known to them and not to the defendants.'

If it had been the duty of the seller to obtain the necessary export licence then clearly he would have had to use his best efforts in an attempt to obtain one. However, the duty was not imposed on the seller and there was no breach by him in this respect.

Comment
See *Pound (A V) & Co* v *Hardy (M W)* [1956] AC 588 (below) where the court did not lay down a hard and fast rule as to who should obtain the export licence, but instead laid the duty on the person who was in the best position which is usually the seller. If the Incoterms are used it is the seller's duty to obtain the export licence.

Carlos Federspiel & Co SA v *Charles Twigg & Co Ltd and Another* [1957] 1 Lloyd's Rep 240 High Court (Pearson J)

• *Property passes on shipment*

Facts
The plaintiffs (Federspiel) purchased cycles from the defendants, fob British port and paid the price of £646 5s.

The defendants went into liquidation and the receiver refused to allow the goods to be shipped unless the plaintiff further paid the price. The plaintiffs claimed that the bicycles had been appropriated to the contract and that property in the goods had passed to them and this was suggested, inter alia, by correspondence between the parties. The receiver on the other hand claimed that it was the intention of the seller that property should pass on shipment.

Held
Property in the bicycles had not yet passed.

Pearson J:

'The intention was that ownership should pass on shipment ... because the emphasis is throughout, on shipment as the decisive act to be done by the seller in performance of the contract. Secondly, it is impossible to find in this correspondence an agreement to change of ownership before the time of shipment
... Thirdly, there is no actual or constructive delivery, no suggestion of the seller becoming a bailee for the buyer. Fourthly,

there is no suggestion of the gods being at the buyer's risk at any time before shipment; no suggestion that the buyer should insist on the seller arranging insurance for them. Fifthly, the last two acts to be performed by the seller, namely sending the goods to Liverpool and having the gods shipped on board were never performed.

[Thus there is] a prima facie interest ... that the property was not to pass at any time before shipment [which] is not displaced by the subsequent correspondence. It follows that there was no appropriation of these goods and therefore the action fails...'

Comment

In this case the court was dealing with an fob contract under which property usually passes on shipment. It must be remembered, however, that it is always necessary to look for the intention of the parties: s17 Sale of Goods Act 1979, *Mitsui & Co Ltd* v *Flota Mercante Grancolumbiana SA, The Cuidad De Pasto and Cuidad De Neiva* [1988] 2 Lloyd's Rep 208 (see below). *Note:* Under s20A Sale of Goods Act 1979 if a buyer pays the price for a specified quantity from an identifiable bulk, the buyer will have ownership in common with other buyers.

Comptoir d'Achat v *Luis de Ridder, The Julia* [1949] AC 293 House of Lords (Lords Porter, Simonds, Du Parq, Normand and MacDermott)

• *Label given to the contract type is not conclusive*

Facts

The parties contracted on cif Antwerp terms for the export sale of grain. They agreed that the seller could demand payment against either a bill of lading and insurance policy or a delivery order and insurance certificate. The seller was to pay for any deficiency in weight delivered. The goods were part of a larger cargo of grain covered by a single bill of lading and policy of insurance. As the seller

was selling to the buyer a proportion of the bulk, the bill of lading and policy of insurance did not conform to the contract because they referred to goods not included in the sale. Therefore, he was bound to perform by using a delivery order and insurance certificate. The buyer paid the price against the tender of those documents. However, when Germany invaded Belgium the ship was diverted from Antwerp to Lisbon where the seller, without the buyer's consent, discharged and sold the goods hoping that the buyer could recover on the policy of insurance evidenced by the certificate. The buyer, instead, brought an action for the money paid.

Held

In considering whether or not a contract is cif, the true effect of all its terms must be taken into account.

Lord Porter:

'The obligations imposed on a seller under a cif contract are well known and in the ordinary case include the tender of a bill of lading, covering the goods contracted to be sold and no others, coupled with an insurance policy in the normal form, and accompanied by an invoice which shows the price ... Against tender of these documents the purchaser must pay the price. In such a case the property may pass, either on shipment or on tender, the risk generally passes on shipment or as from shipment, but possession does not pass until the documents which represent the goods are handed over in exchange for the price. In the result, the buyer after receipt of the documents can claim against the ship for breach of the contract of carriage and against the underwriter for any loss covered by the policy. The strict form of cif contract may however be modified; a provision that a delivery order be substituted for a bill of lading, or a certificate of insurance for a policy, would not ... make the contract concluded upon something other than cif terms, but in deciding whether it comes within that category or not, all the permutations and combinations of provision and circumstance must be taken into consideration. Not every contract which is expressed to be cif contract is such. Sometimes ... terms are introduced into contracts so described which conflict with cif provisions ... the true effect of all its terms must be taken into account through, of course, the description cif must not be neglected ...'

Comment

Unlike the fob contract the cif contract is not a flexible instrument. If the parties to what is supposedly a cif contract move too far away from what the courts consider to be a true cif, the parties take the risk of the courts concluding that in fact the contract is something else, eg an arrival contract. However, see *Henry (D I) v Clasen* [1973] 1 Lloyd's Rep 159 where it was held that the buyer agreeing to be responsible for any surcharge in freight did not destroy the nature of a cif contract.

For the status of ship's delivery orders and a discussion of the delivery document in *The Julia*, see *Waren Import Gesellschaft Krohn & Co v Internationale Graanhandel Thegra NV* [1975] 1 Lloyd's Rep 146.

Concordia Trading BV v Richo International Ltd [1991] 1 Lloyd's Rep 475 High Court (Evans J)

* *Seller's duty to tender documents under fob contract same as that of cif seller*

Facts

In a string contract the plaintiff sellers sold Argentine soya beans to the buyers in 1987 under an fob contract. The contract incorporated the provisions of GAFTA 64 (General Contract Fob Terms for Grain in Bulk), clause 7 of which provided, inter alia, that the bill of lading was to be considered proof of delivery in absence of proof to the contrary. In the normal course of events the sellers would have presented the bills of lading, together with other documents to the buyers for payment. There was, however, nothing expressed in the contract regarding the time when the obliga-

tions to present and pay against the documents should be performed. The issue was whether the breach (failure to present documents) occurred on 5 August when documents were first available or 29 September when discharge began, ie whether the seller's duty in fob was as in cif. Meanwhile the market price of goods or documents dropped. The dispute was referred to arbitration which found for the buyers (ie 29 September). The sellers appealed.

Held

Evans J:

'There is good reason, in my view why the correct inference in the case of fob contracts should be derived from what is "mercantilely reasonable" in those contracts rather than from a direct application of the cif rule. The contracts are of different kinds, and the analogy is not so close that a straight transfer should be made.

Nevertheless, there are compelling reasons why, in my judgment, the duty imposed on the fob seller should be to the same effect as has been established in the case of cif sales. The fob seller is required to obtain shipping documents and to tender them to the buyer, and the buyer is obliged to make payment against the documents as is implicit in the present contract.'

Comment

If the sales contract provides for a time period for the tendering of documents, that time period must be complied with. In the absence of a fixed time period the seller is required to tender the documents within a reasonable period.

Gill & Duffus v Berger & Co Inc [1984] AC 382; [1981] 2 Lloyd's Rep 233 House of Lords (Lords Diplock, Keith of Kinkel, Roskill, Brandon of Oakbrook and Templeman)

* *Failure to accept correct documents is a repudiatory breach*

Facts

The buyers purchased from the sellers a cargo of 'Argentine bolita beans, 1974 crop, cif Le Havre, 500 tonnes'. Payment was to be made against first presentation of shipping documents. A certificate of quality was to be final.

Only 445 tonnes were delivered at Le Havre, the remaining 55 tonnes were carried to Rotterdam. When the documents were first presented for payment they were rejected. They were re-presented and again rejected. The sellers treated the rejection of the goods as a wrongful repudiation of the contract.

The buyers on their part claimed that the certificate of quality applied only to the 445 tonnes and not to the excess which had been carried on to Rotterdam, and that they were entitled to reject the beans for breaches of description and seek damages for non-delivery.

Held

Lord Diplock:

'It has never been contended that the actual shipping documents tendered by the sellers to the buyers, and re-tendered, … did not relate to the whole quantity of 500 tonnes or did not upon the face of them conform to the terms of the cif contract …

That being so, it is, in my view, a legal characteristic of a cif contract so well established in English law as to be beyond the realm of controversy, that the refusal by the buyer under such a contract, to pay to the seller, or to a banker, nominated in the contract if the contract so provides, the purchase price upon presentation at the place stipulated in the contract, of shipping documents which on their face conform to those called for by the contract, constitutes a fundamental breach of contract which the seller is entitled to elect to treat as rescinding the contract and relieving him of any obligatio9n to continue or perform any of his own primary obligations under it … So far as concerns the instant case the relevant primary obligation of the sellers of which they were relieved was any further obligation to deliver to the buyers any of the goods that were the subject matter of the contract …'

Therefore, the buyer had no claim for non-delivery against the seller because the seller ceased to be under his obligation to deliver the goods at the times that the buyer wrongfully refused to accept the correct documents. If the buyer could, however, prove that even had the documents been accepted, the seller would have been unable to deliver goods in conformity with the contract description, then the measure of damages to which the seller would be entitled by reason of the non-acceptance would be reduced by the extent of that lack of conformity.

'If the seller sued the buyer for his failure to pay the price of the goods against tender of conforming shipping documents, the buyer, if he could prove that the seller would not have been able to deliver goods under those shipping documents that conformed with the contract of sale, would be able to displace the prima facie measure of damages by an amount by which the value of the goods was reduced below the contract disconformity; but this goes to a quantum of damages alone.'

Glencore Grain Rotterdam BV v *Lebanese Organisation for International Commerce (LORICO)* [1997] 2 Lloyd's Rep 386 Court of Appeal (Nourse and Evans LJJ, Sir Ralph Gibson)

• *Fob sale – letter of credit*

Facts

Glencore entered into a contract with LORICO on fob Iskenderun terms for a consignment of Turkish soft milling wheat supplied to Glencore by TMO. Payment was to be by irrevocable letter of credit which was to be opened prior to the loading of the cargo on board the nominated vessel.

In turn, LORICO on-sold the consignment to Hoboob on c & f terms which required LORICO to provide their buyers with bills of lading which were marked 'freight pre-paid'.

When opening the letter of credit in favour of Glencore, LORICO stipulated that 'freight pre-paid' bills of lading would be required. However, as Glencore's contract with LORICO was on fob terms, Glencore indicated that they could not accept such payment terms and insisted that the letter of credit should call for presentation of bills of lading marked 'freight payable as per charterparty'. Nevertheless, the letter of credit which was opened called for 'freight pre-paid' bills of lading.

Meanwhile, the nominated vessel was late arriving at Iskenderun and Glencore, facing a late shipment penalty from their suppliers, TMO, insisted on an extra payment from LORICO. When LORICO refused, Glencore refused to load and LORICO sought damages for Glencore's refusal.

Held

Judgment for Glencore.

The first issue before the court was whether the buyers under a contract on fob terms are entitled to open a letter of credit in favour of the sellers which requires the sellers to present 'freight pre-paid' bills of lading in order to receive payment from the buyer's bank. Unless the contract provides otherwise, the buyers must ensure that a conforming letter of credit is opened and in place at the beginning of the shipment period. Once the buyers have satisfied this requirement, the obligation is upon the sellers to load the contract cargo on board the ship nominated by the buyers. In an fob contract, the contract of carriage and freight terms are agreed between the carrier and the buyers. Thus, in the present case, as fob sellers, Glencore were under no obligation to pay the freight and, as such, could not obtain 'freight pre-paid' bills of lading from the carrier unless they took the risk of paying the freight themselves (which, of course, Glencore were not obliged to do) or if payment of the freight were guaranteed in a way acceptable to the carrier. LORICO's assurance that the freight would be paid prior to completion of loading was not sufficient. Therefore, the terms of the letter of credit

requiring Glencore to provide 'freight pre-paid' bills of lading was contrary to the underlying concept of the fob contract. In such circumstances, LORICO were in breach for failing to open a conforming letter of credit.

The second issue was whether Glencore could rely on LORICO's earlier breach (failure to open a conforming letter of credit) to justify their own refusal to load, even if Glencore did not rely on that reason at the time. The established rule is that a party to a contract who has refused performance and has given the wrong reason for such refusal may later rely on a valid reason, so long as that valid reason is not one which, if it had been put forward at the relevant time, could have been put right by the other contracting party. Longmore J (at first instance) held that it would be unjust to allow Glencore 'to go back to an old ground which was not pursued at the time when it might have been possible for the buyers to do something about it'. However, LORICO's duty under the terms of their contract with Glencore was to open a conforming letter of credit in favour of Glencore by the beginning of the shipment period. Because the nominated vessel was late in arriving at Iskenderun, the shipment period had already started by the time Glencore refused to load. Of course, the letter of credit which had been opened was not conforming, but by then there was nothing LORICO could have done since the beginning of the shipment period had already passed. Longmore J was wrong not to allow Glencore to rely on LORICO's breach as a defence to the claim brought against them for refusal to load.

Groom (C) Ltd v Barber [1915] 1 KB 316 (Atkin J)

• *Construction of cif contract as to insurance clause*

Facts

A contract of sale on cif terms contained the condition 'war risk for buyer's account'. The issue before the court, after the carrying ship had been sunk by a German cruiser, was whether it was a seller's obligation to secure war risk insurance but at the buyer's expense, or whether war risk was a concern of the buyer alone, and that if he wanted war risk insurance he had to take out the policy.

Held

The seller under such a clause was under no obligation to effect war risk insurance. All he is required to do is to ship or buy afloat contract conforming goods, then deliver to the buyer within a reasonable time from the date of shipment the shipping documents. The bill of lading, the invoice and the insurance policy will entitle the buyer to obtain, on arrival of the ship, delivery of the goods, or, in case of their loss, will entitle him to recover on the policy their value if they have been lost by a peril agreed to be covered, and in any case will give him a claim against the ship in respect of misdelivery or wrongful treatment of the goods.

Comment

This case construes a specific term of the contract of sale as to what the marine insurance policy tendered under a cif contract should contain when it provides for 'war risk for buyer's account'. Well established law as to the seller's obligations under a cif contract are clearly stated. Indeed, the case of *Bidell Brothers* v *E Clemens Horst Co* [1912] AC 18 (above), probably the leading case in this area of the law, was cited six times.

Kwei Tek Chao v *British Traders & Shippers* [1954] 2 QB 459 High Court (Devlin J)

• *There are two rights of rejection: the right to reject the goods and the right to reject the documents*

Facts

The defendants, a British firm, agreed to sell goods to the plaintiffs, Kwei Tek Chao, cif Hong Kong, shipment continental port.

Payment was to be made by confirmed letter of credit, against the defendants' documents, including a 'shipped' bill of lading. Shipment was to take place not later than 31 October.

The goods were not shipped until 3 November. The sellers presented forged bills of lading showing the goods to have been shipped within the agreed shipping period. This forgery was perpetrated by the forwarding agents at the port of loading and without any knowledge by the sellers.

The buyers accepted the goods when they arrived, even though they knew that they had been shipped outside the agreed period. The market price of the goods fell. The buyers then discovered that the bills of lading were forged and they sued the sellers for the return of the contract price on the basis that the forged bills were a nullity.

Held

Judgment for the plaintiff.

Devlin J:

'There is not, in my judgment, one right to reject; there are two rights to reject. A right to reject is, after all, only a particular form of a right to rescind the contract. Wherever there is a breach of condition there is a right to rescind the contract, and if there are successive breaches of different conditions committed one after the other, each time there is a breach there is a right to rescind in respect of that breach. A right to reject is merely a particular form of the right to rescind, which involves the rejection of a tender of goods or of documents; and a rightful rejection of either is a rescission which brings the contract to an end.

Here, therefore, there is a right to reject documents, and a right to reject goods, and the two things are quite distinct. A cif contract puts a number of obligations upon the seller, some of which are in relation to the goods and some of which are in relation to the documents. So far as the goods are concerned, he must put on board at the port of shipment goods in conformity with the contract description, but he must also send forward documents, and those documents must comply with the contract. If he commits a breach the breaches may in one sense overlap, in that they flow from the same act. If there is a late shipment, as there was in this case, the date of the shipment being part of the description of the goods, the seller has not put on board goods which conform tot he contract description, and therefore he has broken that obligation. He has also made it impossible to send forward a bill of lading which at once conforms with the contract and states accurately the date of shipment. Thus the same act can cause two breaches of two independent obligations.

However that may be, they are distinct obligations, and the right to reject the documents arises when the documents are tendered and the right to reject the goods arises when they are loaded and when after examination they are found not to be in conformity with the contract. It may be that if the actual date of shipment is not in conformity with the contract, and the error appears from the documents, the buyer, by accepting the documents, not only loses his right to reject the documents, but also his right to reject the goods, but that would be because he had waived in advance, reliance on the date of shipment.'

Held

The sellers were not liable for the fraud of the forwarding agents. The buyers had separate and distinct rights to reject both goods and documents. The right to damages when the seller presented an incorrect bill of lading vested when the bill was tendered. That right was not affected by an action which might be taken by the buyer on a subsequent breach of contract in a case where the seller failed to deliver goods in accordance with the contract. The true measure of damages was the difference between the contract price and the value of the goods when the buyers discovered the sellers' breach of obligation.

Comment

This is a frequently cited case on the duality of the seller's obligations under a cif contract –

one relates to documents and the other to goods. This duality of obligations is mirrored by the buyer's opportunity to reject the documents and the goods.

Manbre Saccharine Company Ltd v *Corn Products Company Ltd* [1919] 1 KB 198 (McCardie J)

* *Tender of documents relating to goods already lost*

Facts

By a contract of 16 October 1916, the defendants sold to the plaintiffs 4,200 x 280 lb bags of American pearl starch, price 16s 6d per cwt, cif London. Shipment was to be December 1916 to January 1917 at sellers' option, cash against documents.

Bags of 140 lbs and 220 lbs were shipped aboard the Algonquin. On 12 March 1917; the ship and all her cargo was lost when she was sunk by a German submarine. Two days later the sellers tendered documents which did not include a policy of insurance. The sellers instead wrote a letter to the buyers stating that the buyers were covered by insurance in accordance with a policy in their possession. On receiving the letter and documents, the buyers immediately replied that they could not accept them as a delivery against the contract as: (i) the ship carrying the cargo had sunk on 12 March; and (ii) the sellers must have known that fact before they wrote their letter on 14 March.

Held

Judgment for the buyers.

The sellers of goods on cif terms can effectively tender appropriate documents to the buyers in respect of goods shipped on a vessel which, at the time of tender, the sellers know have been totally lost.

McCardie J:

'If the vendor fulfils his contract by shipping the appropriate goods in the appropriate manner under a proper contract of carriage, and if he also obtains the proper documents for tender to the purchaser, I am unable to see how the rights or duties of either party are affected by the loss of ship or goods, or by knowledge of such loss by the vendor, prior to actual tender of the documents. If the ship be lost prior to tender but without the knowledge of the seller it was, I assume, always clear that he could make an effective proffer of the documents to the buyer. In my opinion, it is also clear that he can make an effective tender even though he possess at the time of tender actual knowledge of the loss of the ship or goods. For the purchaser in case of loss will get the documents he bargained for; and if the policy be that required by the contract, and if the loss be covered thereby, he will secure the insurance moneys. The contingency of loss is within and not outside the contemplation of the parties to a cif contract. The views I have expressed are, I feel, in full accord with the observations of Atkin J in *C Groom Ltd* v *Barber* [above] as to the requirements of a cif contract, and with the judgment of Bailhache J in *Re Weis & Co* v *Credit Colonial et Commercial (Antwerp)* [1916] 1 KB 346. I therefore hold that the plaintiffs were not entitled to reject the tender of documents in the present case upon the ground that The Algonquin had, to the knowledge of the defendants, sunk prior to the tender of documents. This view will simplify the performance of cif contracts and prevent delay either through doubts as to the loss of ship or goods or through difficult questions with regard to the knowledge or suspicion of a vendor as to the actual occurrence of a loss …'

The buyers therefore were not entitled to reject the documents by reason of their having been tendered after the goods were lost at sea. They were however entitled to reject the documents tendered.

First, the sellers tendered no insurance policy at all. McCardie J:

'All that the buyer can call for is delivery of the customary documents. This represents the measure of the buyer's right and the extent of the vendor's duty. The buyer cannot refuse the documents and ask for the actual goods, nor can the vendor withhold the documents and tender the goods themselves.'

Second, the insurance held did not cover the goods as described in the invoice. The sellers were in fact in breach of their sale contract which was for the sale of starch in 280 lb bags and, as stated in the invoice, some was shipped in 220 lb bags and some in 140 lb bags. The size of the bags was part of the description of the goods, so the substitution of a different size by the seller constituted a breach of contract. McCardie J:

'Even if the [defendants] had tendered the policies actually held by them I should still have held the tender bad, for they were policies which covered a quantity of goods outside those mentioned in the bills of lading and invoices sent to the [plaintiffs]. In my opinion a purchaser under a cif contract is entitled to demand, as a matter of law, a policy of insurance which covers and covers only the goods mentioned in the bills of lading and invoices …

Unless the purchaser gets a policy limited to his own interest he would become one only of those who are interested in the insurance; and he is entitled in my view, to refuse to occupy a position which may give rise to obvious complications.'

Comment

All three of the holdings of this case are in accordance with previously accepted law. All emphasise the documentary nature of the seller's performance under a cif contract. See also *Bidell Brothers* v *E Clemens Horst Co* [1912] AC 18 (above), *Golodetz (M) & Co Inc* v *Czarnikow-Rionda Co Inc, The Galatia* [1980] 1 All ER 501 and *Groom (C) Ltd* v *Barber* [1915] 1 KB 316 (above). Although Mc Cardie J referred to Atkin J in *Groom* v *Barber*, it was not clear in that case whether the seller knew of the loss at the time of tender.

The obligation to tender an insurance policy under a cif contract was considered in *Orient* v *Brekke and Howlid* [1913] 1 KB 531. Shipment from Bordeaux of a quantity of walnuts cif Hull had taken place and the plaintiff sellers had sent the defendant buyer an invoice and a bill of lading but no insurance policy. The defendants therefore refused to pay the contract price due thirty days after delivery. The plaintiff, who admitted that there might be an obligation to tender an insurance policy, sought to argue that the buyer had not asked for one specifically and that since the goods had arrived safely, an insurance policy was immaterial and unnecessary. The plaintiff further argued that since the failure to take out the insurance policy was not fatal to the passing of property in the goods, he was still entitled to the contract price. The court took the view that it is essential that a buyer has the goods insured in his favour so that he can dispose of them and secure himself against loss and applied the decision reached two years earlier in *Biddell Bros* v *E Clemens Horst Co* [1912] AC 18 (see above) which had held that it was for the seller to arrange 'insurance on the terms current in the trade, which will be available for the benefit of the buyer', and that it was only on tender of all the documents that there was a delivery against which the buyer must pay the price. Accordingly, the court held that the defendants were entitled to judgment on the grounds the plaintiff's failure to obtain insurance was evidence that he could not effect delivery cif since he could not perform his obligation of delivering all necessary documents to the buyer.

Mash Murrell v *Joseph Emanuel*
[1962] 1 WLR 16 Court of Appeal (Ormrod, Harman and Pearson LJJ)

• *Duration of merchantability*

Facts
The plaintiffs purchased 2,000 bags of Cyprus potatoes shipped at Limassol. The vessel called in at Famagusta in order to load and discharge other cargo, during which time the hatches of the hold containing the potatoes were left open and the ventilation system was not working properly. On arrival the potatoes wee found to be unfit for human consumption.

Held
Section 14 of the Sale of Goods Act 1893 implied a term as to merchantability. The section required not only that the goods should be of merchantable quality at the outset but should remain fit for their purpose and thus merchantable throughout the course of transit and for a reasonable time thereafter.

The defendants were not in breach of s14 since on balance of probability the inference to be drawn from the extended opening of the hold and the lack of ventilation was that the deterioration was the result of these conditions of carriage and not a breach by the seller at the outset.

Comment
Section 14 of the Sale of Goods Act 1979 has been amended and goods sold in the course of business must now be of satisfactory quality, but the principle in the above case would still apply, in that goods must be of satisfactory quality for a reasonable period of time.

Mitsui & Co Ltd v *Flota Mercante Grancolumbiana SA, The Cuidad De Pasto and Cuidad De Neiva*
[1988] 2 Lloyd's Rep 208 Court of Appeal (Purchas and Staughton LJJ, Sir George Waller)

• *The intention of the parties is important in determining when property in goods passes*

Facts
A consignment of frozen prawns was loaded on board The Ciudad de Pasto. Five bills of lading were issued in which Vikingos were named as the shipper and Mitsui Japan were named as the notified party. Vikingos had sold the goods fob to Columbia Fisheries who had in turn sold the goods to Mitsui Japan on arrival terms.

Mitsui USA, a subsidiary of Mitsui Japan, paid 80 per cent of the value of the prawns when they were ready for shipment.

When the goods arrived in Japan they were found to be damaged and when the plaintiffs claimed against the defendants, one of the questions for the court was, did the plaintiffs have title to sue?

Held

In the bills of lading the goods were deliverable to the order of the sellers and the property in the goods did not pass to the buyers until the price had been paid. The sellers were in fact reserving the right of disposal: s19 Sale of Goods Act 1979. There was no evidence to suggest that the buyers were intended to acquire property before presentation of the bills of lading under the letter of credit. The term 'fob' does not necessarily decide when property is to pass. On the facts the presumption in s19 Sale of Goods Act 1979 was not displaced.

Comment

This is one of many cases that focused on the circumstances under which property passes, and the consequences arising from its passing or not passing. Reservation of the right of disposal until the price is paid under s19 Sale of Goods Act 1979 is a frequently litigated issue.

Panchaud Freres v *Etablissements General Grain* [1970] 1 Lloyd's Rep 53 Court of Appeal (Lord Denning MR, Winn and Cross LJJ)

• *A buyer who does not reject documents when she/he could have done so will be taken to have waived that right*

Facts

Buyers purchased 5,500 tons of Brazilian grain cif Antwerp. Shipment was to take place during June/July.

The buyers refused to accept the goods when they arrived on the ground that the wrong quantity had been delivered and the numbers delivered did not correspond with the number in the bill of lading.

The buyers had previously accepted documents in respect of the goods. Amongst these was a bill of lading dated 31 July. However, a certificate of quality in respect of the goods stated that they were loaded on 10–12 August. The question to be determined by the court was whether in taking up the shipping documents without making any objection, the buyers had waived their right to reject the goods on the ground that they were not shipped within the agreed period of shipment.

Held

Lord Denning MR:

'The present case is not a case of "waiver" strictly so called. It is a case of estoppel by conduct. The basis of it is that a man has so conducted himself that it would be unfair or unjust to allow him to depart from a particular state of affairs which another has taken to be settled or correct …

If a man, who is entitled to reject goods on a certain ground, so conducts himself as to lead the other to believe that he is not relying on that ground, then he cannot afterwards set it up as a ground of rejection … If he did not trouble to read [the bill] but instead took up the documents and paid for them, he could not afterwards reject the goods on the ground of late shipment … he had the full opportunity of finding out from the contract documents what the real date of shipment was; and yet he did not trouble to do so …

It seems to me that this case falls within that principle. If the buyers had read the shipping documents when they took them up and paid for them – as they could and should have done – they would have read this certificate of quality and seen that the date of shipment was really August 12th: and that someone had put July 31st on to the bill of lading so as to make it appear that the goods had been shipped in accordance with the contract, whereas, in fact they had not. If the buyers choose not to read the documents, they must put up with the consequences. They must be treated as if they had read them. This was clearly the view of the Committee of Appeal of the London Corn Trade Association Ltd and, in a commercial matter like this, I like to hear the view of commercial men, just as Lord Mansfield did with his special jurymen.

The Committee of Appeal held the buyers "cannot be deemed to have been unaware" that the maize was loaded between August 10th and 12th 1965. By taking up the documents and paying for them, they are precluded afterwards from complaining of the late shipment or of the defect in the bill of lading. That seems to me to be the finding of the Committee of Appeal, and I see no error in law in it. They used the word "waiver" but that does not matter. The buyers are precluded, by their conduct, from relying on the late shipment as a ground for rejecting the goods.'

Comment
The duality of a buyer's right to reject under a cif contract can be lost if, as here, the buyer is put on knowledge that the date of shipment contained in the documents is incorrect.

Pound (A V) & Co Ltd v *Hardy (M W) & Co Ltd* [1956] AC 588 House of Lords (Viscount Kilmuir LC, Viscount Simmonds, Lords Morton of Henryton, Reid and Somerville of Harlow)

• *Obligation to secure export licence under fob or fas contract*

Facts
By a contract made in England, buyers agreed to buy from sellers some Portuguese turpentine fas buyers' ship in Lisbon, the destination known to be a port in East Germany. Under the law of Portugal, turpentine could not be exported without an export licence which could only be obtained through the sellers suppliers who were not known by the

buyers. The sellers applied unsuccessfully to the appropriate government authorities for a licence to export to the desired port so that the goods could be delivered fas the ship chartered by the buyers. Both parties claimed that the other was in default in failing to get the licence.

Held
There was no general rule that where there was a prohibition of export without licence, under an fob or fas contract, the buyer must supply a ship into which or alongside which the goods could legally be placed. The obligations depended on the contract and the surrounding circumstances in each case. Here, the sellers knew the desired destination and only their suppliers, whom had not been disclosed to the buyers, could apply for the necessary licence. Therefore, it was for the sellers to do their best to obtain the licence through the suppliers and as they could not do so, further performance of the buyers was excused.

It was clearly held that it is not necessarily the buyer's obligation to secure any fob or fas contract but the obligation depended on the circumstances surrounding the contracts. The distinction between this case and the earlier *Brandt* case (*H O Brandt & Co* v *H N Morris & Co Ltd* [1917] 2 KB 784), was succinctly put by Viscount Kilmuir LC at p601, where he said:

'In my opinion it is necessary to remember in comparing *Brandt*'s case with any other in the field (1) that the parties had not contracted with reference to an existing licensing system; (2) that a United Kingdom licensing system overtook their contract; (3) that either party could have applied to the British authorities; (4) that the buyers alone knew the facts which it was necessary to state when a licence was applied for.'

Comment
This case, read together with the *Brandt* case, makes it clear that there is no universal rule about the securing of export licences under fob

or fas cases. Rather, each case must be decided on the basis of its own factual situation.

Proctor and Gamble Philippines Manufacturing Corporation v Kurt A Becher GmbH & Co KG [1988] 2 Lloyd's Rep 21 Court of Appeal (Kerr, Croom-Johnson and Nicholls LJJ)

• *Loss of right to reject*

Facts

The parties had entered into a contract on cif terms. The goods had been shipped in conformity with the shipment period and did otherwise conform to the contract, but the bill of lading was technically in breach of an express obligation under clause 6 of the GAFTA terms because it was in fact misdated.

The buyers had expressed their doubts about the real date of shipment but had nonetheless accepted the documents presented and accepted the goods on arrival. The buyers sought to claim damages for the difference between the price they had paid upon tender of the shipping documents and the price they received from their buyers shortly after delivery in July. Their submission was based on the principle that the misdated bill had wrongfully deprived them of their right to reject the documents and the goods and that, therefore, they were entitled to damages based on what their financial position would have been if they had rejected the bad tender. They were not claiming that the unmerchantable bill of lading had precluded them from completing the sale of the goods whilst afloat and they did not present any evidence to the arbitrators to establish that their loss was sustained as a result of the bad tender of the bill of lading.

Held

The buyers were not entitled to damages because they had suffered no financial loss. The price they had paid was for the goods received which did conform to the contract in

all respects, including as to the date of shipment.

The buyers had not lost their right to reject the documents and the goods by reason of the breach of clause 6.

Nicholls LJ:

'Had there been no breach of cl 6 the buyers would have had no right to reject the bill of lading or the goods. What the buyers lost, in the event, was the opportunity to exercise one of the remedies (rejection) afforded by the law in respect of the breach. They lost the opportunity to exercise that remedy, not because of the breach of cl 6, but because they did not know of the existence of the breach at the time. But, as I have sought to indicate, having lost the opportunity to exercise the remedy of rejection in respect of the breach, thenceforth the buyers' remedy in respect of the breach was confined to recovering the actual financial loss, if any, suffered by them by reason of the breach.'

Damages are not a question of making comparison between what the financial position of the buyers is having accepted a bad tender, and what it would have been if they had rejected the documents. Nicholls LJ continued:

'In particular, it was submitted, first, that since the tender of the bill of lading was a bad tender, the comparison is to be made between the financial position of the buyers (a) having accepted the bas tender and (b) having rejected the bad tender. I cannot accept this formulation. The comparison is between the financial position of the buyers in the events which happened (viz having accepted the bad tender) and what their financial position would have been if the bill of lading had stated accurately the date of shipment (viz having accepted a good tender.'

Damages in a case such as this are a comparison of:

1. what the financial position of the buyers is in the events which have happened, ie the difference in the price paid to the sellers and the price received from the buyers; and

2. what their financial position would have been if the bill of lading had stated accurately the date of shipment, ie what the market value for the goods would have been in respect of a conforming bill of lading at the time it was tendered and accepted.

The application of criterion 2 looks at the position at the point in time that the bill was tendered and accepted. On the facts of this case, the lack of conformity on the document was not the reason for any loss sustained because if that bill had been conforming it would not have affected the sale (the goods were shipped to dates) and the market value of the goods on arrival, therefore, would not have been any different to that which the buyers received.

The buyers, therefore, were unable to prove loss as at the time the bill was tendered. They had based their claim on the difference between the price they had paid on presentation of the documents and the price they had received from their buyers on arrival of the goods. Their claim that the bill of lading had become unmerchantable emerged as an alternative claim in the course of argument of the appeal and Nicholls LJ did not think it to be a matter for a remission to the arbitrators to hear further evidence:

'Neither before the arbitrators nor before the judge did the buyers claim that pending the arrival of the cargo in Rotterdam and its delivery to the buyers they had suffered loss by reason only of the bill of lading being unmerchantable because of an inaccuracy in it. What was claimed was the difference in price between the price paid by the buyers on tender of shipping documents in April (plus additional shipping costs also paid by the buyers) less the proceeds of sale of the goods when sold by the buyers shortly after delivery in July. This being so, it is too late for the buyers now to take this point of view, which would have required evidence before the arbitrators. Nor would it be right for their to be a remission to the arbitrators to hear further evidence on this point which was always available to the buyers.

Putting aside, therefore, any claim for damages based solely on the unmerchantability of the bill, if the proper comparison is made, between the buyers' financial position in the events which happened and what their financial position would have been if the bill of lading had stated the actual date of shipment, the answer is plain: the buyers suffered no financial loss. They paid the contract price and they received goods which conformed in all respects, including as to date of shipment. Hence they are entitled to no damages ...'

Pyrene Co Ltd v *Scindia Navigation Co Ltd* [1954] 2 QB 402 High Court (Devlin J)

• *Definition of fob contracts – application of the Hague Rules*

Facts

The plaintiffs sold machinery fob London to the Indian government. During loading and before it had crossed the ship's rail, it fell from the ship's tackle and was damaged. The liability of the carrier for that damage was limited by art IV r5 of the Hague Rules.

At the time of damage a bill of lading had not been issued to the shipper, nor had property passed in the goods.

The shipowner admitted liability. The shipper claimed that the Hague Rules had not started to apply because the bill of lading had not been issued. However, even if they did apply it was argued that they could not apply to the plaintiff shipper who was not a party to the contract of carriage, this being an fob shipment.

Held

Devlin J:

'Although art I(e) of the Rules stated that they applied when the goods are "loaded" on the vessel, this did not mean that the Rules could not apply when the goods had actually crossed the ship's rail. Similarly in art II "loading" covered the whole operation.

The fact that the bill of lading had not

been issued did not prevent the Rules from applying. Therefore it would be absurd to suppose that the parties intend the terms of the contract to be changed when the bill of lading is issued; for the issue of the bill of lading does not necessarily mark any stage in the development of the contract ... Whenever a contract of carriage is concluded and it is contemplated that a bill of lading will, in due course, be issued in respect of it, that contract is from its creation 'covered' by a bill of lading, and is therefore from its creation a contract of carriage within the meaning of the Rules and to which the Rules apply.

It was the intention of all parties involved in the contract of carriage that the seller should participate in that contract in so far as it affected him, therefore, they were parties to the contract and, as against them the shipowners were entitled to limit their liability.

There is no difficulty in principle about the concept of an fob buyer making a contract of affreightment for the benefit of the seller as well as for himself ... The fob contract has become a flexible instrument. In ... the classic type, the buyer's duty is to nominate the ship and the seller's is to put the goods on board for the account of the buyer and procure a bill of lading in terms usual in the trade. In such a case the seller is directly a party to the contract of carriage, at least until he takes out a bill of lading in the buyer's name.

Sometimes, the seller is asked to make the necessary arrangements; and the contract may then provide for his taking the bill of lading in his own name and obtaining payment against the transfer, as in a cif contract.

Sometimes the buyer engages his own forwarding agent at the port of loading, to book space and to procure the bill of lading ... In such a case the seller discharges his duty by putting the goods on board, getting the mate's receipt, and handing it to the forwarding agent to enable him to obtain the bill of lading. The present case belongs to this third type, and it is only in this type that

any doubt can arise about the seller being a party to the contract.

Comment
Some academics use different labels for the various types of fob contract and some break the fob contract down into two main types. What is clear, however, is that the fob contract is indeed flexible unlike the cif contract.

Sharpe (C) & Co Ltd v *Nosawa & Co* [1917] 2 KB 814 (Atkin J)

• *Date for measuring damages for non-delivery under cif contracts*

Facts
Merchants in Japan sold goods to be shipped in June, cif London. Shipping documents, if sent with reasonable dispatch, would have reached London on 21 July. The goods themselves would have arrived on 30 August. The goods were never shipped.

Held
The delivery intended by the contract was a constructive delivery by tender of the shipping documents as soon as possible after shipment and, therefore, there was a breach of contract on 21 July. The measure of damages was to be measured by the difference between the contract price and the market price on 21 July. As it was impossible to buy similar goods coming forward on a June shipment, but possible to buy such goods on the spot, a merchant in these circumstances acting reasonably would have bought goods on the spot.

Comment
This case is one of a number which have held that under a cif contract the contract is one for the shipment of goods within a defined time window, to be performed in part by the tender of appropriate documents. In the event of a failure by the buyer to ship the goods, damages for non-delivery under s51 Sale of Goods Act 1979 are to be ascertained as of

such date as the documents would have been received if they had been sent timeously.

Wimble, Sons & Co v Rosenberg
[1913] 3 KB 743 Court of Appeal (Vaughan Williams, Buckley and Hamilton LJJ)

• *Risk will pass as normal if failure to comply with s32(3) Sale of Goods Act does not affect ability to insure*

Facts
The plaintiffs sold 200 bags of rice fob Antwerp, to be shipped as required by buyers, cash against bill of lading. The defendants instructed the plaintiffs to send the rice to Odessa and left the choice of vessel to them.

The printed form upon which the instructions were issued ordinarily contained a request for necessary particulars of the shipment so as to enable the buyer to insure. On this occasion it contained no such request.

The cargo was shipped accordingly. The buyer had not insured it, it being his practice not to do so until he received the slip containing all the relevant details. The ship stranded and became a total loss on the morning after she sailed.

The buyers refused to pay the price on the basis that the sellers had not complied with s32(3) Sale of Goods Act 1893. That section required the seller to give the buyer sufficient notice of the details of the sea transit in question to enable the buyer to insure. If he fails to do so then the goods remain at his risk throughout the sea transit.

Held
Appeal allowed.

Buckley LJ:

'Subsection 3 requires the seller to give such notice to the buyer as will enable the latter to insure. These words will be satisfied if either:

the buyer is already in possession of knowledge of all the facts which it is necessary to know in order that he may insure the goods, in which case, nothing is wanting to enable him to insure them, or

if such notice (if any) as has been given him, completes his knowledge of the facts so as to enable him to insure …

From the [contract of sale], the buyer knew the particulars of the goods and the port of loading, but not the port of discharge. It was for him to name the port to which he wished the goods to be shipped …

It seems to me that no notice to enable the buyer was wanted for he already had ability; he had all materials necessary to enable him to insure. But if this is not so and the seller was under an obligation to give such notice, etc then I think he had done so. The contract itself … was sufficient notice.'

It is important to note that it is no defence to a claim by a buyer under this section that he had sufficient knowledge to enable him to take out a general insurance because that would be equivalent to say that in every case, even without the knowledge of the particulars, the buyer is in possession of all the information which enables him to insure.

2   Methods of Financing

Alan v El Nasr Import and Export
[1972] 2 QB 189; [1972] 2 All ER
127 Court of Appeal (Lord Denning
MR, Megaw and Stephenson LJJ)

• *The seller may waive failure to open the agreed credit*

Facts
Egyptian buyers agreed to purchase coffee from Kenyan sellers. Payment was to be made 'by confirmed irrevocable letter of credit to be opened at sight one month prior to shipment', and the currency was to be Kenya shillings. Shipment was to take place during September/October.

The buyers opened a credit in pounds sterling which was subsequently confirmed to the sellers. The confirmation made it clear that the credit was in sterling and did not conform to the agreed requirements. Nevertheless, the sellers, both by their words and conduct accepted the credit as opened.

When sterling was devalued the buyers claimed that they were still owed a sum of money by the buyers. The buyers denied this, claiming that the credit as opened in pounds sterling had been accepted by the sellers who had by their conduct agreed to waive the requirement of payment in Kenyan shillings or agreed to vary it.

Held
Judgment for the buyers.

Lord Denning MR:

'... the sellers by their conduct, waived the right to have payment by means of letter of credit in Kenyan currency and accepted instead a letter of credit in sterling. It was, when given, conditional payment, with the result that, on being duly honoured, the payment was no longer conditional. It became absolute and dated back to the time when the letter of credit was given and acted upon. The sellers have therefore received payment of the price and cannot recover more ...

I am of the opinion that in the ordinary way, when the contract of sale stipulates for payment to be made by confirmed irrevocable letter of credit, then, when the letter of credit is issued and accepted by the seller, it operates as conditional payment of the price. It does not operate as absolute payment.

It is analogous to the case where, under a contract of sale, the buyer gives a bill of exchange or cheque for the price. It is presumed to be given not as absolute payment, nor as collateral security, but as conditional payment. If the letter of credit is honoured by the bank when the documents are presented to it, the debt is discharged. If it is not honoured, the debt is not discharged, and the seller has a remedy in damages against both bank and buyer.'

Comment
This case emphasises that it is not enough for the buyer to open a letter of credit in favour of the seller. Payment will only be made on the condition that the letter of credit works and therefore the buyer must ensure that a reliable solvent paymaster is used: see *Sale Continuation* v *Austin Taylor* [1967] 2 Lloyd's Rep 403.

Any implied agreement of absolute payment in letters of credit is to be considered in the light of all the circumstances of the case and the designation of, and agreement to, a particular bank as the issuing bank is only one of the factors to be taken into account: see *Man (E D & F)* v *Nigerian Sweets and Confectionery* [1977] 1 Lloyd's Rep 50 (below).

Banque de l'Indochine v *Rayner*
[1983] QB 711 Court of Appeal (Sir John Donaldson MR, Kerr LJ and Sir Sebag Shaw)

• *Meaning of 'payment under reserve'*

Facts
A contract of sale existed between P and D for which payment was to be made by irrevocable credit. The tendered documents did not comply with the credit and the bank refused to make payment. The seller disputed the alleged discrepancies and the bank offered them payment under reserve. As the documents were subsequently refused by the issuing bank, who were not prepared to reimburse the paying bank, the paying bank sought a return of its money from the seller.

The sellers refused to repay the paying bank saying that they were under no obligation to do so unless one or more of the specified discrepancies was a valid ground for refusing payment in the first instance.

Held
The Court affirmed the decision of Parker J (below). Payment under reserve meant that the beneficiary would be bound to repay on demand if the documents were subsequently rejected by the issuing bank or the buyer, on its own initiative or on the instructions of the buyer respectively, for the same reasons that the paying bank had rejected them.

In this case the issuing bank relied on at least one of the discrepancies noted by the correspondent confirmer which made payment.

Parker J (at first instance):

'By making payment for goods under

reserve, a bank merely reserves their right to get the money back if it is subsequently shown that it is not contractually payable at the date of payment, and they are not entitled to demand their money back in any event.'

Comment
'Payment under reserve' means that the payment is made subject to qualifications or that none of the reasons advanced for the alternative of non-payment were valid.

Bolvinter Oil SA v *Chase Manhattan Bank* [1984] 1 WLR 392 Court of Appeal (Sir John Donaldson MR and Griffiths LJ)

• *When payment out should be injuncted*

Practice note
Sir John Donaldson MR set out the circumstances in which a bank can justifiably refuse to pay out under an irrevocable documentary credit. He said that the unique value of such a method of payment was that the beneficiary would be completely satisfied that whatever disputes might thereafter arise between him and the bank's customer in relation to performance or existence of the underlying contract, the bank was personally undertaking to pay him, provided that the specified conditions were met.

'In requesting his bank to issue such a letter … the customer is seeking to take advantage of this unique characteristic. If, save in the most exceptional cases he is to be allowed to derogate from the bank's personal and irrevocable undertaking, given, be it again noted, at his request, by obtaining an injunction, restraining the bank from honouring that undertaking, he will undermine what is the bank's greatest asset, however large and rich it may be, namely its reputation for financial and contractual probity…

Judges who are asked … to issue an injunction restraining payment by a bank under an irrevocable letter of credit ... should ask whether there is any challenge to the validity of the letter. If there is not, or if the challenge is not substantial, prima facie no injunction should be granted and the bank should be left free to honour its contractual obligation ... The wholly exceptional case where an injunction may be granted is where it is proved that the bank knows that any demand for payment already made or which may thereafter be made will already be fraudulent. But the evidence must be clear both as to the fact of fraud and as to the bank's knowledge. It would certainly not be sufficient that this rests upon the uncorroborated statement of the customer, for irreparable damage can be done to a bank's credit in the relatively brief time which must elapse between the granting of such an injunction and an application by the bank to have it discharged.'

Comment

It is only in the rarest situation that a bank will be enjoined to pay under a letter of credit. That is where it is proven that a demand for payment to be made is fraudulent and was so to the knowledge of the bank.

Bunge Corporation v *Vegetable Vitamin Foods Ltd* [1985] 1 Lloyd's Rep 613 High Court (Neil J)

* *Time of opening credit*

Facts

V Ltd were the purchasers of a cargo of crude palm oil cif Bombay. Shipment was to take place in April 1978 and payment was to be made by confirmed documentary credit opened by V Ltd on 16 March.

B refused to ship the goods on the basis that the credit had not been opened in time. V Ltd claimed that from the words in the contract all that they had to do was give their bank instructions to open the credit and that this had been done by 16 March; they did not have to ensure that the notification of the opening of the credit and its confirmation reach the seller.

Held

It was not acceptable to say that the letter of credit was opened when it was issued by the issuing bank. Every documentary credit involves three contracts: one between the buyer and the issuing bank; one between the issuing bank and the seller; and one between the confirming bank and the seller.

The credit could only really be said to have come into existence if there had been communication to the seller by the banks under the second and third contracts. It was incorrect to say that the buyer had satisfied his obligation simply by giving a mandate to the issuing bank in accordance with which the credit is then opened.

On the evidence the credit had been opened by 16 March and there would be judgment for V Ltd.

Comment

As can be seen from this case, the courts place a great deal of importance on the time by which a letter of credit must be opened. Furthermore, the opening of a credit includes the requirement that it be communicated.

Although it is usual to imply a term that credit has to be opened by the start of the shipping period, that implication may be displaced where it is evident that this was not the intention of the parties or where the sellers, by their conduct, elect to keep the contract alive: see *State Trading Corporation of India Ltd* v *Compagnie Francaise d'Importation et de Distribution* [1983] 2 Lloyd's Rep 679 (below).

Discount Records Ltd v *Barclays Bank Ltd* [1975] 1 All ER 1071 High Court (Megarry J)

* *The court will consider allowing a buyer to avoid payment on an irrevocable credit on the basis of a fraud only where a sufficiently grave case of fraud can be made out*

Facts

The plaintiffs ordered a specific quantity of records and cassettes from a French company and gave signed instructions to Barclays Bank for an irrevocable confirmed documentary credit with full cash cover available until a stated date. The credit was made to the second defendant bank which instructed the third defendant bank, in Paris, which in turn directed opening of an irrevocable letter of credit with a fourth bank, also in Paris.

The goods were not shipped until 12 days after the latest shipment date and between those two dates Barclays had notified an official of the plaintiffs of discrepancies between the goods described in the advice of presentation and the plaintiff's instructions. After making enquiries from the French company, the bank had been able to reassure the official concerned and the second defendant bank then instructed the third bank in Paris to accept bills. Barclays debited the plaintiffs and placed the full credited sum in a new deposit account in the joint names of the plaintiffs and Barclays.

The defendants delivered a consignment of 94 cartons of goods. According to the plaintiffs' evidence, two cartons were empty, five were filled with rubbish, several had had their serial numbers altered and the remainder mostly contained non-contractual items. The plaintiffs sought to cancel the credit and to obtain an injunction to restrain the two defendant banks from paying the draft or any sum pursuant to the irrevocable credit opened on the plaintiff company's request, until judgment or further order, on the grounds that the defendants had been fraudulent and that the plaintiffs were thus entitled to release from their obligation to pay.

Held

The court refused grant an injunction on the grounds that fraud was merely alleged and not proved. Fraud must be 'established' or 'a sufficient case had to be made out'. Unless and until this was done, it would not be proper to allow an irrevocable credit to be effectively revoked.

Megarry J recognised the difficulty of establishing fraud where the injunction is sought against the bank, rather than against the seller, the beneficiary of the credit. In such actions the judge will hear the buyer's side but the bank is not in a position to put forward the seller's arguments. He considered that a convenient solution would be for the buyer to seek an injunction inter partes against the seller, preventing the latter from drawing on the credit. Moreover, as regards the two defendants, the plaintiffs real claim, if justified, was against Barclays Bank for breach of contract.

Megarry J:

'I do not think that this is a case for an injunction at all. It cannot harm the plaintiffs in any way if the seller is paid so long as the money does not come out of the plaintiff's fund ... If Barclays have acted in breach of contract, the plaintiffs will have their claim against them ... I would be slow to interfere with banker's irrevocable credits, and not least in the sphere of international banking, unless a sufficiently good cause is shown; for interventions by the court that are too ready or too frequent might gravely impair the reliance which, quite properly, is placed on such credits.'

As the evidence stood the fraud, though alleged, had yet to be established. A further consideration was that the draft might be in the hands of a holder in due course. No injunction could be granted to prevent the holder in due course of the bills of exchange drawn and negotiated under the letter of credit from seeking to enforce the drawee/acceptor's undertaking in the draft. Megarry J was of the view that this promise was itself independent of the undertakings, both in the letter of credit and in the underlying contract of sale.

The sellers had relied on the American case of *Sztejn* v *J Henry Schroder Banking Corpn* (1941) 31 NYS 2d 631, there being an absence of English authority on the point, to establish that fraud affecting the commercial transaction and the obligation to pay may amount to an exception to the autonomy of the credit. In that case it had been alleged that the seller had shipped rubbish and then passed his draft for collection. Megarry J found the case to be 'plainly distinguishable' in relation both to established fraud and to the absence in that case of any possible holder in due course and said:

> 'Shientag J [in *Sztejn*] referred to the well established rule that a letter of credit is independent of the primary contract of sale between the buyer and the seller, so that unless the letter of credit otherwise provides, the bank is neither obliged nor allowed to enter into controversies between the buyer and seller regarding the quality of the merchandise shipped. However the learned judge distinguished mere breaches of warranty of quality from cases where the seller had intentionally failed to ship any of the goods ordered by the buyer. In relation to the latter case, at p634, the learned judge uttered a sentence upon which the plaintiff placed great reliance:
>
> > "In such a situation, where the seller's fraud has been called to the bank's attention before the drafts and documents have been presented for payment, the principle of the independence of the bank's obligation under the letter of credit should not be extended to protect the unscrupulous seller."
>
> However it is important to note that in the *Sztejn* case the proceedings consisted of a motion to dismiss the formal complaint on the ground that it disclosed no cause of action. That being so the court had to assume that the facts stated in the complaint were true. The complaint alleged fraud, and so the court was dealing with a case of established fraud. Accordingly the matter has to be dealt with on the footing that this is a case in which fraud is alleged but has not been established. I should add that on the facts required to be assumed in the *Sztejn* case the collecting bank was not a holder in due course who would not be defeated by the fraud, but was merely an agent for the fraudulent seller ....
>
> I do not say that the doctrine of [the *Sztejn* case] is wrong or that it is incapable of extension to cases in which fraud is alleged but has not been established, provided a suf-

ficient cause is made out. That may or may not be the case. What I do say is that the present case falls far short of establishing any ground upon which it would be right for the court to intervene by granting the interlocutory injunction claimed.'

Comment
Megarry J did not rule out the possibility that the allegation of fraud affecting the commercial transaction and the obligation to pay might operate as an exception to the autonomy of the credit. Rather, he was at pains to point out, that nothing in the circumstances of the present case constituted a sufficiently grave cause for granting the injunction claimed. However, to decide otherwise would become a question of policy requiring the court to balance the necessity for maintaining the well established rules for the autonomy of the credit against the undesirability of assisting a seller who had fraudulent intention. The comments of Megarry J in respect of the alternative actions open to the plaintiffs is pertinent to this debate. Even where a sufficiently grave case of fraud can be made out, in an injunction of this type there will remain the possibility that the draft might be in the hands of a holder in due course. There can be no exception to the independence of an irrevocable credit if it would have the effect of precluding the bank from paying a bill of exchange drawn under the credit when it has been negotiated to a third party who holds the bill as a holder in due course.

Equitable Trust Co of New York v *Dawson Partners Ltd* (1927) 27 Ll LR 49 (Viscount Sumner)

• *Documents that are 'almost the same' should be refused*

Facts
The court considered the duty of the bank in taking up documents. The credit called for a certificate to be signed by experts. The bank paid against a document signed by one expert.

Held

The bank was not entitled to reimbursement.

Viscount Sumner:

> 'It is both common ground and common sense that in such a transaction the accepting bank can only claim indemnity if the conditions on which it is authorised to accept are, in the matter of the accompanying documents, strictly observed. There is no room for documents which are almost the same or which will do just as well. Business could not proceed securely on any other lines. The bank's branch abroad, which knows nothing officially of the details of the transaction thus financed, cannot take upon itself to decide what will do well enough and what will not. If it does as it is told, it is safe; if it declines to do anything else, it is safe; if it departs from the conditions laid down it acts at its own risk.'

Comment

Article 13 of the Uniform Customs and Practice for Documentary Credits (UCP) (No 500, 1993 Revision) states that the bank is under a duty to take reasonable care in checking the documents presented under a letter of credit. The bank has a reasonable time not to exceed seven banking days. The bank's duty is to ensure that the documents conform with the terms of the credit and with the instructions given by the applicant of the credit. If a bank accepts documents which do not correspond with the credit instructions it will not be entitled to reimbursement. With regard to the doctrine of strict compliance also see: *Rayner (J H) & Oilseeds Trading Co Ltd* v *Hambros Bank Ltd* [1943] 1 KB 37 (below).

Forestal Mimosa v *Oriental Credit Ltd* [1986] 1 Lloyd's Rep 329 Court of Appeal (Croom Johnson and Balcombe LJJ, Sir John Megaw)

- *Where the parties have expressly incorporated the Uniform Customs and Practice for Documentary Credits, they will be bound by the terms of all of its articles unless they expressly agree otherwise*

Facts

Pakistani companies purchased and sold 'wattle mimosa extra' from the plaintiff. Payment was to be made by irrevocable letter of credit to be issued by a bank in Dubai and confirmed by Oriental Credit. The sellers were to present a bill of exchange drawn on the buyer, together with agreed documents, and payment was to be deferred 90 days from the date on the bill of lading. The credits expressly incorporated the Uniform Customs and Practice for Documentary Credits (UCP) (1983 Revision).

The buyers refused to accept the bill of exchange saying that they were only prepared to accept drafts remitted to them under a collection arrangement and not if presented for payment under documentary credit. The bank refused to make payment on the drafts duly presented by the sellers claiming, inter alia, that their words printed in the credit excluded the provision in art 10(b)(iii) of the UCP (1983 Revision). It was their contention that the words 'by acceptance of … drafts drawn (on the buyers)' made it clear that this is when the credit was to become available and that, accordingly, the bank was responsible for payment only if the buyer had accepted the bill of exchange.

The sellers sought summary judgment against the bank for acceptance and payment of the drafts.

Held

By expressly incorporating the UCP (1983 Revision) the parties had agreed to make their credit subject to art 10(b)(iii) of those rules which provided that under a credit where drafts are to be drawn by the beneficiary, there is an obligation on the bank to be responsible for acceptance and payment of the drafts.

They could have excluded individual provisions of the rules if they wished but had not chosen to do so, and neither the bank's own words printed in the credit nor the provision of art 10(b)(iii) required such an exclusion to be implied.

The words in the credit were not inconsistent with art 10(b)(iii) and both made it clear that the obligation of the bank was to give acceptance and payment on maturity, irrespective of the behaviour of the buyer. Since the bank had not done so, and there was no basis for the refusal, it had no defence to summary judgment.

Comment
The was one of the first cases to consider the deferred payment credit introduced by the 1983 rules. Prior to its introduction the only way that a bank could defer its obligation to make payment to the beneficiary was by allowing him to draw on a time bill of exchange. Under the deferred payment credit the bank agrees to make payment only on some future date that is either specified in the credit or determined in accordance with some formula prescribed by the credit. There is no need, therefore, for a bill of exchange. By confirming its acceptance and giving a definite undertaking that payment would be made Oriental Credit guaranteed its acceptance and was liable to pay.

Gian Singh v *Banque de l'Indochine*
[1974] 2 Lloyd's Rep 1 Privy Council (Lords Wilberforce, Diplock, Cross of Chelsea and Kilbrandon, Sir Henry Gibbs)

• *Bank need not check authenticity of documents*

Facts
Payment under an irrevocable documentary credit was to be against documents which included a certificate signed by one 'Balwant Singh ... holder of Malaysian passport E.13276'.

The bank accepted the documents presented and payment was made against them. The applicant then brought an action against the issuing bank on the ground that the certificate was a forgery.

Held
The applicant's appeal was dismissed.

The bank was entitled to be reimbursed by the buyer because it had exercised reasonable care in examining the documents, which appeared to be correct on their face. This sufficed despite the forgery.

Provided that the documents appear on their face to be correct and the bank has exercised reasonable care in examining them, this will suffice despite the forgery and entitle the bank to accept the documents and pay against them and be reimbursed by the buyer.

Lord Diplock commented on the duties of a paying bank in taking up and paying against documents, and their obligation to check their authenticity:

'The fact that a document presented by the beneficiary under a documentary credit is in fact a forgery which otherwise conforms to the requirement of the credit, does not of itself prevent the issuing bank from recovering from its customer, money paid under the credit. The duty of the issuing bank ... is to examine the documents with reasonable care to ascertain that they appear on their face to be in accordance with the terms and conditions of the credit. The express provision to this effect in Article 1 of the Uniform Customs and Practice for Documentary Credits, does no more than re-state the duty of the bank at common law. In business transactions financed by documentary credits, banks must be able to act promptly on presentation of the documents. In the ordinary case, visual inspection of the actual documents presented is all that is called for. The bank is under no duty to take any further steps to investigate the genuineness of a signature which, on the face of it, purports to be the signature of the person named or described in the letter of credit.'

Glencore International and Another v Bank of China [1996] 1 Lloyd's Rep 135 Court of Appeal (Sir Thomas Bingham MR, Saville LJ and Sir John Balcombe)

• *Doctrine of strict compliance – only the invoice must contain every detail required – Uniform Customs and Practice for Documentary Credits (1993 Revision) had been complied with*

Facts

Glencore sold a consignment of aluminium ingots to buyers cif Zhangjiagang terms. Payment was to be by irrevocable letter of credit which was subject to the Uniform Customs and Practice for Documentary Credits (UCP) (1993 Revision).

Glencore tendered documents to the advising bank who, in turn, presented them to the Bank of China. However, the buyers, probably wishing to avoid a loss caused by a fall in the market price of aluminium, instructed the Bank of China to reject the documents on the grounds that:

1 the commercial invoice described the origin of the goods as 'Any Western Brand – Indonesia (Inalum Brand)', whereas the letter of credit described the origin merely as 'Any Western Brand';
2 the goods were not properly described in the packing list; and
3 the beneficiary's certificates were not original documents, nor marked as original, as required by art 20(b) of the UCP (1993 Revision).

At first instance Rix J held that the Bank of China was right to reject. Glencore appealed.

Held

The appeal was dismissed.

On the question of the commercial invoice
Sir Thomas Bingham MR, who delivered the decision of the Court of Appeal, disagreed with Rix J (at first instance) on the description of the goods. The provision in art 37(c) of the UCP (1993 Revision), which the Bank of China sought to rely on, had been satisfied. It states: 'The description of the goods in the commercial invoice must correspond with the description in the credit.' The word 'correspond' does not impose a requirement for the wording in the invoice to be identical. In the instant invoice the words 'Any Western Brand' described the goods in a broad generic way and the additional words 'Indonesia (Inalum Brand)' merely identified the precise brand of goods within that broad generic description. The inclusion of those additional words did not create any inconsistency or alteration in the meaning as had occurred in *Bank Melli Iran* v *Barclays Bank (Dominion, Colonial and Overseas) Ltd* [1951] 2 Lloyd's Rep 367 where the words 'new' and 'new, good' had different meanings in the truck trade.

On the question of the packing list
The Bank of China had claimed that the packing list was defective as it did not contain a description of the goods. However, the UCP (1993 Revision) provides that not every document in the set of documents presented must contain every detail required. The only exception to this is the commercial invoice. With regard to the other documents, it will be sufficient if all the required details can be gleaned from the set of documents taken as a whole, there being a clear link between each document: see further *Midland Bank v Seymour* [1955] 2 Lloyd's Rep 147 (below). On the facts, a clear linkage was present and the packing list satisfied the requirements of the UCP.

On the question of the beneficiary's certificates
The beneficiary's certificates had been produced by Glencore on a word processor and then photocopied as required on the same type of A4-size paper as the original printout from the word processor. One such document was signed by a representative of Glencore and included in the tendered documents. While,

in one sense, the documents, as they were created by Glencore, could be considered originals, they were nonetheless produced by one of the means set out in art 20(b) UCP (1993 Revision) and, as such, were subject to the provisions of that Article. It contains an exception to the general rule that original documents are required by providing:

> 'Unless otherwise stipulated in the credit, banks will also accept as an original document(s) a document(s) produced or appearing to have been produced:
> (i) by reprographic, automated or computerised systems;
> (ii) as carbon copies;
> provided that it is marked as original and, where necessary, appears to be signed.'

The document in question had merely been signed and not 'marked as original'. Such marking is required in order to comply with the provision in art 20(b) and the signature alone will not suffice. As the Court of Appeal pointed out:

> ' ... a signature on a copy does not make an original, it makes an authenticated copy, and art 20(b) does not treat a signature as a substitute for a marking "as original".'

The argument put forward by the Bank of China had been described by Rix J as 'very technical' and one that might appear to lack merit. However, the doctrine of strict compliance does require consideration of the party's merits and his decision that the beneficiary's certificates were defective was upheld by the Court of Appeal.

Hong Kong and Shanghai Banking Corp v *Kloeckner & Co Ltd AG*
[1989] 2 Lloyd's Rep 323 Queen's Bench Division (Commercial Court) (Hirst J)

• *Similar rules on remedies and procedures apply to actions based on letters of credit as to those based on bills of exchange and both forms of payment are similar to cash.*

Facts
The issue in the case was whether the plaintiff bank was entitled to rely on a 'no set-off' clause. The bank financed Gatoil, who traded on the market for crude oil and Kloeckner, another dealer, 'fronted' Gatoil's purchases by providing for their onsale with back-to-back contracts. The financing was conducted in three ways.

First, for Gatoil's purchases of wet cargoes (physical cargoes of oil) the bank paid Gatoil's suppliers by letters of credit and received in return pledges of the bills of lading. Kloeckner gave the bank corresponding undertakings to pay the bank on delivery to them of the bills of lading. These expressly precluded set-off as a defence to claims by the bank.

Second, for dry cargoes (forward contracts), the bank advanced money to Gatoil and, in return, Gatoil assigned the proceeds from the forward contracts matching its purchases. Kloeckner undertook to pay the bank any difference in price.

Third, the bank provided Gatoil a standby letter of credit facility in favour of Kloeckner to cover Gatoil's liabilities to Kloeckner on the dry cargo transactions.

Their dispute arose when Kloeckner fell into financial difficulties. The plaintiff bank claimed $8 million as the balance due from Kloeckner on wet cargo transactions and applied for O.14 summary judgment. Kloeckner denied liability, claiming that with the bank's knowledge an employee of Kloeckner had made the relevant contracts without authority. Under the standby letter of credit facility in favour of Kloeckner, the bank admitted liability of $10 million and Kloeckner counter-claimed this in the bank's action on the wet cargo transactions. Kloeckner also challenged the propriety of the no set-off clause in the wet cargo contracts. The bank's reply and defence to counterclaim pleaded Kloeckner's liability under the wet cargo transactions as a set-off and defended the no set-off clause.

Held

The bank were entitled to rely on the no set-off clause. The decision of the Court of Appeal in *Halesowen Presswork* v *Westminster Bank* [1971] 1 QB 1 was followed.

Letters of credit are similar to bills of exchange and therefore resemble cash. There could therefore be no reason why the bank could not set-off as a defence liquidated sums due and arising directly out of the same transactions under the normal rules of equity.

The court distinguished cases where the autonomy of the letter of credit prevented no set-off against claims on letters of credit from the underlying transactions. The bank's claims to set-off in the instant case were different. They involved the liability of the beneficiary of the letter of credit to the bank. This was a question of the banker-customer relationship, not of claims between buyer and seller on the underlying sale.

There was no reason why liabilities under the banker-customer relationship could not be set-off. Obligations arising under letters of credit were no different from any other aspect of the banker-customer relationship. What was well established by the rules of equity was that banks could not set-off debts arising out of the banker-customer relationship against liabilities to customers. The customer, however, could set-off any liquidated claims arising directly out of the same transaction giving rise to his liability to the bank.

Howe Richardson Scale Co Ltd v *Polimex-Cekop and National Westminster Bank Ltd* [1978] 1 Lloyd's Rep 161 Court of Appeal (Roskill and Cumming-Bruce LJJ)

• *Performance bonds, like letters of credit, are independent of other contracts and any other issues*

Facts

The sellers entered into a contract with the buyers, the first defendants, for the sale and delivery of equipment on a contract price of £500,000 of which £25,000 was payable in advance on presentation of a guarantee by the seller's bank (the second defendants). A further £50,000 was to be paid by irrevocable confirmed credit. The balance of the price was payable under a financial agreement made with the second defendants' bank.

The plaintiff sellers, on receiving the advanced payment, completed the manufacture of the goods and, in due course, received a substantial sum of money under the financial agreement. However, on the grounds that the delivery had not been completed by the date specified in the bank's guarantee, the buyers (the first defendants) claimed repayment of the advance payment. The bank refused saying that it was bound to honour its obligations under the guarantee and the sellers applied for an injunction to restrain the buyers from claiming under the guarantee.

Held

The Court of Appeal applied the principles laid down in *American Cyanamid Co* v *Ethicon Ltd* [1975] 1 All ER 504 and found that the balance of convenience was against the grant of the injunction requested by the buyers.

The bank was under an obligation to perform its requirements under a particular contract. This obligation did not depend on the resolution of any dispute between the parties to the contract, but on whether the event giving rise to the obligation to pay had arisen.

The bank felt that it was under an obligation to make a settlement with the sellers. It would be wrong for the court to interfere with that since to do so would involve the bank in an enquiry as to whether or not the parties had properly fulfilled their obligations under the contract of sale.

Comment

Performance bonds are like confirmed irrevocable letters of credit: see *Owen (Edward) Engineering Ltd* v *Barclays Bank International Ltd* [1978] 1 All ER 976 (below).

Malas (Hamazeh) & Sons v *British Imex Industries Ltd* [1958] 2 QB 127 Court of Appeal (Jenkins, Sellers and Pierce LJJ)

• *Credit will remain as an absolute obligation to pay where the dispute on the underlying transaction does not involve fraud*

Facts

The plaintiffs were a Jordanian firm who entered into a contract with British Imex for the purchase of steel rods to be delivered in two instalments, each of which was to be paid by a separate irrevocable confirmed credit. The bank opened two credits in favour of the defendants and the defendants were paid on the first shipment of the goods. The plaintiffs then alleged that the goods were defective and applied for an ex parte injunction to prevent the defendants, their servants, agents or assigns, from drawing on the second letter of credit.

Held

The Court of Appeal refused to grant the injunction. Jenkins LJ took the view that a confirmed credit constituted an absolute obligation on the bank to pay 'irrespective of any dispute there may be between the parties as to whether the goods are up to contract or not' because 'a vendor of goods selling against a confirmed credit is selling under the assurance that nothing will prevent him from receiving the price.' Jenkins LJ went on to say that the system of financing goods by irrevocable credits 'would break down completely if a dispute as between the vendor and the purchaser was to have the effect of "freezing" ... the sum in respect of which the letter of credit was opened.'

A distinction must be drawn between the seller's contract with the buyer and the bargain between the banker and the seller. The latter agreement imposes an absolute obligation on the bank to pay the buyer irrespective of any dispute with the former.

Jenkins LJ:

'It appears to me that when the first consignment of steel rods arrived they were, according to the plaintiffs, by no means up to contract quality and many criticisms were made on that score. That is a matter in issue between the parties. In the meantime, the plaintiffs wish to secure themselves in respect of any damages to which they may be entitled when this dispute is ultimately tried out, by preventing the defendants from dealing with this outstanding letter of credit ... It seems plain enough that the opening of a confirmed letter of credit constitutes a bargain between the banker and the vendor of the goods which imposes upon the banker an absolute obligation to pay, irrespective of any dispute there may be between the parties as to whether the goods are up to contract or not. An elaborate commercial system has been built up on the footing that bankers' confirmed credits are of that character, and, in my judgment it would be wrong for this court, in the present case to interfere with that established practice.'

Sellers LJ added that he thought the court could interfere in cases where there had been a fraudulent transaction.

Man (E D & F) v *Nigerian Sweets and Confectionery* [1977] 1 Lloyd's Rep 50 Queen's Bench Division (Ackner J)

• *Any implied agreement of absolute payment in letters of credit is to be considered in the light of all the circumstances of the case*

Facts

Payment for 1,100 metric tons of sugar was to be against bills of exchange drawn on the issuing bank but the documents, which were correct when presented, were never paid against, even though the buyers had put the bank in funds for the amount in question. The bank then went into liquidation.

The sellers sought payment from the buyers direct who claimed that all their liabilities to the seller had been discharged. Their refusal to make payment was on the grounds that payment was to be made by documentary credit and the banker had been put in funds expressly for the purpose.

Held

The court took the view that any implied agreement of absolute payment in letters of credit was to be considered in the light of all the circumstances of the case.

Ackner J cited *Alan v El Nasr Import and Export*:

' ... a letter of credit is not to be regarded as absolute payment unless the seller stipulates, expressly or impliedly, that it should be so. He may do so impliedly if he stipulates for the credit to be issued by a particular bank in such circumstances that it is to be inferred that the seller looks to that particular banker to the exclusion of the buyer.'

Ackner J held that on the basis of the contract the buyers were still liable to pay the sellers:

'It seems to be clear ... that the sellers did not stipulate for the credit to be issued .... in such circumstances that it was to be inferred that they looked to that particular bank to the exclusion of [the buyers].'

By finding that the letters of credit did not operate as absolute payment by the buyer, but only as conditional payment, it followed that, since they were not honoured, the debt had not been discharged:

'The respondent's liability to the sellers was a primary liability. This ... was suspended during the period available to the issuing bank to honour the drafts and activated when the issuing bank failed ...
    The sellers' remedy in such circumstances is to claim from the buyers either the price agreed in the contract of sale or damages for breach of their contractual promise to pay by letter of credit.'

Midland Bank v *Seymour* [1955] 2 Lloyd's Rep 147 High Court (Devlin J)

• *Compliance may be gauged from all the documents providing each is correct and complete in itself and the documents are consistent with each other*

Facts

The sellers, a Hong Kong company, sold a cargo of duck feathers to the defendant, a British importer. Payment was to be made by documentary credit against documents consisting of an invoice, a bill of lading and a certificate of origin.

    The tendered documents as a whole provided all details relating to price, weight and condition of the goods and both the bill of lading and the invoice gave the shipping mark. The bill of lading, however, noted the cargo as '12 bales Hongkong duck feathers', whereas the invoice described the goods as 'Hongkong duck feathers – 85 per cent clean' and gave the quantity of the goods as '12 bales each weighing about 190 lbs'. The letter of credit was unhelpful in that its words were ambiguous as to whether the defendants required particular details to be contained in any particular documents or in the documents as a whole. Accordingly, the documents were rejected for lack of compliance.

Held

The bank was entitled to pay against such documents providing that each document, in itself, was valid and that, taken as a whole, the documents were consistent with each other. There would be sufficient compliance with the letter of credit if the body of the bill of lading contained a proper description of the goods.

Devlin J:

'The set of documents must contain all the particulars and, of course they must be consistent between themselves, otherwise they would not be a good set of shipping documents. But here you have a set of documents … [each of] which not only is consistent with itself, but also incorporates the particulars that are given in the other – the shipping mark on the bill of lading leading to the invoice which bears the same shipping mark and which would be tendered at the same time, which sets out the full description of the goods.'

However, Devlin J made it clear that where a bank was given instructions by its customer it was obliged to strictly comply with that mandate.

The doctrine of contra preferentum was argued but Devlin J took the view that it did not apply because the defendants themselves had created the ambiguity in the mandate by the way in which they had completed the bank form when they applied for the credit to be opened.

Comment

The approach of considering all the documents together rather than separately has been approved by the courts as a practical and sensible approach: see *Soproma SpA* v *Marine & Animal By-Products Corporation* [1966] 1 Lloyd's Rep 367 (below).

Moralice (London) Ltd v *E D & F Man* [1954] 2 Lloyd's Rep 526
Queen's Bench Division (McNair J)

• *The de minimis rule under letters of credit*

Facts

The plaintiffs sold 500 metric tonnes of sugar to an Iraqi buyer, 'cif Tripol and insurance to Baghdad'. Payment was to be made against documents in accordance with an irrevocable credit established by the buyer with a London bank. It was provided that 'invoices must describe the goods exactly as above'. The plaintiffs made a purchase from the defendants of 'about 500 tonnes' of bagged sugar in order to implement the sale to the Iraqi

buyer. The plaintiffs were notified by the defendants that documents were ready to be taken up, but that they would show a short shipment of three bags.

The bank refused to permit the plaintiffs to draw against the credit except upon an indemnity being given in respect of the discrepancy. The defendants agreed to indemnity the plaintiffs against 'any consequences which may arise from there being three bags short shipped.' The plaintiffs were paid by the bank upon agreement by the plaintiffs to indemnify the bank against the consequences of accepting documents showing a discrepancy.

The buyer refused to accept the documents. The bank demanded repayment by the plaintiffs of the whole sum paid against the credit. A compromise agreement was reached whereby the bank agreed to accept the documents upon payment by the plaintiffs of £500.

Held

The fact that the plaintiffs were prepared to pay the defendants, although they (the plaintiffs) honestly believed, albeit mistakenly, that they had a right to avoid payment, was ample consideration to support the defendants' indemnity agreement.

The bank was entitled to reject documents which did not exactly comply. The de minimis rule would have applied to such short shipment as between buyer and seller, but the rule could not be applied in accordance with the tender of documents under a letter of credit. The payment of £500 to the Iraqi buyers, who were thereby induced to accept delivery, was a reasonable compromise by the plaintiffs of their liability to the bank.

Comment

This case, following *J H Rayner & Oilseeds Trading Co Ltd* v *Hambros Bank Ltd* [1943] 1 KB 37, Court of Appeal, which is known for the discrepancy involving 'Coromandel groundnuts' and 'machine shelled groundnuts', makes clear the availability of the de minimis rule as between buyer and seller under a contract of sale, and its unavailability in the context of the tender of documents under a documentary credit.

The Uniform Customs and Practice for Documentary Credits (No 500), art 49, allows for a tolerance level but not when dealing with individual items or packages.

Owen (Edward) Engineering Ltd v *Barclays Bank International Ltd* [1978] 1 All ER 976 Court of Appeal (Lord Denning MR, Browne and Geoffrey Lane LJJ)

- *Performance bonds are like confirmed irrevocable letters of credit*

Facts
English sellers entered into a contract to supply and erect glasshouses in Libya. The Libyan buyers were to open an irrevocable letter of credit in favour of the sellers. The sellers told their English bank to give a performance guarantee. The English bank instructed a Libyan bank to issue a performance bond in favour of the buyers for a certain sum and gave their guarantee payable on demand without proof of conditions to cover that sum. The Libyan bank issued a bond accordingly. The sellers received no confirmed letter of credit and refused to proceed with the contract. The buyers demanded payment on the guarantee. The sellers obtained an interim injunction to prevent the English bank from paying on the guarantee. On the application of the English bank, the injunction was discharged.

On appeal by the sellers.

Held
A performance bond was very like a letter of credit, and it was settled that banks must honour letters of credit. Notwithstanding that the sellers were not in default, banks had to honour their bond: they were not concerned with relation between buyer and seller, and there was no need for the bank to inquire into the validity of the buyer's claim. The appeal would be dismissed.

Comment
Performance bonds, like letters of credit, are independent of other contracts and any other issues: see *Howe Richardson Scale Co Ltd* v *Polimex-Cekop and National Westminster Bank Ltd* [1978] 1 Lloyd's Rep 161 (above).

Rayner (J H) & Oilseeds Trading Co Ltd v *Hambros Bank Ltd* [1943] 1 KB 37 Court of Appeal (MacKinnon and Goddard LJJ)

- *The bank must comply with the mandate without question*

Facts
Rayner sold a consignment of groundnuts to Danish buyers. The buyers contacted their bank and ordered them to open a credit in favour of the sellers on production of an invoice describing the goods as Coromandel groundnuts and a bill of lading describing the goods as Coromandel groundnuts in bags. The plaintiffs presented the documents to the bank who refused to make payment on the grounds that the bill of lading did not comply with the description in the credit.

Held
In determining whether the documents comply with the credit, the bank will have no regard to trade custom.

MacKinnon LJ:

'In the margin of the bill of lading are the marks "OTC CRS Aarhus" and then it says, "6,330 bags machine shelled groundnut kernels, each bag said to weigh 1,771 lbs net".

The defendants refused to accept the draft and they did so upon the ground that the terms in the letter of credit called for documents which covered a shipment of ... Coromandel groundnuts, whereas in this case the bill only described the goods as "machine shelled groundnut kernels ... CRS" (which means Coromandel in the trade).

The bank can say to the beneficiary: "these are the terms upon which we will pay" and if they have only been authorised by their customer to pay on certain terms, they must see that those terms are included in the notification which they give to the beneficiary, and must not pay on any other terms. If they do pay on any other terms they run the risk of their customer refusing to reimburse them. It does not matter whether the terms imposed by the person who requires them to open the credit are reasonable or unreasonable, … the bank is not concerned with that. The bank … must do exactly what its customer requires it to do, and if the customer says, "I require a bill of lading for Coromandel groundnuts", the bank is not justified … in paying against a bill … for anything except Coromandel groundnuts, and it is no answer to say: "You know perfectly well that machine shelled groundnut kernels (CRS) are the same as Coromandel groundnuts" … whether Hambros knew or not that there was this trade description (CRS) is nothing to the point …'

Comment

This case is an example of the doctrine of strict compliance in practice. Despite the fact that the bank may know a trade term, if the description in the documents is not the same as the description in the mandate and the credit instructions, the bank should reject the documents.

Whilst the bank is obliged to comply with the instructions given by the customer without question, if that mandate is unclear about whether particular details should be contained in any particular document, the court may instead gauge compliance by reference to the documents looked at as a whole rather than by reference to the documents separately. This has been approved by the courts as being a practical and sensible approach provided that each single document is correct and complete in itself and the documents as a whole are consistent with each other: see *Midland Bank* v *Seymour* [1955] 2 Lloyd's Rep 147 (above), and *Soproma SpA* v *Marine & Animal By-*

Products Corporation [1966] 1 Lloyd's Rep 367 (below).

Soproma SpA v *Marine & Animal By-Products Corporation* [1966] 1 Lloyd's Rep 367 Queen's Bench Division (Commercial Court) (McNair J)

• *Tender of documents under a letter of credit*

Facts

A contract of sale was entered into on 3 August 1962, between New York sellers and Italian buyers for 1,000 tonnes of 'Chilean fish fullmeal, steam-dried, minimum 70 per cent protein, 10 per cent max fat … free of Salmonella at time of shipment, as per sample sent … Shipment September/October 1962 in seller's option. Price: US $20 per metric ton September. US $139 per metric ton October. Cost and Freight Savona … Payment: Against letter of credit, confirmed, irrevocable with M. Bank, New York.' The credit also referred to shipment temperature of 37.5°C.

Various documents were tendered under the contract. The buyers wrote to their bank that as documents showed 67 per cent protein they could not accept the documents. Additionally the sellers tendered a 'freight collect' bill of lading accompanied by a freight receipt showing that it had been paid instead of a freight paid bill of lading, and the bill showed a temperature of 100°F. Following the rejection of the documents, substitute documents were tendered directly to the buyers.

Held (inter alia)

In the law relating to documentary credits, there is no place for the operation of the de minimis rule. Here, while the credit required bills of lading to state temperatures to be 37.5°C and the bill of lading stated the temperature to be 100°F, a discrepancy of .5°F, this constituted a breach of the obligations imposed by the letter of credit.

The statement describing the goods as 67 per cent protein was defective as under the Uniform Customs the description in the invoice must correspond exactly with that in the credit and here it did not.

It is not open to a seller, whose documents were initially rejected by the bank, to resubmit new documents directly to the buyer as it is the buyer's obligation to provide the seller with a solvent and reliable paymaster, who could be sued by the seller if necessary.

Comment
This case considers and reaches holdings on a number of important issues relating to documentary credits. It is probably best known for the holding that in the law relating to documentary credits, the de minimis principle has no place, and the holding that under a documentary credit the documents must be tendered directly to the bank which cannot be bypassed.

Stach (Ian) Ltd v *Baker Bosley Ltd*
[1958] 2 QB 130 High Court
(Diplock J)

• *Credit should be opened by start of shipping period: illustration of string contracts*

Facts
Stach, steel merchants, contracted with Baker Bosley for the sale to them of 500 metric tons of metal plate at US $205 per ton. The goods were to be delivered fob Benelux port, destination Canada, payment by confirmed irrevocable letter of credit, divisible and assignable to the plaintiffs' nominees in West Germany.

The defendants, who were having difficulty in obtaining a letter of credit from their own sub-buyers, failed to open a credit in favour of the sellers. The plaintiffs wrote them a letter requesting the credit to be opened immediately. The defendants never in fact opened the credit and the sellers eventually sold their goods elsewhere at a price below the contract price.

Held
It was the duty of the buyer to open the credit at least by the start of the shipping period.

Diplock cited the decision in *Pavia* v *Thurmann-Neilson* [1952] 2 QB 84:

'I think that when a seller is given a right to ship over a period and there is machinery for payment that machinery must be available over the whole of that period.'

He also gave a clear summary of the mechanism of string contracts:

'Both the plaintiffs and the defendants are merchants dealing in steel ... neither of them was a manufacturer or stockist or user of steel; they were both middlemen.

... their method of carrying on business was to enter into practically simultaneous contracts of purchase and sale and to rely upon the banker's credits opened by the buyers to enable them to pay the purchase price to the person from whom they had in turn bought.

... their ultimate user under the terms of the contract of sale opens a transferable divisible credit in favour of his seller for his purchase price; his seller in turn transfers so much of the credit as corresponds to the purchase price to his seller' or more probably, if his own contract with another merchant calls for a transferable, divisible credit, procures his own banker to issue a back-to-back credit – that is to say, he lodges the credit in his own favour with his own banker, who in turn issues a transferable divisible credit for the amount of the purchase price to his own seller; and so on, through the string of merchants until the banker of the last merchant in the string issues the credit in favour of the actual manufacturer or stockist ...'

The measure of damages in the event of failure is as follows:

'In accordance with the judgment in *Trans Trust SPRL* v *Danubian Trading Co Ltd* [1952] 2 QB 297; [1952] 1 All ER 90 in a case of this kind where there is a string of contracts which it is known (as it was known in this case) can only be financed by a letter of credit from the ultimate buyer, prima facie, the measure of damages is the loss of profit on the transaction, since the defendants must have known that their failure to provide the letter of credit would make it impossible for the plaintiffs to carry out the transaction, just as failure on their own buyer's part to provide a letter of credit made it impossible for the defendants themselves to carry out the transaction. I think, therefore, that probably the right basis is loss of profit.'

Comment
The requirement that the letter of credit be opened at the latest by the first day of the shipment period gives certainty to what can be a troublesome issue. It is of course open to the parties to the contract to specify otherwise, for example before the start of the shipment period.

State Trading Corporation of India Ltd v Compagnie Francaise d'Importation et de Distribution
[1983] 2 Lloyd's Rep 679 Queen's Bench Division (Commercial Court) (Lloyd J)

• *Documentary credit – time of opening*

Facts
The buyer and seller entered into contracts in 1978 for the shipment of Indian tapioca chips between February and March and March/April 1979.

In January 1979 the contracts were amended and the documentary credits were required to be opened and confirmed 'immediately and no later than 15 January 1979'. This date had already passed at the time of amendment but the buyers did instruct the bank to confirm the credits on the same day as the amendment took place. However, due to a bank strike the sellers were only given confirmation of the credits on 5 March, after the shipping period.

On 2 March, the sellers contacted the buyers stating that they would not ship the goods because the credits had not been opened and there was no contract between them.

Held
Although it is usual to imply a term that credit has to be opened by the start of the shipping period, that implication may be displaced where it is evident that this was not the intention of the parties or where the sellers, by their conduct, elect to keep the contract alive.

Lloyd J took the view that the amendment specifically required the credit to be opened 'immediately' and that the amendment was not intended to be understood as requiring the buyers to open the credit immediately up to the 15 January and not any later.

Since the date of confirmation required by the amendment had already passed, that could not be complied with but there was no reason why the buyers could not carry out the duty specifically required of them to open the credit immediately.

The buyers had complied with this instruction. The sellers were not entitled to treat the contract as repudiated on 2 March. They had, any event, by their conduct, elected to keep the contract alive.

United City Merchants v Royal Bank of Canada
[1983] 1 AC 168 House of Lords (Lords Diplock, Fraser of Tullybelton, Russell, Scarman and Bridge of Harwich)

• *Payment to be made to beneficiary innocent of fraud*

Facts
The plaintiffs sold manufacturing equipment to a Peruvian company. The parties agreed on a scheme to circumvent exchange control regulations then in force. Payment was to be by documentary credit issued in Peru and confirmed in London by the defendants. Unknown to the plaintiffs the goods were shipped outside the shipping period required

by the credit and independent loading brokers fraudulently inserted an earlier date in the bill. The defendants refused to make payment against the documents when presented by the plaintiffs.

Held
Appeal allowed.

Where a seller wishes to draw on credit he must present the correct documents. If they are correct then the bank is contractually bound to pay against them. This obligation exists independently of alleged breaches of the sale contract. The parties deal in documents and not in goods. The irrevocable documentary credit is intended to give the seller the assurance that he will be paid against correct documents and before he loses control of the goods as represented by those documents.

The general obligation to make payment is subject to the qualification that the bank need not pay against documents which the seller fraudulently presents in order to obtain payment, those documents containing expressly or by implication material representations of fact which he knows to be untrue: *Sztejn* v *J Henry Schroder Banking Corpn* (1941) 31 NYS 2d 631. The unscrupulous and dishonest seller should not be allowed to rely on the irrevocability of the credit to carry out a fraud.

In this case, however, the fraud was not perpetrated by the seller but by a third party. The seller was ignorant of it. The bank contended that if the documents contain a misstatement of a material fact then they need not pay and knowledge on the part of the beneficiary is irrelevant. If that was so the exception in favour of fraud would be irrelevant. If there was fraud and the seller beneficiary was not a party to it then he was entitled to payment. The general rule that the bank was under a duty to take up documents which conformed on their face with the credit, was subject only to the exception of fraud but not, as here, fraud of which the seller was innocent.

The question should be left open as to what would happen if a document presented by a beneficiary has been forged by a third party and that forgery is such as to make it a nullity and therefore without any value for the purpose of a cash advance by the confirming bank. That was not the case here – the bill of lading was valid and transferable receipt despite the fact that it had the wrong date. It was still evidence of the contract of carriage.

Comment
It is now accepted that if the beneficiary is a party to the fraud, the bank should not pay. This case however leaves open the question of what makes the beneficiary 'a party' to the fraud. Also left open is the question of what should happen if a beneficiary presents a forged document to the bank. Fraud therefore remains a difficult issue for a bank when dealing with documents under a letter of credit. It is difficult to obtain an injunction to prevent payment under a letter of credit if fraud is merely alleged: see *Discount Records Ltd* v *Barclays Bank Ltd* [1975] 1 All ER 1071 (above). It may be possible to get a freezing injunction to freeze the proceeds of the letter of credit until the fraud issue is heard at full trial, but only if there is a pre-existing cause of action: see *The Veracruz I* [1992] 1 Lloyd's Rep 353.

3 Bills of Lading

Annefield, The [1971] 1 Lloyd's Rep 1 Court of Appeal (Lord Denning MR and Phillimore LJ)

• *The words 'all disputes under this contract' are ineffective to incorporate an arbitration clause into contract contained in bill of lading*

Facts
Goods were damaged in the course of transit. The arbitration in the charterparty provided that 'all disputes arising out of this contract should be referred to arbitration'. The incorporation clause provided that 'all the terms, conditions, and exceptions of the charterparty including the negligence clause are incorporated herewith'.

The cargo owners failed to institute arbitration proceedings. Some five years after the discharge of the goods they issued a writ and the shipowner applied for a stay of proceedings.

Held
The Court of Appeal granted the shipowner a stay of proceedings.

There was no specific incorporation of the arbitration clause in the bill of lading. Therefore, there could only be effective incorporation of the arbitration clause into the bill of lading if the clause in the charterparty itself made provision to do so. This had not been done. The words 'all disputes under this contract' in the arbitration clause referred to the charterparty contract and did not amount to an express incorporation.

Phillimore LJ described the decision in *The Merak* (see below) as 'unusual' but the court nonetheless substantially took up Russell LJ's reasoning and applied his test.

Lord Denning proposed amended to the test:

'I would follow the test laid down by Lord Justice Russell in *The Merak* ... but I would adapt it slightly. I would say that a clause which is directly germane to the subject-matter of the bill of lading (that is to the shipment, carriage and delivery of goods) can and should be incorporated into the bill of lading contract, even though it may involve a degree of manipulation of the words in order to fit exactly the bill of lading. But if the clause is one which is not thus directly germane, it should not be incorporated into the bill of lading contract unless it is done explicitly in clear words either in the bill of lading or in the charterparty.'

Comment
The notion that there may be 'a degree of manipulation of the words' where the shipment is directly germane to the shipment, carriage and delivery came under scrutiny in *Miramar Maritime Corporation* v *Holborn Oil Trading Ltd* [1984] 1 AC 676 (HL).

Diamond Alkali Export Corporation v F L Bourgeois [1921] 3 KB 443 King's Bench Division (McCardie J)

• *Nature of proper bill of lading and policy of marine insurance*

Facts
Goods sold cif Gothenburg were shipped from

an American port. The sellers tendered, along with an invoice:

1. a document purporting to be a bill of lading containing the notation 'Received in apparent good order and condition … to be transported by the SS Anglia, now lying in the port of Philadelphia … or failing shipment by said steamer in and upon a following steamer …';
2. a certificate of insurance issued by an American insurance company, which, as the certificate declared, 'represents and takes the place of the policy and conveys all the rights of the signed policy holder … as fully as if the property was covered by a special policy direct to the holder of the certificate.'

It was provided that payment would be made against documents under a confirmed letter of credit. The documents were rejected by the buyer.

Held

The documents were properly rejected by the buyer in that:

1. What purported to be a bill of lading was really not one at all. For a document to be considered a bill of lading, it must state that the goods were actually shipped on board a named vessel. The 'received for shipment' form will not suffice. Ample authority starting from the case of *Lickbarrow* v *Mason* (1787) Term Rep 685 made that point abundantly clear.
2. The certificate of insurance was not a proper insurance document for tender under a cif contract. What English law requires, as contrasted to American law, is a policy of insurance. A consistent line of authority is cited to the effect that a mere statement by the seller that it holds the buyer covered under a named policy of insurance will not suffice under English law.

Comment

This case revisits and reaffirms just what con-

stitutes a good tender of documents under English law. They are no less than a shipped bill of lading and a policy of insurance. Lesser documents need not be accepted by the buyer. However, if the contract of sale provides that certificates of insurance may be tendered instead of the actual policy itself, the seller may then tender such certificates. It should be noted that under the Uniform Customs and Practice for Documentary Credits (No 500), insurance certificates may be tendered for the purpose of receiving payment under a documentary credit, and where floating policies of marine insurance are used, the tender of certificates making reference to the policy under which they were issued is acceptable.

Federal Bulk Carriers Inc v C Itoh & Co Ltd, The Federal Bulker
[1989] 1 Lloyd's Rep 103 Court of Appeal (Dillon, Bingham and Butler-Sloss LJJ)

• *Ineffective incorporation of arbitration clause into contract contained in bill of lading*

Facts

The owner of The Federal Bulker let it on a voyage charter to the charterer. The bills of lading issued under it were negotiated to Itoh. They had been issued in the normal course in the form envisaged by the charterparty and contained an incorporation clause which stated, 'All terms and conditions and exceptions as per charterparty … and any addenda thereto to be considered as incorporated herein as if fully written.' The arbitration clause in the charterparty referred to 'all disputes arising out of this contract'.

On taking delivery of a cargo of soya beans, Itoh complained of damage to that cargo and brought arbitration proceedings against the shipowners. The shipowners sought a declaration that the arbitration clause was not incorporated in the bills of lading.

Held

The incorporation clause in the bill of lading was insufficient to incorporate a charterparty arbitration clause. The decision in *The Varenna* [1983] 2 Lloyd's Rep 592 makes it clear that the court's task is to ascertain the intentions of the parties as expressed in the written document and that the court is not in any way concerned to construe the charterparty or ascertain the intentions of the parties to that contract save in so far as the terms of the charterparty have been effectively incorporated in the bill of lading contract. If the language of the incorporation clause is too general and fails to state what it is that is to be incorporated, the terms of the charterparty will not be incorporated into the bill of lading contract.

Bingham LJ:

'I deal at the outset with a point strongly made by Mr Hirst for the cargo-owners in reliance on the words in the bill of lading "as if fully written". Those are words not found, I think, in any of the decided cases and it was submitted by Mr Hirst that their presence strengthened the case for incorporation.

For my part, I cannot agree. It is clear beyond argument, whether expressly stated in the bill of lading or not, that any provision which is incorporated is to be treated as if fully written. But an express statement to this effect does not, in my judgment, assist in determining what is to be incorporated and what is not.'

The matters stated to be incorporated did not include the term 'clauses' and instead stated 'terms, conditions and exceptions'. The arbitration clause was not an 'exception' in the charterparty so that part of the incorporation clause was of no meaning here. The question, therefore, was whether an arbitration clause could be said to either a 'term' or a 'condition'. The Court took the view that the test laid down by the House of Lords in *Thomas* v *Portsea* [1912] AC 1 and the later authorities that had relied on that test, supported neither of these interpretations. There could be no

argument that the words in question had been used in a different context. The authorities were clear that general language of the kind used in this incorporation clause was not sufficient to incorporate an arbitration clause.

The language of the arbitration clause itself was also held inapt for incorporation in a bill of lading.

Bingham LJ:

'Looking at the incorporating words and cl 11 alone, this Court is I think bound to conclude that the cargo owners cannot show that cl 11 should be incorporated, because the incorporating words and the arbitration clause in the charterparty are exactly the same as those in *The Annefield* [1971] 1 Lloyd's Rep 1 where the Court of Appeal held affirming Mr Justice Brandon, that the arbitration clause was not incorporated. ...

In this case the words in the charterparty are "any disputes under this contract". Those words, in this context, meant: "under this charterparty contract". They do not include the bill of lading contract. In any case they are not so explicit as to bring in disputes under the bill of lading.'

Comment

The test for the incorporation of an arbitration clause is strictly applied. The rational for this is commercial necessity. The bill of lading is a negotiable commercial instrument and it may come into the hands of a holder who has no knowledge and no ready means of knowledge of the terms of the charterparty. If the parties desire to bring in an arbitration clause, it must be done explicitly in one document or the other. To be sure, they should spell out the arbitration clause in the bill of lading.

Golodetz (M) & Co Inc v *Czarnikow-Rionda Co Inc, The Galatia* [1980] 1 All ER 501 Court of Appeal (Megaw, Shaw and Walter LJJ)

• *The test for a 'clean' bill of lading is not whether it would be acceptable to a bank under a documentary credit advice – the bill must not qualify that the goods are in apparent good order and condition*

Facts

The sellers had agreed to sell sugar c & f free out of Iran and chartered a vessel to carry the sugar from Kandia in India to Iran. Four days after the vessel had arrived in Kandia, and when the sugar was partly loaded, fire broke out, destroying 200 tonnes of it. The remainder of the sugar was carried to its destination.

Under the terms of the contract of sale the sellers were entitled to be paid the price on tender of a clean 'on board' bill of lading. Instead of tendering one set of bills of lading to the buyers as originally intended by the parties, the sellers tendered two bills of lading; one in respect of the 200 tonnes of sugar which had been lost and the other in respect of the balance of the consignment. They were in the standard form, which by printed clauses acknowledged the shipment of sugar in apparent good order and condition. The bill relating to the lost sugar had added to it a typewritten notation stating that the cargo covered by the bill had been discharged because it had been damaged by fire and/or water.

The buyers accepted the bill relating to the delivered sugar but rejected the bill of lading relating to the lost sugar on the ground that it was not a 'clean' bill of lading and that the loss of the sugar should fall on the sellers. The sellers claimed that the typewritten note did not prevent it being a clean bill of lading and that they were entitled to be paid the price of the 200 tonnes of sugar which had been lost.

Held

Appeal dismissed. Decision of Donaldson J [1979] 2 All ER 726 affirmed.

The bill of lading was 'clean' and the buyers should have accepted it. There was nothing in it to qualify the admission that *at the time of shipment* the goods were in apparent good order and condition.

While there was a further requirement in law that to be 'clean' a bill of lading must be a document that would ordinarily and properly be accepted in the trade as being a merchantable document, there was no evidence to suggest that this particular bill with its typewritten notation would not have been accepted in the trade as being an appropriate document.

Megaw LJ:

'I have no doubt but that the learned judge was right in saying that, on the correct approach in law, this bill of lading, with the typewritten notation on it, is a "clean" bill of lading in the proper sense of that word; and therefore, if indeed the arbitrators' finding that it was not a "clean" bill of lading is a finding which has got to be treated as using the word "clean" in its proper legal sense, the arbitrators had erred in law. That is the view the learned judge took.

However, counsel for the buyers, as I have said, submits that, on the construction of the award as a whole and by reference to various documents which passed between the parties, and, I think he also submits, as a matter of ordinary good sense, the arbitrators ought, by way of necessary inference, to be taken as saying that the bill of lading was not "clean" in the sense that it was not a document which would ordinarily and properly have been accepted in the trade as being an appropriate document. That there is such a requirement in relation to bills of lading is, I think, sufficiently clear. The authority in that regard which is usually quoted, and which was quoted by the learned judge in this case, is a passage from the speech of Lord Sumner in *Hansson v Hamel & Horley Ltd* ([1922] 2 AC 36 at 46, [1922] All ER Rep 237 at 241). The passage cited by the learned judge contains these words:

"These documents have to be handled by banks, they have to be taken up or rejected promptly and without any opportunity for prolonged inquiry, they have to be such as can be re-tendered to sub-purchasers, and it is essential that they should so conform to the accustomed shipping documents as to be reasonably and readily fit to pass current in commerce."

Donaldson J unreservedly accepted that

proposition. He said that if the arbitrators had found that a bill of lading in this form was not acceptable in the trade his decision "would, of course, have been differen". In that event he would have upheld their decision on this issue. But the learned judge found himself unable to take the view that that was what the arbitrators were to be treated as having said, either by the words that they used or by any inference that could properly be drawn in respect of them from the award as a whole or any relevant matters referred to therein. ...

... In my judgment, accepting the conclusion of the learned judge, the arbitrators here must be taken, incorrectly as a matter of law, to have held that the bill of lading in question was not '"lean" by reason of the notation referred to.'

Comment

The buyers had submitted that there was a practical and a legal test. The practical test founded on whether the bill of lading in this form would be acceptable to the banks generally as a 'clean' bill of lading and this was dismissed as not being the true test for a 'clean' bill both by Donaldson J and the Court of Appeal. Donaldson J defined the legal test in the following terms:

'As between the shipowner and the shipper the crucial time is shipment. The shipowner's prime obligation is to deliver the goods at the contractual destination in the like good order and condition as when shipped. The cleanliness of the bill of lading may give rise to an estoppel and the terms of the bill of lading contract may exempt the shipowner from a breach of this obligation, but everything stems from the state of the goods as shipped. As between the seller and cif or c & f buyer the property and risk normally pass upon the negotiation of the bill of lading but do so as from shipment. Thus, the fact that the ship and the goods have been lost after shipment ... is no reason for refusing to take and pay for the documents. ...

The bill of lading ... casts no doubt whatsoever on the condition of the goods at [the time of shipment] and does not assert that

at that time the shipowner had any claim whatsoever against the goods. It follows that in my judgment this bill of lading, unusual though it is, passes the test of cleanliness.'

Gullischen v *Stewart Brothers*
(1884) 13 QBD 317 Court of Appeal
(Lord Coleridge CJ, Brett MR and
Bowen LJ)

• *Obligation in charterparty on consignee relating to carriage and discharge of goods was incorporated into bill of lading*

Facts

The defendant shipper was issued with two sets of bills of lading as shipper of the goods and as consignee. The bills provided that the holder of the bill should pay 'freight (and demurrage) and all other conditions as per charterparty).'

A clause in the charterparty provided for cessation of shipper's liability as follows:

' ... as this charterparty is entered into by the charterers on account of another party their liability ceases as soon as the cargo is on board, the vessel holding a lien upon the cargo for freight and demurrage.'

The vessel was delayed at the port of discharge and the shipowner brought an action for demurrage.

Held

The plaintiff was entitled to maintain the action for demurrage. The contract in the bill of lading and the contract in the charterparty were consistent as to demurrage at the port of discharge; it was an obligation on the consignee of the goods. That obligation was incorporated into the bill of lading since it incorporated all the conditions of the charterparty applicable to the receipt of goods at the port of discharge. The cessation clause had not been incorporated into the bill of lading; it had to be rejected as inapplicable in reading the bill of lading.

Brett MR:

'In all probability the defendants would have been liable for demurrage upon the charterparty if it had contained no clause for cesser of liability; but that clause is inserted and their liability would have ceased if they had done nothing more than load the ship. They took, however, two sets of bills of lading. The contract by a bill of lading is different from a contract by charterparty, and the defendants are sued upon the contract contained in the bill of lading. It would be absurd to suppose that their liability upon the bills of lading would cease upon the loading of the cargo. What is their liability upon the loading of the cargo? It is to pay freight and "other conditions as per charterparty". Upon the terms of the charterparty the consignees were to pay demurrage at a certain rate; that is a condition which is incorporated in the bills of lading. But the clause as to cesser of the charterer's liability is not incorporated ... but the contracts in the charterparty and in the bill of lading are consistent as to demurrage.'

Kum and Another v *Wah Tat Bank and Another* [1971] 1 Lloyd's Rep 439 Privy Council (Lords Upjohn, Devlin and Pearson)

• *Mate's receipt can be document of title*

Facts

T Ltd had shipped rubber from Sarawak to Singapore. The shipments were financed by W Bank against bills of exchange and mate's receipts issued by the charterers of the vessels which carried the goods. The consignee of the goods was stated on the mate's receipt as being O Bank, agents for W Bank.

Upon arrival of the goods, the charterers released them to T Ltd who did not produce the mate's receipt and managed to obtain the goods by giving indemnities to the charterer.

W and O Banks claimed for conversion of the goods which they said were wrongly released. They said that the mate's receipts were equivalent to documents of title because it was trade custom to treat them as such.

Therefore, since the O Bank was named as consignee in the mate's receipts, the defendants were estopped from denying their right to the goods.

The Malaysia Court of Appeal had held that a document of title to goods could be created by trade custom and it had been shown that in this area of trade between Singapore and Sarawak a mate's receipt was equally used as a document of title in the same way as a bill of lading. This was not affected by the fact that the mate's receipt had the words 'not negotiable' written on it.

Whilst they accepted that where there was trade custom supporting the treatment of mate's receipts as documents of title, which was neither uncertain nor an unreasonable practice, in these circumstances the mate's receipts could not constitute a document of title as it bore the words 'not negotiable'.

Held

The Privy Council upheld the Court of Appeal on the ground that the shipment of the goods constituted a delivery to the ship as bailee for the banks, thereby pledging the goods to the banks.

Lord Devlin:

'The form of mate's receipt used is similar to a bill of lading and there is no difficulty about treating it as an equivalent ... it is quite a natural development, first for the mate's receipt to become more elaborate and then for merchants to feel that in certain cases, the bill of lading can be dispensed with ... but where the words "NOT NEGOTIABLE" ... are part of the printed form, their presence on a mate's receipt which is to be used simply as such, may be superfluous but it is not incongruous. The only meaning whether it be a popular or a legal meaning, that can be given to this marking is that the document is not to pass title by endorsement and delivery ...

The rule is plain and clear that inconsistency with the document defeats the custom ... whichever way the argument for the

respondents is put, it amounts in the end to a submission that the force of custom should expel from the document words that are on it; this is not permissible by law ...'

Comment
It is of course usually the bill of lading that is seen as a document of title: see *Lickbarrow* v *Mason* (1787) 2 Term Rep 63. As multi-modal transport develops new documents are introduced which perhaps will become more common than the traditional bill of lading. *Kum* v *Wah Tat Bank* demonstrates that the courts are willing to consider other documents if commercial usage requires this. Developments are also taking place as a result of the UN Convention on Multimodal Transport and the ICC Rules on Multimodal Transport Documents.

Leduc & Co v *Ward and Others*
(1888) 20 QBD 475 Court of Appeal (Lord Esher MR and Fry LJ)

- *Construction of liberty to deviate clause*

Facts
The plaintiffs (endorsees of a bill of lading) shipped 3,123 bags of rape seed onto a ship owned by the defendants from the port of Fiume to Dunkirk. The bill of lading provided that the ship had 'liberty to call at any ports in any order, and to deviate for the purpose of saving life or property'. After commencement of the voyage, the ship deviated 1,200 miles to Glasgow and was lost with all cargo by reason of perils of the sea.

The plaintiffs sued the defendants for non-delivery of the goods and evidence was admitted to show that at the time the bill of lading was issued, the plaintiffs knew that the ship was intended to proceed to Glasgow.

Held
Such evidence was not admissible to vary the terms of the bill of lading which called for a voyage direct from Fiume to Dunkirk, subject to the liberty to call at ports substantially

within the course of the voyage. Glasgow being totally out of that route, was not such a port. The ship, therefore, was lost while deviating from the route contracted for and the excepted perils clause (including perils of the sea) did not exonerate the defendants from liability as to non-delivery of the goods.

As expressed by Lord Esher MR, at p481:

' ... if the only voyage mentioned is from the port of shipment to the port of destination, it must be a voyage on the ordinary track by sea of the voyage from the one place to the other. So here, if the description of the voyage had been merely from Fiume to Dunkirk. I think the contract would have been for a voyage on the ordinary sea track of a voyage from Fiume to Dunkirk, and any departure from that track in the absence of necessity would be a deviation.'

Comment
This basic and often relied upon case established that liberty clauses in contracts of carriage would be narrowly construed. The deviations allowed would be only ones along the ordinary sea track of the voyage contracted for, and that track would be determined by whether it was a sailing ship or a motor vessel as well as geographical considerations.

Merak, The [1964] 2 Lloyd's Rep 527 Court of Appeal (Sellers, Davies and Russell LJJ)

- *Incorporation of charterparty arbitration clause into contract contained in bill of lading*

Facts
The plaintiffs' timber was shipped under a bill of lading which stated that the voyage was 'as per charterparty dated the 21st April'. The bill contained a clause incorporating 'all the terms, conditions, clauses and exceptions ... contained in the said charterparty'. The terms of the charterparty included an arbitration clause.

In the course of the voyage the cargo was damaged. The plaintiffs, who were indorsees of the bill of lading, were unaware of the arbitration clause in the bill of lading and eventually brought a court action for cargo damage. The writ was issued just within the 12-month period of the discharge of the goods. The shipowner, relying on the arbitration clause alleged to be incorporated in the bill of lading, and, therefore, on s4 Arbitration Act 1950, moved for a stay of proceedings. In opposition to the application the plaintiffs relied, as one of their grounds, on the claim that there was an ineffective incorporation of the arbitration clause into the bill of lading.

Held

The arbitration clause was incorporated into the bill of lading and, therefore, a stay should be granted.

The incorporation clause itself did not refer to cl 32, the arbitration clause, but the Court nonetheless found it to be sufficiently widely drafted to be effective to incorporate the arbitration clause from the charterparty. Indeed, their Lordships took the view that the incorporating language was very comprehensive. Russell LJ described it as being language of 'the most ample width possible to imagine', and Davies LJ described it as 'all embracing'. This was in part because cl 32 of the charterparty itself expressly applied to disputes arising out of the bill of lading by stating that 'any dispute arising out of this charterparty or any bill of lading issued hereunder, shall be referred to arbitration'. This left no doubt that both the charter and the bill of lading issued under it were subject to the clause. On this point the Court distinguished the House of Lords decision in *Thomas v Portsea Steamship Co Ltd* [1912] AC 1. In that case there was a similarly wide incorporation clause which made no mention of the arbitration, but the wording of the arbitration clause in the charterparty contained a significant difference to that in the instant case. It provided that 'any dispute or claim arising out of any of the conditions of this charter shall ... be

settled by arbitration'. It referred, therefore, only to disputes under the charter. These words, even when taken together with the general words of incorporation in the bill of lading, were insufficient to subject disputes arising out of the bill of lading contract to arbitration.

Russell LJ:

'I think the true view of *Thomas v Portsea* is that it shows that clauses which are directly germane to shipment, carriage and delivery may be incorporated by general words though the fact that they are found in the charterparty may involve a degree of verbal manipulation to fit exactly a bill of lading, but that where there is a clause whose subject matter is not thus directly germane such as an arbitration clause, it is not permissible to construe general words of incorporation as extending to a clause, which does not in terms relate to a bill of lading.'

A different issue was that it was too late for the plaintiffs to start arbitration proceedings. Commencement of an arbitration is a 'suit' and instituting proceedings under an arbitration agreement is equivalent to bringing an action for the purposes of art III(6) Hague-Visby Rules, with the result that it is subject to the limit on actions of one year from the time when the goods were or should have been delivered.

Comment

The Merak is authority for the proposition that reference to 'clauses' is enough at the first stage to permit incorporation of an aptly drafted arbitration clause but subsequent authorities suggest that the decision is confined to its own special facts. The test laid down by Russell LJ has been followed, and adapted, in later cases: see, for example, *Federal Bulk Carriers v C Itoh & Co Ltd, The Federal Bulker* [1989] 1 Lloyd's Rep 103 (above), *The Annefield* [1971] 1 Lloyd's Rep 1 (above), *Miramar Maritime Corporation v Holborn Oil Trading Ltd* [1984] 1 AC 676 (HL). Arbitration clauses are traditionally given a restrictive interpretation and the courts look for an explicit and precise incorporation of it. A bill of lading is a negotiable instrument and a holder in course may have limited knowledge of its terms: see Bingham LJ in *Federal Bulk Carriers* v *Itoh, The Federal Bulker*. Certainty is therefore important: see Lord Denning MR in *The Annefield* (above).

Shinhan Bank Ltd v *Sea Containers Ltd & Another* [2000] 2 Lloyd's Rep 406 Queen's Bench Division (Commercial Court) (Longmore J)

• *The term 'clean receipt' is the same as 'clean' for a bill of lading and the issue of false receipts is a deceit*

Facts
The first defendants, Sea Containers Ltd (SCL) purchased 35,000 containers to be manufactured in three separate factories from Win Corporation in China. The arrangement for payment was that Win would present to the bank a draft bill of exchange to be accepted by SCL payable 60 days from bill of lading date, together with SCL invoices and clean receipts evidencing receipt of the containers by SCL. With the knowledge of SCL, Win made arrangements with their bank whereby the bank were prepared to advance the price to Win on that basis on the maturity date of the bill of exchange but before payment by SCL.

SCL issued and signed 'clean receipts' for the containers before the majority of the containers specified in the receipts and accompanying lists had, in fact, been received by them. They did this to enable Win to obtain further supplies from the factory which made the containers. The bank was not told of the variation of the contract. However, Win agreed with SCL that SCL would not have any obligation to pay unless they received the containers and accepted the bills of exchange.

Win presented the documents to the bank and obtained a discounted sum representing the price, but became insolvent before most of the containers specified in the clean receipts were delivered to SCL. SCL refused to accept the relevant bills of exchange in respect of containers not received. The bank brought proceedings against SCL alleging that issue of the clean receipts in respect of containers not actually received was deceit or, alternatively, negligence.

SCL denied fraud claiming:

1. that they did not know the clean receipts were going to be presented to the bank, and
2. that they did not know that the full terms of the contractual relationship between themselves and Win were not to be made known to the Bank.

SCL denied any negligence, asserting that the bank was itself negligent in paying out on the documents without the security of an accepted bill of exchange.

Held
SCL were liable to the bank in deceit and negligence for issuing clean receipts.

On the issue of deceit
Longmore J found that any reasonable businessman would take the receipts as meaning that the containers had been received by or on behalf of SCL:

'... it does not seem to me that any sensible businessman (or even sensible lawyer) would conclude that the words "we acknowledge acceptance of" under the heading "Clean Receipt" would mean "We expect to receive but have not yet received." The obvious conclusion is that, for whatever reason, the place and date of delivery is not stated not that the words mean the opposite of what they say.'

When the receipts were issued SCL had not received the containers. The receipts were, therefore, false. Longmore J had no doubt in his mind that Mr Ward, the employee of SCL who authorised the issue, knew that what they recorded was not in fact true and, in issuing them, was willing that they should be understood as meaning that the containers had been received. The final question to answer was whether Mr Ward knew or intended that the receipts would be shown to and acted upon by Win's bankers. There could be no argument that SCL did not expect the receipts to be presented and paid against. When Mr Ward authorised the issue on behalf of SCL he was aware that the bank were prepared to pay Win against issue of clean receipts before the bills of exchange were accepted. He therefore knew, or should have known as a reasonable businessman, that his authorisation of issue of clean receipts for containers not yet received, and the likely reliance on them by the bank, would result in Win being paid against them before SCL had received the containers. The elements of deceit had thus been established. Ward knew that the receipts would be shown to the bank, that they were false and that the bank would pay against them.

On the issue of whether SCL had been negligent

SCL relied on the test of assumption of responsibility asserting that neither they nor Mr Ward, on their behalf, assumed any responsibility for the correctness of the receipts. Longmore J considered at some length the purpose and status of a document that described itself as a 'clean receipt' and dismissed the defendants assertion that the documents they had issued were in some way of a different class or type to the traditional bill of lading:

'Receipts are commercial documents; any businessman knows that it is irresponsible (to say the least) to issue a receipt for goods which have not, in fact, been received. If a receipt is to be used as part of an international trade transaction, it is even more irresponsible. It is by no means unimportant that these receipts were headed "Clean Receipts". The word "clean" is a well known adjective in commercial documentation as meaning that the document has no qualification or clausing. The commonest qualification or clausing in international trade documents such as receipts relates to the condition of the goods at the time of receipt. If a clean receipt is given that means not merely that the goods have been received but they have been received in good order and condition or apparent good order and condition in the case of goods which cannot be readily examined at the time of receipt.

All this is axiomatic in relation to bills of lading; one of the primary purposes of a bill of lading is for the shipowner to acknowledge receipt of the goods; if he issues a clean bill of lading he is acknowledging the receipt of the goods in apparent good order and condition; that acknowledgement constitutes a representation to the world (and, in particular, to banks) that the goods have been received in that condition ...

The issuer of a receipt assumes a responsibility that it is true so far as he knows .... and if he knows or should know that it will be shown to third parties such as bankers, he is under a duty of reasonable care to ensure that it represents the true facts.'

Longmore J also considered the threefold requirements adopted by Lord Bridge of Harwich in *Smith* v *Bush* [1990] 1 AC 831 and held:

1. it was reasonably foreseeable by Mr Ward that the bank would suffer loss if the receipts were untrue;
2. there was a sufficiently proximate relationship between the bank and SCL; and
3. it is just and reasonable that SCL should owe the bank a duty of care.

Since Mr Ward did not take reasonable care to ensure that the representation that the containers had been received was true and the bank relied on the false clean receipts, the claim in negligence was also made out.

On the issue of whether the bank had been negligent

Any negligence of the bank is no defence to any claim in deceit once the elements of that tort are established but it can, in theory, be relevant to a claim which is itself merely in negligence. The bank relied on the receipts. They had not acted negligently by entering into the documents against acceptance arrangement to make advance payment to Win before the bills of exchange were accepted. Nor were they negligent in failing to compare the false clean receipts with earlier genuine receipts or in not obtaining the security of accepted bills of exchange, and particularly when SCL had approved such arrangement.

Comment

Longmore J's judgment contains a great deal of interesting statement about the purpose of documents in the international trade transaction. It is the veracity of those documents that is vital to the smooth efficient running of international commerce and in this respect Longmore J noted the words of Cresswell J in *Standard Chartered Bank* v *Pakistan National Shipping Corporation (No 2)* [1998] 1 Lloyd's Rep 684; affirmed [2000] 1 Lloyd's Rep 218:

> '… false bills of lading are a cancer in international trade. A bill of lading is issued in international trade with the purpose that it should be relied upon by those into whose hands it properly comes – consignees, bankers and indorsees. A bank … relies on the veracity and authenticity of the bill. Honest commerce requires that those who put bills of lading into circulation do so only when the bill of lading, as far as they know, represents the true facts.'

Silver v *Ocean Steamship Co Ltd* [1930] 1 KB 416 Court of Appeal (Scrutton, Green and Slesser LJJ)

- *Duty of carrier to inspect goods and unload them carefully*

Facts

By two bills of lading dated 25 May 1927, of which the plaintiffs were endorsees, the defendants acknowledged to have shipped on board their ship two parcels consisting respectively 16,000 and 6,334 tins of frozen eggs for carriage from Shanghai to London. The bills of lading stated that the tins were 'shipped in good order and condition'. Upon arrival and inspection, the plaintiffs claimed that a very

large number of tins were gashed and/or perforated and/or punctured, and the contents had depreciated in value.

The defendants denied that the tins were shipped in good order and condition and denied that they were delivered in any condition other than that in which they were received. The defendants claimed that if any of the tins were delivered damaged, that damage arose or resulted from the act or omission of the shippers, or from the inherent vice or defect of the goods, or from insufficiency of packing.

It was found that many of the cases were dented or perforated, some of the perforations being gashes and some merely pinholes.

As expressed by Scrutton LJ, at p429:

> 'These tins were at first stacked on a wooden tray, with very slight sides. It was found that some tins slid off or fell unpleasantly near the heads of people working below, who not unnaturally protested and the ship adopted a system of discharging in nets. When the tins were first placed in the net the bottom tier stowed flat. But as soon as the net was hoisted the flat tier disappeared and the tins were pressed together. The Chief Officer of the ship admitted that there was a chance of damage at that stage. But when the net was lowered into the lighters and set down the chance of damage became almost a certainty.'

Held

By issuing clean bills of lading, the carrier was estopped from claiming that the goods were received other than in good order and condition, and that by issuing such bills of lading, the carriers were not entitled to claim that the damage was caused by insufficient packing or by the inherent vice or defect of the goods within the meaning of the exceptions provided for by art IV r2 of the Schedule to the Carriage of Goods by Sea Act 1924.

Comment

It must be concluded from this case that:

1. a carrier acts at its peril in issuing a clean

bill of lading in circumstances where a full and proper inspection of the goods is not carried out; and

2. after loading, the carrier owes the shipper a duty of care with regard to the carrying and discharge of the goods. Here, in the process of discharge, to quote one witness, at p438, with reference to the tins they 'shot all over the place when the net opened' and as put by another witness, at the same page, 'when the net opened the tins spilt all over the show'.

SS Ardennes (Cargo Owners) v SS Ardennes (Owners) [1951] 1 KB 55
High Court (Lord Goddard CJ)

• *The parties can reach oral agreement on contract of carriage – bill of lading only evidential agreement*

Facts
The plaintiffs contracted with the defendant carriers for the carriage of 3,000 cases of mandarin oranges on the Ardennes from Cartegena, Spain to London. The bill of lading had a printed clause which contained a liberty to call at intermediate ports, to proceed by any route directly or indirectly and to overcarry. However, in a bid to evade an increase in import duty in England due on 1 December, the plaintiffs reached an oral agreement with the defendants that the vessel proceed directly to London.

In the event, the vessel went via Antwerp and did not arrive at London until 4 December. By this time there was not only the increase in import duty to pay but there had also been a fall in the market price for mandarin oranges. The plaintiffs claimed damages consisting of the loss of profit on the oranges and the amount of extra duty which they had to pay for their importation.

The defendants sought to rely on the liberty clause in the bill of lading, contending that the bill of lading represented the true contract between the parties and that evidence of an oral agreement could not be given where it was inconsistent with the terms of the bill of lading.

Held
Judgment for the plaintiffs.

The bill of lading is only evidence of the contract of carriage. Other evidence could be admissible in rebuttal. The cargo owner was therefore entitled to prove that the contract entered into did in fact contain a term that the voyage would be direct. The carrier was bound by what actually had been agreed verbally and was in breach of that verbal contract.

Lord Goddard:

'I have no hesitation in finding that there was a promise made to the shippers' representative that the ship should go direct to London, and that they shipped in reliance on that promise. I therefore have now to consider the defence which arises out of the terms of the bill of lading ...

It is, I think well settled that a bill of lading is not in itself the contract between the shipowner and the shipper of goods, though it has been said to be excellent evidence of its terms ... The contract has come into existence before the bill of lading is signed by one party only, and handed by him to the shipper, usually after the goods have been put on board. No doubt, if the shipper finds that the bill contains terms with which he is not content, or does not contain some term for which he has stipulated, he might, if there were time, demand his goods back; but he is not in my opinion, for that reason, prevented from giving evidence that there was in fact a contract entered into before the bill of lading was signed, different from that which is contained in the bill of lading or containing some additional term. He is no party to the bill of lading; nor does he sign it. ... the bill of lading is not itself the contract; therefore in my opinion evidence as to the true contract is admissible ...

... the representation that the ship would sail direct to London, would amount to a warranty ... it was a promise that the shipowner would not avail himself of a liberty which would otherwise have been open to him ...'

Trade Star Lines Corporation v *Mitsui & Co Ltd* [1996] 2 Lloyd's Rep 449 Court of Appeal (Evans, Gibson and Brooke LJJ)

• *Mate's receipt and bills of lading both wrongly issued as 'clean' – no indemnity to be implied into the charterparty.*

Facts

The plaintiffs took a time charter of the defendant shipowners vessel, The Arctic Trader. This was on the standard NYPE form and a clause incorporated the Hague Rules into the charterparty and into bills of lading issued under it. The plaintiffs entered into a voyage charterparty with a third party who were sellers of crude salt. Salt shipped by this third party was contaminated by substantial quantities of stone of various sizes, cement, pieces of tarpaulin, and possibly pieces of metal, and this ought to have been sufficiently evident to the master of the ship, an employee of the defendant shipowners, for him to clause the mate's receipts. However, he was persuaded by the shipper's agents to issue 'clean' mate's receipts showing the salt to be 'in apparent good order and condition'. Thereafter, clean bills of lading in accordance with the receipts were issued by other agents of the shipper.

The contamination of the cargo led to difficulties and delays at the first discharging port. The receivers objected to the contaminated condition of the salt and part of the cargo remained on board, and was subsequently discharged with the balance of the cargo at the second discharging port. These delays disrupted the plaintiffs' planned trading programme for the vessel and they suffered consequent loss. The plaintiffs claimed against the defendants for damages on the grounds that there was an implied term in their time charter that the master would issue the receipt correctly, or take reasonable care when issuing

the receipt. This dispute was referred to arbitration and the arbitrators found in favour of the plaintiffs. On appeal, Tuckey J reversed this decision. The plaintiffs now appealed against that decision.

Held

The appeal was dismissed.

The implied term proposed by the plaintiff charterers was not relevant to the terms of their time charterparty. The charterparty and the bills of lading issued under it were expressly made subject to the Hague Rules and therefore to art III r3(3) of those Rules which place the shipper under a duty to issue, on demand, a bill of lading which states "(c) the apparent order and condition of the goods". This requires an accurate statement of fact and amounts to an unqualified or 'absolute' contractual undertaking. Performance of the duty therefore requires more than 'reasonable care' on the part of the shipowner or his master. A term of the type claimed by the plaintiffs would amount to the same absolute contractual undertaking and so be consistent with the duty owed to a shipper when issuing a bill of lading under art III r3(3) of the Hague Rules.

If the time charterer is himself the shipper, then an implied term of the kind suggested by charterers would impose a duty on the master to tell the charterer/shipper what he already knows, namely, the apparent order and condition of the goods which he has shipped. Here the shipper was the voyage charterer of the vessel, but this charter was taken from the plaintiff time charterers who were the party with authority under the charterparty to instruct the master to receive cargo on board. That cargo is loaded by or on behalf of the charterer for the purposes of the charterparty, and a third party shipper should be regarded as the charterer's agent accordingly. It follows from this that whether or not the charterer is also the shipper there is the same objection to implying a term that the master or chief officer will tell the charterer what he already knows, or is deemed to know.

In both cases the charterer's own deemed knowledge of the condition of the salt could be said to be the effective cause of whatever consequences flowed from the misstatement which was made. There may be an argument for saying that a term should be implied in circumstances where the charterer does not, and is unlikely to, know for himself what the apparent order and condition of the goods on shipment was, but that consideration did not arise in this case. Far from requesting the master to sign and issue receipts which contained an accurate statement of the apparent order and condition of the goods, the shippers, or perhaps the charterers' agent, 'persuaded' him to issue receipts which contained an inaccurate statement. When the clean bills of lading were issued, the charterers knew, either themselves or by their agents, including the shippers, that the bills of lading ought to have been claused. In other words, the charterers' losses flowed from the issue of clean bills, which ought to have been claused, and for the purposes of the charterparty that was the responsibility of the charterers themselves. The arbitrator had found, and the Court of Appeal agreed, that the master should have claused the receipts and wrongly failed to do so. However, the Court of Appeal took the opportunity to clarify that in order to imply a term where there is no knowledge on the part of the charterer, it must be clear that the master or chief officer is obliged to sign mate's receipts which state the apparent order and conditions of the goods received on board if requested to do so and if necessary to enable the charterers or their agents to issue bills of lading on behalf of the ship.

A mate's receipt, unlike a bill of lading, does not have a contractual life of its own and has effect only in relation to the charterparty and the shipowner's liabilities as bailee of goods in fact received on board. Under a time charter it acts as a non-negotiable receipt for the goods and delimits the authority which the master or the charterers and their agents have to issue bills of lading on behalf of the vessel. However, cls 8 and 46 of the charterparty provided considerable certainty as to the authorities both of the master and the charterers or their agents to issue bills of lading and, taken together, they clearly envisaged that the master may be requested to issue a mate's receipt and appropriately defined the charterer's right to issue bills of lading on behalf of the master. They ensured that the master was authorised to sign bills 'as presented', and that the charterers, if required, were authorised to sign on behalf of the master, and that in both cases the bills must be in accordance with the mate's receipts.

Comment

Two authorities were considered: *The Almak* [1985] 1 Lloyd's Rep 557 and *The Nogar Marin* [1988] 1 Lloyd's Rep 412. The judgments in both cases were concerned with issues of breach and of causation and of implied indemnities but involved different issues from the present case. The Court of Appeal did not find either case to be inconsistent with the conclusions they had reached.

In *The Almak* a master with authority to sign bills of lading 'as presented' under a voyage charterparty, signed bills presented by independent shippers which bore the wrong date. The charterers alleged that the master's carelessness was in breach of an implied term of the charterparty. Mustill J held that no such term could be implied and in finding that it was just that the charterers should bear the loss he held, inter alia: (1) the master's duty to his employers the shipowners, and possibly to third parties, was not relevant; (2) the term would operate to protect the charterers from the consequences of their own mistake, if they themselves were the shippers, and it should not be implied; (3) they could not be in a better position if the shippers were independent parties; and (4) even if the shipowners were liable, they would be entitled to recover a matching indemnity from the charterers.

In *The Nogar Marin* it was the shipowners who were claiming damages or an indemnity from the charterers alleging that they were in breach of an implied term of the voyage charterparty arising out of the presentation of clean receipts or bills for the master to sign. The charterers had shipped the goods for their own account for which the master issued clean mate's receipts which ought to have been claused. Clean bills of lading were then issued by the ship's (not the charterers') agents. The shipowners suffered loss when the vessel was arrested by receivers who were misled by the clean bills of lading as to the apparent order and condition of the goods. The shipowners' claim failed. Mustill LJ found the mate's receipt to be a simple non-negotiable receipt with no contractual effects and as the charterparty did not stipulate for it to be signed 'as presented' or indeed at all, it was not part of the mechanism established by the charterparty. In the present case the Court of Appeal noted that this was different from the mate's receipt in question since cls 8 and 46 of the charterparty indicated circumstances where the receipt did have a necessary part to play, but pointed out that if that finding was wrong the judgment of Mustill LJ on this point in *The Nogar Marin* provided an additional reason for holding that there is no obligation under the charterparty with regard to signing the receipt.

Waren Import Gesellschaft Krohn & Co v Internationale Graanhandel Thegra NV [1975] 1 Lloyd's Rep 146 Queen's Bench Division (Kerr J)

• *Where a ship's delivery order is permitted by the contract, only documents which perform the functions of a shipped bill of lading as closely as possible will be good tender*

Facts
The sellers agreed to sell certain quantities of Thailand manioc chips cif Rotterdam. Payment was to be cash against documents. The shipping documents were to include a full set of 'on board bills of lading and/or ship's delivery orders'.

The sellers shipped one cargo load of chips. They then wished to perform their obligations to the buyers by splitting the bill of lading and tendering to the buyers delivery orders which were addressed to the agents of an associated company (T Co) of the sellers at Rotterdam asking them to deliver the chips to the order of the sellers. The buyers rejected the delivery orders on the ground that they were not ship's delivery orders as required by the contract and refused to pay the price.

Held
The delivery orders which had been tendered fell far short of what was required. First, they were addressed to persons who were not in possession of the goods. Second, they contained no undertaking by anyone that the goods would be delivered to the buyers but merely an instruction to the addressee to deliver the goods to the order of the sellers.

Kerr J:

'In *The Julia* [1949] AC 293 a cif contract entitled the sellers to tender delivery orders instead of bills of lading. While the goods were still in transit the sellers tendered a delivery order addressed to their agents at the port of discharge, and the buyers accepted and paid against this document because of a long prior course of dealing between the parties. The document was in fact more favourable to the buyers than the delivery orders in the present case in that (a) it instructed the agents to deliver the goods to the buyers or to the bearer of the document whereas the present delivery orders instruct the agents to deliver the goods to the order of the sellers, and (b) before transmission to the buyers the delivery order was endorsed by the agents with an undertaking that they would honour its terms, which is absent in the present case. Despite these features and despite the long prior course of dealing on the basis of such documents between the parties it was unanimously held by the House of Lords that the document was not good tender under the contract and that upon the seller's failure to deliver the goods to them the buyers were entitled to recover the price they had paid ...

... I do not think it is necessary or desirable to attempt to define "ship's delivery order" exhaustively. They must, however, in my judgment be documents issued by or on behalf of shipowners while the goods are in their possession or at least under their control and containing some form of undertaking that they will be delivered to the buyers (or perhaps to bearer) on presentation of the documents. If they contain such an undertaking, then it appears to me to be irrelevant whether the documents were originally issued by the shipowners or their agents, or whether they began their life by being addressed to the shipowners or their agents with instructions to deliver to the buyers followed by a re-issue of the documents by the shipowners or their agents incorporating such an undertaking. In either event such documents will attain as far as is possible the object of a cif contract performable by means of ship's delivery orders by placing the buyers as nearly as possible in the same position as if they had been given bills of lading ...'

Comment

See *Comptoir d'Achat* v *Luis de Ridder, The Julia* [1949] AC 293 referred to by Kerr J above which found that on the basis of the documents tendered the contract, although purporting to be cif, was in fact not.

4 Carriage of Goods by Sea (1): Charterparties

Ben Shipping Co Ltd v *An Bord Bainne, The C Joyce* [1986] 2 All ER 177; [1986] 2 Lloyd's Rep 285 Queen's Bench Division (Commercial Court) (Bingham J)

• *There is no breach of contract if the shipper presents to the master for signature a bill of lading which conforms with the terms of the contract*

Facts

The owners of The C Joyce let her to the charterers under a voyage charterparty on the Gencon form for the carriage of a cargo of dried milk powder from Amsterdam to South Africa. The charterparty contained a clause that the shipowners were not to be liable for any loss or damage to the cargo even if caused by the negligent navigation of the master. However, the bills of lading to be issued under the charterparty were to contain a clause subjecting the voyage and therefore the contract to the Hague-Visby Rules (a clause paramount). Bills of lading in accordance with the charterparty were presented by the shippers to the master who duly signed them.

On discharge of the vessel in South Africa claims were made by the holders of the bills of lading alleging damage to the cargo and short delivery. In due course proceedings were issued in South Africa. The shipowners settled the cargo owner's claims and then sought an indemnity from the charterer. They based their argument on the fact that cl 2 of the Gencon charter gave them a defence to any cargo claims brought against them by the charterers, other than those arising out of unseaworthiness.

Held

Bingham J rejected the shipowners argument and held that cl 2 of the Gencon form gave the shipowners no rights of indemnity against the charterer.

It was clearly stated that the bills of lading signed under the charter should include a clause subjecting the contract to the Rules. The shipowner was therefore expressly subject to the liability imposed by the Rules to an indorsee of the bills of lading, and if the shipowners wanted an indemnity from the charterers in that eventuality they should have asked for one in the charterparty.

In order to recover an indemnity the shipowners have to establish that the charterers gave the order in breach of the charter. Since the contract terms contained no hint that the parties intended the owners to be indemnified, and the implication of such a term was not necessary to give the contract business efficacy, there was no ground for the implication of an indemnity clause into the charterparty.

Bingham J:

'The charterers were not in breach of contract in tendering for signature bills containing a clause paramount. They would strictly have been in breach had they issued bills in any other form. By the same token the charterers did not request the owners to do anything which the owners had not expressly bound themselves to do. I find nothing in the ratio of the authorities which helps the owner here.'

He distinguished *Krüger & Co Ltd* v *Moel Tryvan Ship Co Ltd* [1907] AC 272 (see below). The shipowner had argued that the

Krüger right to an indemnity ought to be implied into the charterparty. However, in that case the charterers were in breach of the charterparty by tendering a bill of lading which conflicted with the terms of the charterparty, whereas in the present case the charterers were obliged to tender a bill of lading which imposed the liability of the Hague-Visby Rules on the shipowner.

Bingham J:

' ... the first ground of liability depends on a finding that the charterers were in breach of contract in tendering bills for signature which conflicted with their obligations under the charterparty. Crucial to both grounds of decision was the finding of disparity between the bills which the charterers were under the charterparty entitled to present. From this finding the conclusion naturally follows, and it matters little whether the owners claim damages for breach of contract of which an indemnity will be the measure, or an indemnity arising from the loss which they have suffered from complying with the charterers' request to do something which they were not obliged to do under the charterparty.'

Comment

The findings of Bingham J were approved in *The Nogar Marin* [1988] 1 Lloyd's Rep 412.

Eridania SpA v *Rudolf A Oetker and Others, The Fjord Wind* [2000] 2 All ER (Comm) 108 Court of Appeal (Clarke and Stuart-Smith LJJ, Sir Murray Waller)

• *Obligation as to seaworthiness under voyage charter*

Facts

The Fjord Wind was chartered to Oetker under a time charter and then voyage chartered by them to Eridania for the carriage of soya beans. While on a voyage under the latter charter, The Fjord Wind experienced serious engine problems and was eventually put out of action for three months. The owners gave notice to the holders of the bill of lading and the sub-charterers that the voyage had been frustrated. The cargo was transhipped into a substitute vessel.

The cargo owners brought a claim against Oetker and the shipowners for the consequent delay and expense on the basis of cls 1 and 35 of the charterparty which had been incorporated into the bill of lading. Clause 1 stated:

'That the said vessel, being tight, staunch and strong and in every way fit for the voyage, shall with all convenient speed proceed to [the River Plate] ... and there load ...'

Clause 35 stated:

'Owners shall be bound before and at the beginning of the voyage to exercise due diligence to make the ship seaworthy and to have her properly manned, equipped and supplied ... '

In respect of cl 1 the cargo owners claimed

1. that there was an absolute warranty that the vessel was seaworthy at the beginning of the approach voyage;
2. that the vessel was not seaworthy at that time; and
3. that a breach of warranty was caused by the loss because it was the same unseaworthiness which caused the subsequent breakdown of the vessel and its consequences.

The shipowners contended that cl 1 must be read in the light of cl 35 and that, so construed, the owners' obligation was to exercise due diligence to make the vessel seaworthy so that the nature of the obligation at each stage was the same.

Moore-Bick J ([1999] 1 Lloyd's Rep 307) gave judgment for the cargo interests, holding that the vessel was unseaworthy and that the shipowners had failed to show that they had exercised due diligence. He also found that the shipowners' obligation as to seaworthiness in cl 1 of the charter was qualified so far as the laden voyage was concerned by cl 35 which required Oetker only to exercise due diligence.

The shipowners appealed.

Held

Appeal dismissed.

Cls 1 and 35 had to be taken together to ascertain the intention of the parties.

Clarke LJ commented that it was settled law that:

> '... particular terms of a contract must be construed in the context of the contract as a whole and that all contracts must be construed in their factual matrix or against their surrounding circumstances.'

Accordingly, cl 1 did not stand alone. It imposed a more onerous obligation than cl 35 and was intended to govern the shipowners' obligations during the period prior to the commencement of loading rather than thereafter. It was cl 35 that governed the shipowner's obligations thereafter and the operation of this clause affected the whole operation of cl 1.

Clarke LJ:

> 'If there were no cl 35 it is likely that it would be held that there was an absolute warranty that the vessel should be seaworthy for both the approach voyage and loading.
>
> Yet on any view cl 35 expressly applies "before and at the beginning of the voyage", which must include the loading process. the owners must exercise due diligence to make her seaworthy for the loading process and thereafter they must exercise due diligence to make her seaworthy for the cargo-carrying voyage itself. It follows that cl 35 directly affects the true construction of cl 1 and the question arises whether it was intended to affect the whole operation of the clause. In my judgment, it was. The expression "before and at the beginning of the voyage" is apt to include the whole period before the beginning of the voyage.'

Oetker's obligations in relation to seaworthiness before the approach voyage were not absolute under cl 1 but were limited to an obligation to exercise due diligence before and at the beginning of the cargo-laden voyage. That this reflected the intentions that the parties could be said to have, was to be found in the assumption that they would not have expected a different regime for cargo damage under the charter and bill of lading and would have expected a Hague or Hague-Visby Rules regime to have applied and not an absolute warranty of seaworthiness. Clarke LJ:

> 'It seems to me to be most unlikely that the parties intended liability for damage to cargo caused by unseaworthiness to be different under the charter and under the bill of lading, in circumstances where the bill of lading expressly incorporates all the terms conditions and exceptions of the charter. Yet that would be the effect of accepting the plaintiffs' construction, unless it were held that cl 1 of the charter were incorporated into the bill of lading, which I agree with the judge it was not because, in so far as it is concerned with the approach voyage, it is not germane to the loading and carriage of the cargo.'

Oetker's obligation of seaworthiness was at all stages the same, namely to exercise due diligence to make the vessel seaworthy. Clarke LJ said:

> '... it is extremely unlikely that the parties would have agreed a different regime for cargo damage under the bill of lading and the charterparty. They would be expected to apply a Hague or Hague-Visby Rules regime and not to have agreed an absolute warranty of seaworthiness. In particular they would not be likely to have agreed a different regime for different voyages which were both subject to the same contract in respect of which the charterers were to pay freight.
>
> ... I have reached the conclusion that the correct construction of cls 1 and 35 of the charter when read together in the context of the contract as a whole and in the light of the commercial considerations to which I have referred is that the disponent owners' obligation as to seaworthiness at each stage was the same, namely to exercise due diligence to make the vessel seaworthy.'

The Fjord Wind was unseaworthy when she left the port of loading. The issue of seaworthiness was concerned with the state of the vessel rather than with whether owners acted prudently or with due diligence. The crankpin bearing that failed only hours after putting to sea was the defect that resulted in the engine failure, and when the vessel left the port of loading she was not fit to withstand an ordinary voyage down river. Clarke LJ:

'I agree with the judge that seaworthiness is concerned with the state of the vessel rather than with whether the owners acted prudently or with due diligence. The only relevance of the standard of the reasonably prudent owner is to ask whether, if he had known of the defect, he would have taken steps to rectify it. In the instant case, there can I think be no doubt that he would, if he had known that there was a defect which would cause the bearing to fail as it did, which it seems to me is the relevant state of knowledge for these purposes. It follows that the vessel was unseaworthy when she left Rosario because she was not in a fit condition to withstand an ordinary voyage down the River Parana.'

The owners knew that there was something wrong with the vessel since she had a history of crankpin bearing failures which manifested itself as a propensity for crankpin bearings to fail at intervals. A prudent owner with such knowledge would have taken steps to rectify the defect rather than risk the consequences of another crankpin failure. The consequences that resulted from the failure of a crankin on the voyage in question were, therefore, foreseeable and the plaintiffs were entitled to recover the costs of transhipment and damages for the delay. Clarke LJ continued:

'... the judge was in my opinion right to hold that the vessel was unseaworthy when she left Rosario because there was present a defect which meant that it could not operate on an ordinary voyage, since it failed on the voyage down-river, [with consequences] which were entirely foreseeable. Thus, if the owners had known that such a defect was present the bearing would fail in those circumstances, they would have rectified the defect.'

The defect which led to the failure of the crankpin bearing was never identified and that made it difficult for the owners to show that they had exercised due diligence. The shipowners had attempted to argue that the exercise of due diligence means no more than the exercise of reasonable care and skill and that want of due diligence involves negligence. The Court rejected this argument. Clarke LJ:

'A very thorough investigation was required in order to identify the cause of the problems which had occurred on a number of occasions. ... a bearing failure may have very serious consequences, including the shutting down of the main engine in dangerous circumstances. ... the more serious the possible consequences the greater the effort that must be made to identify the cause of the problem and, if possible, to eradicate it.'

The shipowners could not displace their obligation of due diligence by showing that the engine builders, as their independent contractors, had exercised due diligence by conducting as thorough an investigation as could reasonably have been expected. It is settled law that the duty of due diligence is non-delegable: *Riverstone Meat Co Pty Ltd* v *Lancashire Shipping Co Ltd* [1961] AC 807. Since no evidence was called from the engine builders, it was not possible to say that due diligence was exercised. Clarke LJ:

'I agree with the judge that the owners failed to demonstrate that a proper investigation was carried out. They adduced no evidence from [the independent contractors], with the result that they have not demonstrated what was done, so that it is not possible to say that due diligence was exercised. As I see it, there are three possibilities. The first is that the owners failed to give [their independent contractors] sufficient instructions to carry out a proper and thorough investigation, the second is that [their independent contractors] failed to carry out the owners' instructions and the third is that [their independent contractors] did carry out a proper and thorough investigation but no or insufficient evidence of it was put before the court in order to enable the court to say that due diligence was exercised.'

Waller LJ:

'There was a defect which caused the bearing to fail on a perfectly ordinary voyage down the Parana within a short distance of the loading port. If a prudent owner had known that that defect existed or in the context of this case that such a defect still existed, he would have been bound to remedy the situation or not send the vessel to sea. ...

On the question of due diligence ... I would put the matter simply in this way. There was a problem causing bearing failures which had been identified prior to Durban. The casualty in this case demonstrated that the problem had not been cured. The existence of the problem called as the judge said for detailed investigations in Durban. The owners delegated the making of those investigations to [the independent contractors], but did not produce evidence as to the extent of the investigations carried out by [the independent contractors]. The owners thus failed to discharge the burden of proof that was on them.'

Galaxy Energy International Ltd v *Novorossiyk Shipping Co, The Petr Schmidt* [1998] 2 Lloyd's Rep 1
Court of Appeal (Evans and Peter Gibson LJJ, Sir Christopher Slade)

• *Commencement of laytime under a voyage charterparty – when notice of readiness is tendered*

Facts

The Petr Schmidt was taken on a voyage charterparty on the Asbatankvoy form for a loaded voyage from Tuapse to two discharging ports, Trieste and Venice. Clauses 6 and 30 (the latter a typed addition) required the master of the ship to give a notice of readiness to the charterer when the vessel was ready to load and unload and specified that such notice was to be tendered within 06.00 and 17.00 hours local time. The master was permitted to send the notices by telex or fax. A notice relating to loading was tendered at 00.01 and a notice relating to discharge was tendered at 18.00. At the time of these tenders, the vessel had arrived at the appropriate place within the port in question and was in fact ready to load or discharge as required by the charterparty.

The charterers contended that since these notices were 'tendered' outside the period specified by cl 30 of the charterparty, they were invalid as a notice of readiness and of no effect. They submitted that laytime commenced no earlier than when the loading or discharge operation began. Their claim was dismissed both by the arbitrators and by Longmore J sitting in the Commercial Court ([1997] 1 Lloyd's Rep 284). The arbitrators based their decision on 'constructive tender of the notice of readiness at those times' and as being 'deemed effective when the "office hours" or "specific hours" commence'. Longmore J could see no good reason why a notice given when the vessel was at the required contractual position and ready to discharge should not be regarded as being effective as at the time at which the contract fixed for it to be tendered.

The charterers appealed. The question of law certified by Longmore J was:

'Whether if a clause in a charterparty requires a notice of readiness to be tendered within particular hours of the day and it is, in fact, tendered outside those hours but at a time when the ship is physically ready to load or discharge, it is an invalid notice and a nullity so that a fresh notice has to be given before laytime can begin or whether the notice takes effect when those hours begin.'

Held

Appeal dismissed.

A notice which contains correct and accurate statements of existing fact does not become invalid because it is made at some earlier time than the tender required by the charterparty. Such a notice contains an implied representation that the statement tendered remains accurate when the notice is actually received and read. In this case, that was at 06.00 on the morning after the telex or fax messages were sent and so when 'office hours' began.

Evans LJ referred to and agreed with the recent judgment of Thomas J in *T A Shipping Ltd* v *Comet Shipping Ltd, The Agamemnon* [1998] 1 Lloyd's Rep 675; [1998] CLC 106 (see below) and with the decision in *Transgrain Shipping BV* v *Global Transporte Oceanico SA, The Mexico 1* [1990] 1 Lloyd's Rep 507; [1990] 1 Lloyd's Rep 207. A notice which contains inaccurate statements is invalid and is a nullity so far as the contract is concerned and does not have some kind of 'inchoate' status enabling it to ripen into a valid notice whenever the change of circumstances occurs. In such cases, a fresh notice must be given. Neither of these findings were affected by the decision in the present case. At the time the notices were transmitted, they contained accurate statements: the vessel was at the place required by the charterparty and was ready to load or unload as the case may be. They stated existing fact. They did not state that the vessel would be ready at some future time, which would have the effect of making them an ineffective tender as in *The Mexico 1* (see especially Mustill LJ at p513) and Thomas J in *The Agamemnon* (see below). Evans LJ agreed with the shipowners' submission that the fact that a valid notice was tendered by telex earlier than 06.00 hours did not prevent it from being valid notice which took effect at 06.00 hours and so become a tender in accordance with cl 30:

'The telex message was sent out of hours in the knowledge that it would remain on the receiver's machine until the following day when it would be available for office staff to deal with when they began work at or after

06.00. It seems to me that this is a clear case of "tender" at that time. Neither the fact that the message was "received" by the charterer's machine at the same time as it was sent, nor the possibility that the office staff might take it off their machine and even deal with it before 06.00, prevents this from being a "tender" at 06.00 for the purposes of clause 30. If the notice was given by a letter hand-delivered the previous evening, to be dealt with the next day, or posted through the office door at some time during the night, or left with a messenger to be handed to the office staff when they arrived at 06.00, then in my view the position would be exactly the same. These were different methods of achieving a "tender" at 06.00. If clause 30 referred to the notice being "received", as clause 6 does, then the position would be clear, just as it would be if the requirement was that the notice should be "given", meaning presumably "tendered and received", which is the word sometimes used (cf the Gencon charterparty (revised 1922 and 1976) Part II clause 6(c)).'

The primary requirement is that the notices should be statements of existing fact. Evans LJ quoted from the judgment of Lord Denning in *The Tres Flores* [1974] 1 QB 264; [1973] 2 Lloyd's Rep 247 at p249:

'In order to be a good notice of readiness, the master must be in a position to say: "I am ready at the moment you want me, whenever that may be ...".'

The master of The Petr Schmidt was in that position. The notices sent accurately stated it and contained an implied representation that those statements were accurate at the time the notice was sent. It did not follow that this implied representation of present readiness later became invalid. Evans LJ again used his letter analogy:

'In such a case, the implied representation is that the statement remains accurate when the notice is tendered. Again, the letter analogy is useful, and it is expressly permitted by the terms of clause 6. A letter written at (say) 18.00 refers to the vessel's condition at that time. It cannot be tendered to the charterer's agents until 06.00 on the following day, or at least until some time, short or long, after it is written. The letter-notice is not invalid, in my judgment, merely because the statement was made before the time of tender, nor can it be said that clause 30 requires that the letter must be written, as well as tendered, during office hours.'

Peter Gibson LJ was in entire agreement with Evans LJ that tender was made at the commencement of office hours on the next working day and on the fact that this accorded with cls 6 and 30 he said:

'The mere fact that there is a time gap between the Master declaring his ship's readiness and the receipt of the notice does not invalidate the notice, provided that it remains as true at the moment of receipt as at the moment of declaration. Clauses 6 and 30 should be read together and the receipt by the Charterers of the notice can be said to be the counterpart of the tender by the Owners. Realistically, the notice was received when there was someone in the Charterers' office to read and act upon it at the opening of office hours.'

Sir Christopher Slade, who agreed with the judgments of Evans and Peter Gibson LJJ, added some brief observations on the purposes of the clauses in the charterparty:

'Laytime under this charterparty was expressed to begin on the expiration of six hours after receipt of the notice of readiness. The commercial purpose of the second sentence of clause 30, as I would infer, must have been to ensure that the charterers or their agents should not be saddled with the receipt of a notice of readiness, and the consequent commencement of laytime, between 17.00 hours and 6.00 hours, that is to say outside what might be regarded as office hours.'

He thought the decision reached by the Court to be:

'... entirely consistent not only with this commercial purpose but also with the

wording of clauses 6 and 30, which I think should be read together. The wording of clause 6 makes it clear that the time of the giving of the notice plus the receipt thereof are the relevant factors for the purpose of the clause.'

Comment

The charterers argued that Longmore J was wrong to introduce the distinction between invalidity for what may be called a substantive reason, ie because the notice is incorrect in a material respect, and a notice which although valid in itself is tendered in breach of some 'timing provision' as to when a valid notice may be tendered. Their argument was that a notice outside of office hours should be treated as non-contractual. Since the tender of these notices was found to be valid tender, it became an issue that did not arise but Evans LJ and Sir Christopher Slade did take the opportunity to comment on what the legal position might be if cl 30 had stipulated tender in office hours alone. Evans LJ was 'inclined to agree' that this would have made the notice non-contractual and invalid under cl 30 for the same reasons that Thomas J found the notices to be invalid in *The Agamemnon*. Likewise, if the notice was taken to the charterers' offices outside of hours and not left but taken away, then that would not amount to a valid tender until tendered the next day. He commented that the phrase 'invalid' notice of readiness was a phrase of ambiguous meaning and said:

'It may in a sense be correct to say that a notice given outside the contractual hours is invalid but only in the sense that it does not *comply with the contract*.' (emphasis added)

Sir Christopher Slade did not regard the notices of readiness in the present case as 'non-contractual' (ie as having been originally 'tendered' outside the permitted hours), but thought that even if they did not comply with the strict wording of cl 30, the finding of their validity would not alter and they would still fall to be treated as valid notices.

Georgian Maritime Corporation v Sealand Industries [1997] 2 Lloyd's Rep 324 Queen's Bench Division (Commercial Court) (Mance J)

• *Charterers obligation to specify place for delivery of vessel*

Facts

The respondents time chartered the claimant owners vessel on an amended ASBATIME form. The vessel was to be delivered 'in charterers option' and 'as the charterers may direct' to the respondents' 'berth Hong Kong or dropping last outward sea pilot'. Lines 34–45 of the charterparty stated the owners general obligations as to delivery and cl 3 provided for delivery and re-delivery with quantities of bunkers as set out in cl 56. Clause 14 gave the respondents the option to cancel the charter should the vessel 'not have been delivered on or before 10 August 1995 12.00 hours'. The respondents purported to exercise this option when notice given by the master failed to specify the place of delivery and the vessel was not in fact at their berth at Hong Kong with the stipulated bunkers at the agreed time. The claimants argued that the vessel had been put at anchorage by noon on 10 August and that, despite various requests, no instructions had been forthcoming from the charterers as to berth, and that bunkering was complete at 14.00 hours.

The arbitrator rejected the owners' claim for wrongful cancellation of the charter, holding that the charterers were entitled to cancel the charter: (i) for non-delivery of the vessel by the time stipulated in cl 14; and (ii) because the vessel was not with stipulated bunkers and in a deliverable state when delivery should have occurred.

The claimants appealed on two grounds:

1. that the respondents identification of a place for delivery was a pre-condition of the claimants duty to deliver; and
2. that the claimants failure to have the stipulated quantities of bunkers on board did not entitle the respondents to exercise an option to cancel under cl 14.

Held

Appeal allowed.

On a true construction of the charterparty, the respondents' obligation to select a place for delivery of the vessel was a precondition to the claimants' duty to deliver and to the respondents right to cancel for non-delivery. The claimants depended on and were not in a position to fulfil their obligation to deliver unless and until the respondents identified a place of delivery.

Mance J:

'The making of delivery depends under lines 34–45 upon charterers identifying where delivery is to take place. The only charterparty agreement is that time runs from the placing of the vessel at charterers' disposal at the place so selected by charterers. There is no basis on which even owners, still less charterers when they were in default of selection, can claim to treat delivery as having been made on any other basis or at any other place. ...

Unless and until charterers select such a place, owners cannot deliver in accordance with the charter, although they may have a claim for damages against time charterers for failure duly to select the place for delivery (see eg *Anders Utkilens Rederi* v *Co Tunisienne de Navigation of Tunis, The Golfstraum* [1976] 2 Lloyd's Rep 97, where the damages claimed consisted of lost hire). In the present case, the time for delivery never arose, and there is thus no basis on which charterers could assert, in the context of the cancelling clause, that the vessel was due to be, but had not been, delivered.'

It was irrelevant that the claimants may not have made such delivery if they had been informed by the respondents that delivery was to be at their Hong Kong berth. To allow such an argument would inevitably lead to charterers raising speculative arguments after the event as to whether owners would hypothetically have been able to fulfil their obligations to deliver. The correct view to take was that the charterer may have a claim in damages for failure to duly select a place of delivery. In the present case, the respondents had no such claim because delivery never became due. Mance J continued:

'It does not assist charterers to argue that, if they had identified a place for delivery, owners would not have delivered the vessel in time and in the right condition at that place. The operation of the cancelling clause depends on delivery actually being due and not being made when due. Charterers' contention that they were under no obligation to select the place for delivery, since it was clear that owners would not be able to deliver in the right condition and in time at any place so selected, has no basis. In practical terms, it would lead after the event to speculative arguments whether charterers were right about this. In principle, there is no way in which charterers were relieved of their obligation to identify the place for delivery, merely because they considered, however correctly, that owners would be unable to effect delivery there by the time specified in the cancelling clause. It was not suggested that any inability in fact to deliver there by that time with the agreed bunkers (or any indication that there may have been of any intention to deliver there by that time without the agreed bunkers) involved any breach of charter, still less a breach of condition or repudiation by owners which, if duly treated as such, could have relieved charterers from further performance. The effect of the cancelling clause was simply that charterers would have a right to cancel, and owners would be vulnerable to loss of the charter, if, and only if, due delivery was not made by the time specified in the clause. Costs of any steps taken to effect an abortive tender (if delivery is tendered late and charterers cancel) fall on owners, not on charterers. In the present case, charterers' failure to identify any place for delivery means in my judgment that delivery never became due at all, and charterers' claim to invoke the cancellation clause was unjustified.'

The claimants failure to have on board, at the time for delivery, the bunkers in the quantities referred to in cl 3 and stipulated in cl 56 did not invalidate any delivery which was or could have been made. It was not proper to construe the charter as providing cancellation by reason only of failure to meet the conditions in cl 56.

'Clause 14 as amended applies simply "should the vessel not have been delivered" by that time. It is common ground that this must at least refer back to the provisions of lines 34–45, expressly dealing with delivery. If the vessel on delivery was not, by the time stipulated in clause 14, "ready to receive container with clean-swept holds and tight, staunch, strong and in every way fitted for container service, having water ballast and with sufficient power to operate all cargo-handling gear simultaneously (and with full complement of officers and crew for a vessel of her tonnage)", her delivery could thus be rejected and the charterers could cancel.'

If a cancellation clause is to be intended to relate to specific obligations, this has to be made clear.

'The conjunction of a cancelling clause and primary delivery provisions like lines 34–45 is natural and familiar. If the cancelling clause had been intended to relate to other specific obligations, such as the obligation to have certain quantities of bunkers on board on delivery, this could have been made clear. It would have been easy to include a specific reference to compliance on delivery with clauses 3 and/or 56 in either lines 34–45 or clause 14 itself. It may be, as charterers submit, that there could be advantages in terms of simplicity and certainty in such a link. On the other hand, there could be objections in terms of rigidity and the expansion of the right to cancel to circumstances where the discrepancy in bunkers was of no conceivable relevance. If a vessel to be "delivered" under clause 14 requires bunkers complying with clauses 3 and 56, I can see no scope for any qualification limiting the requirement to circumstances where the discrepancy is of "real commercial significance".'

A cancelling clause such as the one contained in cl 14 was a forfeiture clause which should not be applied lightly and caution was appropriate before extending its application by reference to specific provisions of a charterparty. The correct analysis for this charterparty, and the natural and familiar one for any charterparty, was that cl 14 had to be read in conjunction with the general obligations concerning delivery laid out in lines 34–45 and in cl 3 rather than in conjunction with the specific obligations as to quantities of bunkers etc stipulated in cl 56. Mance J considered the decisions in *Noemijulia Steamship* v *Minister of Food* [1951] 1 KB 223, *The Madeleine* [1967] 2 Lloyd's Rep 224 and *The Arianna* [1987] 2 Lloyd's Rep 376 and concluded:

'The proper construction of this particular charterparty is, as I see it, as follows. The obligation regarding bunkers on delivery imposed by clauses 3 and 56 is, if broken, readily capable of giving rise to a claim for damages. There is no reason to treat the charter as conferring in respect of it the more draconian remedy of cancellation which would apply automatically if its performance was directly relevant under clause 14. Properly understood, clause 14 operates by reference to lines 34–45. If the vessel on tender for delivery lacked bunkers, to an extent which meant that she did not comply with some aspect of lines 34–45, cancellation under clause 14 would become a possibility. In that context, the question whether the deficiency was of real commercial significance could arise. In the present case, charterers' only contention before the arbitrator was that mere non-compliance with clauses 3 and 56 automatically entitled them to cancel. They did not seek to justify their cancellation with reference to lines 34–45 at all. The award contains nothing to enable them to do so now, and there is no basis for remission.'

Comment

Mance J added the interesting observation, obiter, that

'… if compliance with clauses 3 and 56

were required, there would be some difficulty in seeing why tender with bunkers in excess of the quantities specified in clause 56 would not justify cancellation, especially since clause 56 requires the vessel "to be redelivered with approx. same quantities as on redelivery" and calls for settlement of any differences between delivery and redelivery quantities at Platts mean price ruling on redelivery. The very fact that this difficulty would exist, whether or not it could then be overcome as a matter of construction, may itself be a further pointer towards the irrelevance of clauses 3 and 56 in the context of clause 14.'

Krüger & Co Ltd v *Moel Tryvan Ship Co Ltd* [1907] AC 272 House of Lords (Lord Loreburn LC, Earl of Halsbury and Lord James of Hereford)

* *Charterer is obliged to present bills of lading in accordance with charterparty and shipowner will not be bound by master's signature on bills which do not conform*

Facts

The parties' charterparty contained a clause exempting the shipowners from liability for accidents in navigation, even when occasioned by the negligence of the master. The master was to 'sign clean bills of lading without prejudice to the charterparty'.

The vessel loaded the charterers' cargo of rice at Rangoon and the charterers' agents presented bills of lading to the master which contained the words 'freight for the said goods and all other conditions as per charterparty' but did not incorporate the exemption given by the charterparty. On the voyage from Rangoon to Rio, and owing to the negligent navigation of the master, there was a total loss of the cargo and the indorsees of the bill of lading, the buyers, recovered the value of the cargo from the shipowners as legal carrier.

Held

The charterers were bound to indemnify the shipowners against the claims of the holders of the bill of lading. The defendant charterers were entitled by their charterparty to tender a bill of lading if they thought it proper to do so but that bill of lading was to expressly incorporate the terms of the charterparty, including the negligence clause. Failure to issue such a bill was a breach of contract which caused the loss to the shipowners in their liability to the buyer.

The charterparty governs the rights and obligations of the charterer and shipowner in respect of the carriage of the goods. In this charterparty contract it had been agreed between the shipowners and the charterers that the shipowner was not to be liable for the master's negligence. The bill of lading in the hands of the charterer merely acts as a receipt for the goods and as a document of title but it performs no contractual function and cannot affect the terms contained in the charterparty.

Lord Halsbury:

'The bill of lading cannot control what has been agreed upon before between the shipowner and the merchant, and what has been expressed in a written instrument which is final and concluded between the parties.'

The primary duty of the charterers is the tender to the master of bills of lading in accordance with the terms of the charterparty. The shipowner is not bound by the master's signature since the master does not have authority to extend the principal's liability in this way.

Lord Loreburn LC:

'In my view the cardinal fact which ought to govern our decision is that under this charterparty the shipowners are not liable for losses caused by the master's negligence in navigating the vessel. When the bills of lading are given they may give rise to rights in persons other than the charterers and on conditions other than those contained in the charterparty; and therefore it is the duty of the charterers who have to present these bills, to provide that they shall not expose the shipowners to risks from which by contract they are to exempt. Nothing has occurred that disentitles the shipowners to this protection. The master, who signed the bills of lading under an excusable error of law, did not waive his principal's right to be so protected, nor did his principal waive it. It is not a case for warranty. It is a case in which, by contract, the shipowners undertook to carry a cargo on the footing that they were not to be liable for the master's negligent navigation and the charterers have made him so liable by the bills of lading. Hence arises the duty to give adequate indemnity.'

Lord James of Hereford:

'That the bills of lading came into existence for the convenience and business purposes of the charterers is also clear. Shipowners have only to carry. They care not for whom, and have nothing to do with the terms upon which the charterers deal with their goods.

But to the charterers it is all-important that they should obtain bills of lading which they can indorse over and so transfer the property in the cargo. Of the terms of such transfer the shipowner knows nothing, and thus from the nature of things and from the course of business the charterers prepare the bills of lading and tender them to the master of the vessel for signature. And so it comes that the charterers, who are controlled by the charterparty and acting under it, have cast upon them the primary duty of tendering to the master bills of lading in accordance with the terms of that document. They had no right to ask the master to sign a bill of lading in any way deviating from the charterparty.'

Comment

The decision provides authority for the implication of a term into the contract of carriage between the shipowner and the charterer that if the master is to sign a bill of lading at the charterer's request, that bill of lading should not be in the form of a contract that would increase the shipowner's liability above that contained in the charterparty. A provision requiring the master to sign bills 'as presented' by the charterer therefore gives the shipowner a corresponding right to be indemnified by the charterer if larger liabilities are incurred to the bill of lading holder than was contemplated in the charterparty. In *Manchester Trust* v *Furness* [1895] 2 QB 539 the Court of Appeal held that this basic rule will not be displaced by a provision in the charterparty making the master the agent of the charterer unless the indorsee of the bill of lading has actual notice of the terms of the charterparty, because mere knowledge of the existence of the charterparty does not give the holder constructive notice of the terms of the charterparty. However, the bill may become the charterer's bill if it is signed with authority on their behalf.

For the position where the charterparty is made expressly subject to the Hague Visby Rules, which do not permit exclusion of liability for negligence: see *The C Joyce* [1986] 2 All ER 177 (above).

Re an Arbitration between Sea and Land Securities Ltd and William Dickinson & Co Ltd, The Alresford [1942] 1 All ER 503 Court of Appeal (Mackinnon, Goddard and Du Parcq LJJ)

• *Time charter – cesser of hire*

Facts

The charterers took The Arlesford for a six-month period. She was not fitted with degaussing apparatus, which was not compulsory at the time, and the charterers suggested that the opportunity should be taken to fit her with it during what was expected to be a long wait to loading when she was at port at Blyth. No agreement was made as to the continuation of the hire while this was being done. The fitting took up nine days before the vessel's turn to load came, and a further one-and-a-half days after she had been loaded. The charter-

ers claimed that the vessel was withheld from their use for those times and withheld a proportion of the time charter hire in respect of that time.

The owners relied on cl 12 of the charterparty which expressly provided for cesser of hire only in the event of deficiency of crew or accidents preventing the working of the ship, except where the damage occurred through the charterers having chosen rivers or ports which caused danger to the ship. In reliance on this clause they contended that the hire was payable throughout the whole contract period.

The owners appealed against the decision of Atkinson J who had found that the vessel had been 'deliberately' withheld from the charterers use.

Held

Decision of Atkinson J ([1942] 1 All ER 88) reversed.

Their Lordships were unanimous in their view that the charterers consented to the ship going into drydock to be fitted with degaussing apparatus, and that, therefore, the vessel was not 'deliberately' withheld. Nothing which the shipowners did was in any way a breach of the contract contained in the charterparty.

First, there was no cessation of hire within the terms of cl 12 of the charterparty. Employment of the vessel for the fitting of degaussing apparatus did not fall within its express terms and there was therefore no cesser of hire for the period occupied in fitting the degaussing apparatus.

Second, the vessel had not been withdrawn from the use of the charterers during the nine days the fitting operation was in process and the ship was waiting to load her cargo. She would in any event have been idle during this period.

Mackinnon LJ:

'Under this contract the shipowners agree to render certain services and do work and labour for the charterers by the agency of their servants and crew. While the ship is waiting at Blyth for her cargo, she is doing everything that the shipowners need do for the charterers. The charterers had said: "You have to load this cargo at Blyth and it is necessary for the vessel to wait for her cargo and whilst waiting for her cargo she is doing the service which you, the shipowners, have promised that she shall perform." I think it is a misuse of language to use such phrases as "the withdrawal of the ship from the use of the charterers" and "deliberately withdrawn from the use of the charterers" merely because during that period the shipowners were doing some work of their own and doing that work of their own at the very suggestion of the charterers themselves. As I suggested during the course of the argument, if, when the vessel is necessarily waiting for her cargo, the shipowners turned the crew off to chip rusty plates or do some painting, or something of that sort, the charterers could not object and say: "If the ship was loaded she ought to be sailing the seas instead of being chipped, or painted, here." The fact is that the ship could not be sailing the seas, because she was where she was in enforced idleness, and it does not matter one-halfpenny to the charterers how the shipowners choose to employ their servants at a time when they cannot be carrying out what they promised to carry out for the charterers, namely, to carry their goods across the sea and to deliver them. For that reason it seems to me to be hopeless for the charterers to claim that during the first period of waiting at Blyth, that is, the first 8 days and 21 hours, they are not liable to pay hire.'

Third, the owners were not in breach of contract for the completion of the operation in the one-and-a-half days after the ship had loaded since the charterers themselves had suggested that the apparatus be fitted. Mackinnon LJ continued:

'The second period, the 1 day and 13 hours which was occupied to complete the fitting of the degaussing apparatus after the cargo was loaded, I think rests on a rather different basis; and it is not so obviously manifest that, in regard to that time, the charterers are not entitled to refuse to pay hire. I think they also fail in their claim there to be relieved

from paying hire in respect of that period. Their obligation to pay hire during the period of this time charterparty is unabated unless, first, there is a clause in the charterparty giving them a right to stop payment during any particular period – and there is none with regard to this period – or, secondly, they may be entitled to set up their claim for damages on the ground that, during this particular period, the shipowners were not carrying out their part of the contract. I do not think it is open to them to make that suggestion and to claim damages in respect of this period of 1 day, 13 hours, because, as I say, it is manifest that the shipowners during that time were only doing that which the charterers had themselves suggested they should do. The charterers suggested that the shipowners should take the opportunity whilst the vessel was necessarily waiting at Blyth to have the degaussing apparatus put in. Of course, the putting in of that apparatus would have to be completed. Another opportunity was taken to complete that operation, and, in taking that opportunity, I do not see that there was any breach of contract on the part of the shipowners—because they were only doing that which the charterers had suggested that they should do, and was something which the charterers had, therefore, entirely approved of their doing.'

Goddard LJ agreed with the findings of Mackinnon LJ and respectfully thought Atkinson J to have 'overlooked the plain facts of the case'. He said that he could 'not understand how it could be said that the shipowners committed any breach of their contract to the time charterers' when the work done had been carried out at the charterers suggestion and with their consent as a 'a good thing' to do to occupy time when she could not take her cargo on board immediately. He pointed out:

'If the facts had been that, when the ship arrived at Blyth, it was found she could not load immediately from some cause or another and the shipowners had said "We are going now to fit degaussing apparatus on the ship," and the time charterers had said

"No, we do not want you to do that; since we cannot load our cargo immediately, we want to send the vessel on another voyage," different considerations would arise.'

T A Shipping Ltd v Comet Shipping Ltd, The Agamemnon [1998] 1 Lloyd's Rep 675 Queen's Bench Division (Commercial Court) (Thomas J)

• *Notice of readiness is invalid if the vessel has not reached the place specified in the charterparty for giving notice – subsequently arriving and being ready to load or discharge the cargo does not make the notice valid*

Facts

The Agamemnon had been chartered on the Gencon form and the owners were entitled to give notice of readiness to load if the loading berth was not available when 'so near thereto as she may be permitted to approach'. There was no need for the charterers' agents to accept a notice of readiness because under the provisions of cl 33, time counted whether the notice was accepted or not.

At 23.00 hours on 5 October 1995, the master of the Agamemnon sent the charterers' agents notice of readiness to load at Batton Rouge, a port on the Mississippi River. At this time the vessel was actually lying about 170 miles from Batton Rouge at the South West Pass, an area customarily used as a waiting area for vessels wishing to proceed to one of the ports in the river. The charterers' agents kept in regular contact with the master during the up-river transit and the vessel was under the effective control of the charterers' agents as regards the organisation of pilots for the transit of the Mississippi. The vessel arrived at the general anchorage at Batton Rouge at 10.25 on Saturday 7 October and because the berth to which she was to proceed was occupied, she berthed at 20.30 on Sunday 8 October. Loading commenced the

following morning at 10.15 but was stopped because of a nine-day strike at the port. As a result, the precise time that laytime commenced became crucial to the award the owners were entitled to.

The arbitrators found that the charters' agents were, or ought to have been, fully aware of the vessel's time of arrival at the Baton Rouge anchorage, the nearest anchorage that the vessel was permitted to approach the berth, and that notice of readiness was to be treated as having been given at 10.25 on 7 October. Consequently, laytime commenced at 14.00 on 7 October and expired 45 minutes before the nine-day strike began. On this finding, the owners were entitled to a substantial sum by way of demurrage. If laytime commenced more that 45 minutes later, then the strike would have started whilst the vessel was still on laytime and the amount of demurrage recoverable would have been a very much smaller sum.

The charterers appealed against the award of the arbitrators, arguing that the notice of readiness had been given prematurely and before the vessel's arrival at a point as near to Baton Rouge as she could approach and that as no notice was given when she arrived at that point on 7 October, laytime could not commence before the vessel started to load at 10.15 on 9 October.

Held

Appeal allowed

The test for validity of a notice is whether the condition in the charterparty for the giving of notice has been met and the vessel is, at the time the notice is given, at the point stipulated in the charterparty where notice can be given. The notice of readiness given before the vessel arrived at the Batton Rouge anchorage was not a valid notice of readiness. The vessel had not reached a point as close to the loading berth as she might be permitted to approach; she only reached that point when she arrived at the Batton Rouge anchorage at 10.25 on 7 October. Her subsequent arrival at the Batton Rouge anchorage had no effect on that notice.

For a charterparty on the usual terms, a notice given prematurely and before the vessel's arrival cannot be viewed as an 'inchoate notice' which subsequently takes effect as a valid notice when the vessel arrives ready to load or discharge the cargo. Thomas J rejected the owners' argument that a distinction was to be drawn between the notice as invalid and a 'nullity' because it was untrue and potentially valid or 'inchoate' because it was truthful in its terms but had not been given at the right point in time. In his opinion the notice was not true:

'The notice stated that the vessel was at the correct point at which she was, namely the South Western Pass; that she was in all respects ready to load; the notice also stated that laytime was therefore to commence in accordance with the terms of the charterparty. ...

[The] notice was therefore a statement that the vessel had reached the point which was the nearest to Batton Rouge she was permitted to reach. In that sense, it was not true. ...'

On the basis of this reasoning, Thomas J agreed with and applied the decision of the Court of Appeal in *Transgrain Shipping BV v Global Transporte Oceanico SA, The Mexico 1* [1990] 1 Lloyd's Rep 507 and referred to the judgment of Mustill LJ at p513 in that case:

'Moreover, quite apart from the practical objections to this variant of the argument, it does not meet the fundamental objection that the contract provides for laytime to be started by the notice (which means a valid notice) and in no other way.'

Accordingly, an invalid notice of readiness cannot operate to commence laytime and laytime in this case therefore commenced only on the commencement of loading at the Baton Rouge anchorage. Thomas J clarified his reasoning for this as follows:

'Since the decision in *The Mexico 1* [1990] 1 Lloyd's Rep 507, it has been clear that if, as is normally the case, a charterparty requires that a notice of readiness be given

to start laytime, then a valid notice must be given before laytime can commence. ...

Under this charterparty, a notice of readiness that would be effective to commence laytime could only be given when:

1. The vessel reached the loading berth or, if the loading berth was not available, on the vessels arrival at the point at or off the port or so near to the port as the vessel might be permitted to approach.
2. She was in all respects ready to load.

If those conditions were not fulfilled, the notice of readiness was not a valid notice as it did not that comply with the conditions set out in the charterparty and therefore it did not trigger the commencement of laytime.

When the notice of readiness was given at the South Western Pass, the vessel had not, on the findings of fact made by the Arbitrators, reached a point as close to the loading berth as she might be permitted to approach; she only reached that point when she arrived at the Batton Rouge anchorage at 10.25 on 7 October. Thus at the time the notice was given, the owners had not complied with the terms of the charterparty for the giving of notice. It was not a valid notice and could not operate as the event to trigger the commencement of laytime. Therefore, as in *The Mexico 1*, unless something happened after the notice was given to make laytime start, it never started at all. No further notice was given and nothing further of relevance happened which is raised by the questions before the Court on the appeal.

...

Thus on the principles clearly established by *The Mexico 1*, laytime did not commence when the vessel reached the Batton Rouge anchorage, but only on the commencement of loading. ...

The decision in *The Mexico 1* is quite clear. A notice of readiness which is effective to start laytime running can only be given when the conditions set out in the charterparty for its giving have been met. A notice that does not meet those conditions is not a valid notice.'

An alternative submission of estoppel by conduct for an inchoate notice is found in the decision of Donaldson J in *The Shackleford* [1978] 1 Lloyd's Rep 191 at p198. Thomas J rejected the argument that the reasoning for that decision applied to the facts of the present case noting that it had been 'accurately summarised' in the head note: "under the terms of the charter, the receivers could have rejected or ignored the notice, but they had accepted it and this created an estoppel by conduct so that the charterers could not object that the notice was premature".

Comment

See also *Galaxy Energy International Ltd v Novorossiyk Shipping Co, The Petr Schmidt* [1998] 2 Lloyd's Rep 1 (above) which went on appeal after the judgment in *The Agamemnon* had been given. Thomas J agreed with the decision of the trial judge, Longmore J, in this case and the Court of Appeal later agreed with Thomas J's decision in *The Agamemnon*. The key difference between that case and the present one was that *The Petr Schmidt*, unlike *The Agamemnon*, was at the required contractual position and ready to discharge when the notices were sent. Thomas J agreed with Longmore J that such a notice accurately stated readiness to discharge and was in accordance with the principles as set out in *The Mexico 1*. Those principles are concerned solely with a truthful notice meeting at the time of its tender the conditions stipulated in the charter as to the readiness of the ship. The notice sent by *The Petr Schmidt* did meet those conditions. The notice sent from The *Agamemnon* did not: it was sent when she was not at the point she was required to be at and not ready to discharge, therefore the conditions for giving a valid notice of readiness were not met.

Timber Shipping Co SA v London & Overseas Freighters Ltd [1971] 2 All ER 599 House of Lords (Lords Reid, Morris of Borth-y-Gest, Guest, Donovan and Cross of Chelsea)

• *Time charterers' liability for late redelivery of vessel is the hire rate as specified in charterparty*

Facts

The appellant charterers time chartered the respondent owners' vessel, The London Explorer. Redelivery was to be at Houston, USA, 'on or before 29 December 1968'. Her last voyage, which commenced in good time was from Japan to New Orleans and then to Houston for discharge of her final cargo and redelivery of the vessel. She arrived at New Orleans in good time but was delayed there until 25 February 1969 by a dock strike. On arrival at Houston she met another strike there and lay at anchor until finally able to discharge the remainder of her cargo on 24 April 1969.

Strikes are not covered by the off-hire clause and the charterers admitted that they must make a payment in respect of the whole period up to 24 April 1969. The issue in dispute was the proper basis on which the rate of payment should be assessed. Charter rates had fallen substantially since the date of commencement of the charter and during the period from 28 December 1968 to 24 April 1969 were lower than that payable under the charterparty. The owners contended that they were entitled to the higher rate of hire as set out in the charter for the whole period up to the actual redelivery of the vessel. The charterers contended that the period of hire was 'for 12 months 15 days more or less in charterers' option ...' (it had originally read 'for about' but been amended) so that they were liable on the charter rate to 13 January 1969 at the latest and thereafter liable in damages at the current market rate for their wrongful use of the vessel until its redelivery on 24 April 1969.

Their dispute was referred to arbitrators who found in favour of the owners. The decision of the arbitrators was upheld by the Court of Appeal ([1970] 3 All ER 756; [1971] 1 QB 268). The charterers appealed against the order of the Court of Appeal.

Held
Their Lordships were agreed that the charterers were liable to pay hire at the rate stipulated in the charterparty until the time of actual redelivery on 24 April 1969.

Lord Reid was unable to agree with the appellants' argument that their charter ended on 13 January at the latest by virtue of the deletion of the word 'about' from the relevant clause in the charterparty. If the vessel was still in their use the charterers would not have discharged their obligations to the cargo owners or receivors. He cited *Gray & Co* v *Christie & Co* (1889) TLR 577, as good authority for the proposition that there is a presumption that a definite date for the termination of a time charter should be regarded as an approximate date only and said:

'Parties are of course entitled to make any agreement they choose. But it seems to me to be highly unlikely that any parties would agree that, if the completion of the last voyage is delayed beyond a particular date, by some cause for which neither is responsible, the charterers should have no right at all to give any directions as to the future movements of the vessel. The vessel might then still be in mid-ocean and it would seem odd, to say the least, if the owners then became free to use the vessel as they chose subject only to any liability they might have under bills of lading of the cargo to its consignees.'

Where, as is more usual, the unexpected delay is of fairly short duration, there is no argument that the charter rate is payable for that period of delay. The charterers were suggesting that the same principle did not apply to a long delay and Lord Reid was unwilling to agree that such a principle was acceptable:

'But it seems to me quite unreasonable to say that if the unexpected delay is of reasonable duration then parties are presumed to agree that the charter rate is to apply but not when such delay is of unreasonable duration. On what possible basis could one judge whether the duration of an unexpected delay is reasonable or unreasonable? It seems to me that, unless the parties agree otherwise, it must be presumed because it is businesslike that the charter is intended to continue in operation until the end of a legitimate last voyage – unless of course one of the parties was responsible for the delay.'

The word 'about' in the pre-printed clause of the charterparty reflects the existing law that dates are presumed to be flexible. The substitution of it with a definite margin of '15 days more or less' appeared to be an intention to define the degree of flexibility and to oust the ordinary presumption of flexibility. Lord Reid took the view:

'That means that it would have been a breach of contract if the charterers had sent the vessel on a voyage expected to end on 14 January or any later date. But it does not mean, as the charterers argue, that the charterers were necessarily in breach of contract by failing to redeliver the vessel on or before 13 January. If what I have said earlier is right there still remains the separate presumption that the parties intended that, if unexpected delays on the last legitimate voyage caused redelivery to be delayed beyond the agreed date, the charter should nevertheless continue in operation until the end of the voyage. That presumption appears to me to be fortified by the other provisions in this charter. Clause 4 provides: "That the Charterers shall pay for the use and hire of the said Vessel [at a certain rate] per Calendar Month, commencing on and from the day of her delivery, as aforesaid, and at and after the same rate for any part of a month; hire to continue until the hour of the day of her re-delivery ..." at a certain range of ports. And then there is a provision that the charterers are to give not less than 15 days' notice of the expected date of redelivery. I think that the natural meaning of this clause is that it is to apply until actual redelivery at the end of the last voyage. Accordingly, on this question I am of opinion that the appeal fails.'

It had been suggested that a new contract could be implied for the off-hire period. Lord Reid was firmly of the view that there was nothing in this case from which any new contract could be inferred and said:

'Such a new contract cannot be inferred from what the parties might or probably would or as businessmen might have been expected to do if they had realised the true position. It can only be inferred from what in fact they did and said, or perhaps failed to do, construed in the light of facts known to them.'

Lord Morris also found that hire continued up to the hour of redelivery on the short ground that cl 4 of the charterparty imposed an obligation on the charterers to pay for the use and hire of the vessel at the contractual rate until the hour of the day of her redelivery and that this obligation existed whether or not there was a breach by the charterers in failing to redeliver when they could have done. He said:

'I read the words "the hour of the day of her re-delivery" in cl 4 in the present case as referring to the time of the actual redelivery.
...
There is no finding in the present case that the charterers were in breach. There can be no doubt that the voyage from Japan to New Orleans and Houston was one on which the vessel was reasonably sent. There is no finding that the date of redelivery was in the circumstances not a reasonable one. All the indications are that in the circumstances the continued use of the vessel was with the owners' concurrence. This, however, does not involve that any new contract was made. But the owners treated the charterers as entitled to give orders. Furthermore, time was, in my view, not made of the essence. Quite apart, however, from these various considerations the charterers were liable, under the terms of cl 4, to pay hire at the contractual rate until the time of actual redelivery. On

this issue I would, therefore, dismiss the appeal.'

Comment

The case raises some interesting issues in respect of the obligation for timely redelivery of the vessel under a time charter and whether it should be treated as a breach of contract. Whilst their Lordships were all in agreement that the charterers were liable to pay hire at the rate stipulated in the charterparty until the time of actual redelivery, they differed in their views on whether failure to redeliver on time might amount to a breach of contract. The following provides a summary of this.

First, per Lords Reid and Cross of Chelsea:

1. it could be assumed that by the terms of the charterparty the charters were bound to redeliver the vessel on or before 13 January; and

2. the vessel was on her last legitimate voyage and was expected to arrive on time but did not because of unexpected delays for which neither party was responsible; and

3. in such circumstances the presumption is that the charter should continue in operation until the end of the voyage and in the present case this presumption was fortified by the provision in cl 4 that the hire was to continue 'until the hour of the day of her re-delivery' at one of the specified ports;

4. however, if the charterers had sent the vessel on a voyage that had been expected to end on 14 January or later, then they would have been in breach of contract.

Second, per Lords Morris of Borth-y-Gest, Guest and Donovan:

1. the charterers were not in breach of contract since the final voyage was one on which the vessel was legitimately sent and there was a reasonable expectation that the date of redelivery would, in normal circumstances, have been met;

2. however, the obligation on the charterers to pay for the use and hire of the vessel at

the contractual rate until the hour of the day of her redelivery imposed by the terms of cl 4 of the charterparty, existed whether or not there was a breach by the charterers in failing to redeliver when they should have done;

3. the words of cl 4 could not be read as providing that hire was to continue until redelivery at the end of the period covered by the words '12 months 15 days more or less' so as to make time of the essence: *Watson Steamship Co Ltd* v *Merryweather & Co* (1913) 18 Com Cas 294 distinguished.

Torvald Klaveness A/S v *Arni Maritime Corporation, The Gregos*
[1994] 4 All ER 998 House of Lords (Lords Templeman, Ackner, Mustill, Slynn of Hadley and Woolf)

• *The time at which validity of charterers' order for a final voyage prior to redelivery is to be judged is when the order is to be performed and not when the order is given*

Facts
The charterers, Torvald Klaveness A/S, were bound by the terms of a time charterparty to give orders which would result in the vessel being redelivered to the owners at an authorised port in Europe on or before 18 March. The vessel was in fact redelivered eight days late. On 9 February the charterers instructed the master to proceed to the port of Palua on the Orinoco (Venezuela) to load cargo for carriage to Fos, Italy. On 25 February, in view of delays to river traffic caused by the grounding of a vessel with unusual severity in the Orinoco River, the owners refused to load at Palua and requested fresh orders to enable the vessel to be redelivered on time. On 29 February the charterers refused to give fresh orders and insisted that the order of 9 February for a laden voyage from Palua was valid. The owners treated the conduct of the charterers

in ordering and attempting to insist upon loading at Palua as a repudiatory breach of contract and accepted that repudiation. A 'without prejudice' agreement was entered into and the vessel performed the laden voyage to Fos subject to the charterers paying an agreed higher rate of hire if, at arbitration, it was held that the owners would have been justified in refusing to perform the voyage.

The arbitrator found in favour of the owners. The validity of the order for the final voyage was to be judged as at the time when it fell to be complied with on 25 February and not at the time when it was given on 9 February. The order originally given on 9 February had by 25 February become invalid and the owners were entitled to refuse it. The charterers by giving the order and then refusing to replace it had given an order for a voyage which could not be legitimately given and were thereby in wrongful repudiation of the charter. Evans J ([1992] 2 Lloyd's Rep 40) upheld the award but certified that questions of general public importance were involved. The Court of Appeal ([1993] 2 Lloyd's Rep 335) found in favour of the charterers on the grounds, inter alia, that an order which if complied with would involve some degree of lateness could not in itself be an actual breach of condition or a repudiatory breach. The owners appealed against the decision of the Court of Appeal.

Held
The House of Lords allowed the appeal and restored the award of the arbitrator.

Lord Templeman (concurring in the result) was of the opinion that, in the absence of any provision to the contrary, the time for redelivery in a time charter was of the essence of the contract. The charterer was required by the terms of the charterparty to give orders which ensured that the vessel would be redelivered on time and the owner of the vessel was entitled to treat an order which would not enable the vessel to be redelivered on time as a repudiatory breach of contract. If the owner complied with the order he lost his right to repudiate the contract but was entitled to damages for any late delivery. Since the order to load at Palua, if complied with, would have prevented redelivery on time, that order was one which the charterers were not entitled to give and was a repudiatory breach of contract. The owners were therefore entitled to the increased rate of hire.

Lord Mustill (Lords Ackner, Slynn of Hadley and Woolf agreeing) found that the time 'primarily at least' at which the legitimacy of a charterer's order was to be judged was the time when the order became due for performance and not when the order was given. In the giving of such an order the charterer remains constrained by terms expressly or impliedly accepted by the charterer in the original contract. When the time for performance arrives the owner is obliged to perform a service required by the charterer which conforms with that which the shipowner promised in advance to render. The owner cannot be compelled to perform a service which falls outside the range encompassed by the owner's original promise. Thus, if circumstances change so that compliance with the order calls for a service which in the original contract the shipowner never undertook, the obligation to comply falls away.

Lord Mustill:

'Whatever the charterer may order, a service which falls outside the range encompassed by the owner's original promise is not one which he can be compelled to perform; and this is so as regards not only the duration of the chartered service, but also all the other limitations imposed by the charterparty on the charterer's freedom of choice. There is thus to be a measuring of the service called for against the service promised. As a matter of common sense, it seems to me that the time for such measurement is, primarily at least, the time when performance falls due.
...

[If compliance with an order] will involve a service which lies outside the shipowner's undertaking the latter can say so at once, and reject the order. But if the order is apparently valid its validity is no more than contingent, since the time for matching the service against the promise to serve does not arrive until the nature of the service is definitively known; and this will not usually be until the service is due to begin, or in some instances until it is already in progress. Thus, if and for so long as the service required conforms with those which the shipowner promised in advance to render the specific order creates a specific obligation to perform them when the time arrives. But only for so long as that state of affairs persists. If circumstances change, so that compliance with the order will call for a service which in the original contract the shipowner never undertook, the obligation to comply must fall away. As I see it, the charterers' order in advance amounts to a continuing requirement, the validity of which may change with the passage of time.'

Lord Mustill considered the three grounds on which a shipowner was entitled to treat himself as discharged when called upon by a charterer to perform an extra-contractual service.

The first ground was that the charterer is obliged to give a valid order for the employment of the ship and the giving of an invalid order is by its nature a repudiatory breach. However, the charterer is in breach only when the time for giving an order for the employment of the vessel has expired with no valid order being made. Lord Mustill:

'... it is necessary to distinguish between two propositions: that the charterer is obliged at the appropriate time to give a valid order for the employment of the ship, and that he is obliged never to give an invalid order. At first sight this distinction may seem mere wordplay, but for present purposes it is essential, as may be seen from the example of a charterer who gives a series of orders, all of them invalid and hence ineffectual. The former proposition entails that since an ineffectual order is the same as no order at all, the charterer becomes in breach only when the time for giving an order for the employment of the vessel has come and gone with no valid order having been given. The consequence of the latter is different, namely that every invalid order is in itself a breach of contract, giving the shipowner an immediate and distinct cause of action on each occasion.'

His Lordship had difficulty in accepting the latter proposition. There were some judgments which asserted that an illegitimate order was in itself a breach and the point had been conceded in the Court of Appeal. It was a different matter to say that the giving of an invalid order in every case entitled the shipowner to treat the contract as at an end. He continued:

'It is however quite another matter to say that the duty never to give an invalid order is so fundamental to the working of the contract that the giving of such an order must in every case entitle the shipowner to treat the contract as at an end, even if by rejecting the order he can ensure that it causes him no damage at all. My Lords, although it is well established that certain obligations under charterparties do have the character of conditions I would not for my part wish to enlarge the category unduly, given the opportunity which this provides for a party to rely on an innocuous breach as a means of escaping from an unwelcome bargain. In the present instance I can see no commercial necessity to hold that the issuing of an invalid order is an automatic ground of discharge, and every reason for holding that it does not.'

The second ground was that redelivery after the final date is a breach of contract entitling the shipowner to treat himself as discharged. It follows, therefore, that an order for a voyage which according to a reasonable prediction will lead to late redelivery must necessarily be a repudiatory breach. However, Lord Mustill was of the opinion that timely redelivery is probably not a condition of a time charterparty contract and therefore is not necessarily a repudiatory breach. A short delay in redelivery, for example, will not justify the termination of the contract. His Lordship preferred the view that the obligation was 'innominate'. He stated:

'I turn to the second argument which concentrates, not on the rejected order itself, but on the hypothetical consequences which would have been likely to ensue if it had been obeyed. It runs as follows. The timely redelivery of the vessel is a condition of the contract; an actual late redelivery, whether long or short, would therefore enable the shipowner to treat the contract as terminated; the invalid order actually given, if obeyed, would probably have caused the vessel to be redelivered late; the breach of condition which this would have entailed must be referred back to the invalid order, even though in fact it was not obeyed. At first sight this argument appears to lead straight to the law on anticipatory breach, and in particular to the discussion in *Federal Commerce and Navigation Co Ltd* v *Molena Alpha Inc* [1979] AC 757 of the situation where the threatened breach is not of a fundamental character. On reflection, however, I question whether this analysis is sound, for I am not convinced that the shipowner can at the same time treat the charterer as evincing an intention to commit a breach in the future and yet ensure, by rejecting the order, that no such breach ever takes place.

Quite apart from this however I find it hard to accept that timely redelivery is a condition of the contract. The classification of an obligation as a condition or an 'innominate' term is largely determined by its practical importance in the scheme of the contract, and this is not easily judged in relation to the obligation to redeliver, since the occasions for the cancellation of a charter on the ground of a few days' delay at the end of the chartered service are likely to be few. If the ship is laden when the final date arrives the shipowner will often have obligations to third party consignees which make it impossible for him to cut short the voyage, quite apart from the improbability that he will go to the trouble and expense of arranging for the discharge and receipt of the cargo at an alternative destination, just to save a few days' delay. ...

Even acknowledging the importance given in recent years to time clauses in mercantile contracts (see eg *Bunge Corporation v Tradax SA* [1981] 1 WLR 711 and *Cie Commerciale Sucres et Denrées* v *C Czarnikow Ltd* [1990] 1 WLR 1337) I would incline to the view that this particular obligation is "innominate" and that a short delay in redelivery would not justify the termination of the contract.'

The third ground was that the persistence of the charterers in an illegitimate order was conduct 'evincing an intention no longer to be bound' by the contract, and hence a repudiation of it. Whilst the original order on 9 February did not constitute a repudiation in itself, the charterer was obliged by the charterparty to replace the original order, being ineffectual, with one which it was entitled to give. Thus, whilst the issuing of an invalid order was not an automatic ground of discharge, the charterer's persistence in an order which had become invalid showed that the charterer did not intend to perform its obligations under the charter. That was an anticipatory breach which entitled the owner to treat the contract as at an end. As Lord Mustill explained:

'This argument depends, not on the invalid order which was given, but on the valid order which was not. The original order having become ineffectual the charterers were obliged by cl 11 to replace it with one which they were entitled to give. Whether at the time of the cancellation they had committed an actual breach of this obligation is debatable, but at all events the breach was not final, since (if I correctly understand the arbitrator's reasons) there would have been time if all else failed for the charterers to ballast the vessel back to the redelivery area before the final date, or conceivably to issue an order for a revised laden voyage. But it is plain from the facts stated by the arbitrator that the charterers had no intention of doing this, and that the critical time would pass without any valid orders being given. This is the significance of the changed circumstances which rendered the original order invalid. Not that the order constituted a repudiation in itself, but that the charterers' persistence in it after it had become invalid showed that they did not intend to perform their obligations under the charter. That is to say, they 'evinced an intention no longer to be bound' by the charter. This was an anticipatory breach, which entitled the owners to treat the contract as ended.'

Comment

In giving consideration to the first issue, the date for judging the validity of the charterer's order, Lord Mustill was of the opinion that

'... the inquiry has been led astray by concentrating too much on the order and too little on the shipowner's promise to furnish the services of the vessel, which is what the contract is about.'

In practice the interests of both parties demand that the charterer is entitled to give orders in advance of the time for performance. In order to provide for this, the terms of a charterparty lay down promises the practical implications of which are undefined since they depend on how in the future the charterer decides to employ the vessel. For such orders, the broad promise contained in the charterparty is converted to a series of specific obligations only when the time for performance of an order arrives. In the present case, the crucial date was 25 February when the charterers could have given an order which would have enabled redelivery on time but insisted on an order which did not allow the vessel to be redelivered on time. This order, if complied with, would have prevented redelivery by 18 March and was therefore a repudiatory breach of contract. If the master had accepted the order to load at Palua, the owners would have lost their right to accept repudiation but would have remained entitled to damages for late delivery.

In the Court of Appeal, after a careful discussion of the reported cases which, in the event, he concluded were indecisive Hirst LJ ([1993] 2 Lloyd's Rep 335 at 346) analysed the first issue principally in terms of convenience and concluded that:

'... the legitimacy of the last voyage order has to be established at the date when it is given, having regard not only to the reasonableness at that date of the estimate of the expected duration of the voyage, but also to the reasonableness at that date of making an estimate at all ...'

On the question of whether the giving of the illegitimate order constituted a repudiation of the contract the arbitrator considered that given that the anticipated overrun was only a few days he would, in the absence of authority, have considered that there was no repudiation, but regarded himself as compelled by authority to the opposite view.

Tynedale Steam Shipping Co Ltd v *Anglo Soviet Shipping Co Ltd* [1936] 1 All ER 389 Court of Appeal (Lord Roche, Scott LJ and Eve J)

- *Cesser of hire under a time charter*

Facts

The respondents chartered a vessel from the appellants under a 'Baltime 1920' charter. When arriving into Liverpool carrying a deck-load of timber properly loaded and stowed and securely lashed she was struck by a severe squall and listed sharply to port. The port-side foredeck was lost overboard taking with it the foremast to which the forward winches were attached. Shore cranes and two floating derricks had to be hired to discharge the cargo from the fore-end. The derricks had be berthed between the vessel and the quay which prevented discharge from the after-end. Discharging therefore took six days two hours longer than it would normally have done and the shipowners claimed hire for this period. They also claimed that the cost of hiring the floating derricks was for the charterers' account. The charterers claimed that they were not bound by the charterparty to pay the hire for the period of delay, and that the shipowners were liable for the hire of the floating derricks. Their dispute was submitted to arbitra-

tion and then on a special consultative case stated by arbitrators in which Goddard J found in favour of the charterers on both of their claims. The shipowners appealed.

The 'cesser of hire' provision was in cl 10 of the charterparty and provided:

'In the event of loss of time caused by ... breakdown of machinery, damage to hull or other accident preventing the working of the steamer and lasting more than 24 consecutive hours, hire to cease from commencement of such loss of time until steamer is again in efficient state to resume service.'

Other relevant clauses in the charterparty provided as follows:

Clause 2:   'Owners are to maintain her in a thoroughly efficient state in hull and machinery during service ...'

Clause 3:   'The steamer is to be fitted and maintained with winches, derricks, wheels and ordinary runners capable of handling lifts up to three tons ...'

Clause 12:   'Owners only to be responsible for ... delay during the currency of this charter for loss or damage to goods on board, if such delay or loss has been caused by want of due diligence on the part of owners or their manager, in making steamer seaworthy and fitted for the voyage or any other personal act or omission or default of owners or their manager. Owners not to be responsible in any other case nor for damage or delay whatsoever and howsoever caused even if caused by the neglect of or default by owners' servants.'

Held

This was a standard charterparty used by the Baltic timber trade and in construing it the court must assume that its terms were chosen with full regard to the decisions laid down in cases reported before it was drawn up. Scott

LJ in particular was at pains to reinforce the fact that the commercial world would rely on the court construing the document in accordance with previous case decisions and that it would be wrong to depart from this unless it was 'on account of the wording of the particular instrument compelling such a departure'. He expressed the compelling commercial reasons not to do so in the following terms:

'I do feel this very strongly: that from a commercial point of view the distinction between what causes the charter hire to go off and what causes it to come on again is, to the commercial man, a distinction which is rather apt to worry him; and I am very loathe to construe an ordinary commercial clause in a way that is not simple to the commercial mind if the clause can properly be interpreted in a simple way. And this clause, I think, can be interpreted simply, for this reason: the clause provides that in the event of loss of time caused by damage to hull or other accident preventing the working of the steamer, then hire for a minimum length of time is to cease until the steamer is again in an efficient state to resume the service.

... the word "again" indicates the former state of the ship and the latter state of the ship. The state before she went off hire and the state to which she must have returned before she goes on hire again are intended to be the same. If one turns to clause 1 of the charterparty in which, following on the description of the ship which is given at the outset of the charter, it is laid down that the ship must be "in every way fitted for ordinary cargo service"; and if one has in mind the provision in clause 2: "Owners are to maintain her in a thoroughly efficient state in hull and machinery during service," and that in clause 3: "The steamer is to be fitted and maintained with winches, derricks, wheels and ordinary runners capable of handling lifts up to three tons" – having all those three express provisions of the charter in mind, I think that the stress of clause 10 is on the words "the steamer," meaning the contract steamer, the steamer of the kind described in this contract, which is to be maintained in the manner expressly stated in

the contract; and that when, in substance, the steamer has ceased to be a steamer with those qualifications, then the charter hire goes off and will not re-attach until the steamer is again a steamer with those qualifications – subject always to this: that the qualifications necessary for work in port are not the same as the qualifications necessary for work at sea, as was pointed out by the House of Lords in *Hogarth* v *Miller*. If you take that view, it is a simple interpretation of the clause from the point of view of the ordinary commercial man.'

The shipowners sought to rely on the distinction between a ship that was partly efficient and one that had been totally 'prevented from working'. They contended that so long as the vessel was efficient or able to discharge, however slowly, the cesser of hire clause under its terms was not in operation. Lord Roche considered at length the decision in *Hogarth* v *Miller, Brother & Co* [1891] AC 48. He found the language of the cesser of hire clause in that case to be indistinguishable from the one in the present case with the exception of the word 'stopped' which was used instead of the word 'preventing'. He agreed with the decision of Lord Halsbury LC who had found that the purpose of the clause was clear on its wording: if the hirer of the ship could show there was loss of time, then the clause was there to guard the hire against paying the owner when the working powers of the vessel are interfered with, and the working of the vessel is stopped for more than 48 consecutive working hours. That was the contingency that gave rise to the operation of the clause and would be contemplated by the parties as so doing. In the instant case the vessel was not 'working' because of a 'breakdown of machinery' that was 'preventing' discharge from the forward part of the ship and she was not 'again in an efficient state to resume her service' until the owners put her back into an efficient state in hull and machinery for that purpose. Accordingly, under clause 2 and under clause 10 events had happened which put into operation the cesser of hire clause. Roche LJ summed this up as:

'... if certain events happen, then ipso facto
hire is to cease and is not to begin again until
that state of affairs has ceased to exist.'

Whistler International Ltd v *Kawasaki Kisen Kaisha Ltd* [2000] 3 WLR 1954 House of Lords (Lords Bingham of Cornhill, Nicholls of Birkenhead, Hoffffmann, Hope of Craighead and Hobhouse of Woodborough)

• *Distinction between employment and navigation in a time charterparty*

Facts

Whistler took a time charter of a bulk carrier,
The Hill Harmony, on an amended NYPE
1946 form for an eleven- to thirteen-month
period. For seven to nine months of that period
the vessel was sub-time chartered to Kawasaki
Kisen Kaisha. Kawasaki instructed the vessel
to sail from Canada to Japanese ports and, on
the recommendation of a weather-routeing
service, requested the master to cross the
Pacific by the shorter northerly Great Circle
route. The master, who had previously suffered heavy weather damage on that route, did
not comply with those instructions and proceeded instead by the shorter more southerly
rhumb line route. The voyages took an extra
6.556 and 3.341 days respectively and, under
cl 15 of the charterparty, Kawasaki deducted
hire in respect of the additional days at sea and
the cost of the additional bunkers consumed
on the grounds that they represented damages
for breach of the master's obligation to follow
the charterers' order and directions as to
employment and breach of the obligation to
prosecute the voyages with the utmost
despatch (provided for under cl 8 of the charterparty).

Whistler claimed against Kawasaki for the
amounts not paid and the matter was submitted to arbitration. The arbitrators held that the
routeing instructions given by Kawasaki were
orders as to employment within cl 18 of the

charterparty and were specific course instructions which could not be disregarded without
good reason. The master's previous experience of heavy weather was not a good reason
and did not justify the decision not to follow
the orders.

Clarke J allowed appeals brought by
Whistler and Kawasaki against the arbitrators'
award in respect of sums to be deducted from
the hire ([1998] 4 All ER 286 (QBD)). He held
that an order as to where the vessel was to go
was an order as to employment but that an
order as to how to get there was an order as to
navigation which was a matter for the master
and not within cl 8. The master's decision to
proceed by a different route which resulted in
a financial loss was therefore an act of the
master in the navigation of the ship under art
IV r2(a) of the Hague-Visby Rules, ie an 'act,
neglect or default ... in the navigation ... of
the ship'.

The Court of Appeal dismissed the charterers' appeal ([1999] 4 All ER 199). In the
absence of any special provisions in the charterparty governing or restricting the right of
the master to select the navigational course
between destinations, the master's decision,
made bona fide for the safety of the vessel,
was a decision on navigation, and the arbitrators erred in law in categorising it as an order
as to employment.

Held

The decision of the Court of Appeal was
reversed and the award of the arbitrators
restored. Orders as to the deployment of the
vessel, including the route by which it must
sail, are a matter of the 'employment' of the
vessel, and cannot be disregarded by the
master unless there is good reason to justify
doing so. The fact that heavy weather had
been encountered on previous voyages on that
route did not, in itself, amount to good reason
to refuse to proceed by that route as requested
by the charterer. It did not displace the obligation on the master to proceed with utmost
despatch and there had not been other maritime reason for not taking the shortest and
quickest route which would so displace it.

The obligation on the master to take the shortest route master lies irrespective of any express orders he may receive from the charterer.

Lord Bingham of Cornhill expressed this as follows:

'The starting point in the present case is, in my opinion, the master's obligation to prosecute his voyages with the utmost despatch. Irrespective of any express orders by the charterer, that would ordinarily require him to take the route which is the shortest and therefore quickest, unless there is some other maritime reason for not taking the shortest and quickest route.'

Their Lordships considered in some detail the distinction between the 'employment' and the 'navigation' of a vessel and the difficulty in drawing the line between the two and considered the proper test to be an economic one based on the commercial interests of the shipowner and the charterer. These interests differ and that has an effect on their view on matters relating to the 'employment' and the 'navigation' of the vessel. The shipowners' interest lies with the vessel itself and the asset it represents whereas the charterers' interests have more to do with maximising the earning potential of the vessel during the period of their charter. The true construction of the words 'employment' and 'navigation' must be taken in the context of the charterparty they have entered into. Lord Hobhouse saw them as being different aspects of the operation of the vessel:

' ... the meaning of any language is affected by its context. This is true of the words "employment" in a time charter and the exception for negligence of "navigation" of the ship in the charterparty or contract of carriage. They reflect different aspects of the operation of the vessel. "Employment" embraces the economic aspect – the exploitation of the earning potential of the vessel. "Navigation" embraces matters of seamanship.'

Lord Bingham, in respect of much the same distinction, gave consideration as to what the test might be and said:

'It is not hard to think of orders which plainly relate to the employment of the vessel and others which plainly relate to its navigation. It is much less easy to formulate any test which clearly distinguishes between the two. The charterer's right to use the vessel must be given full and fair effect; but it cannot encroach on matters falling within the specialised professional maritime expertise of the master, particularly where the safety or security of the vessel, her crew and her cargo are involved.'

Comment

The decision establishes that a distinction should be drawn between 'employment' and 'navigation' of the vessel and that the appropriate test for a court when considering that distinction, is an economic one.

5 Carriage of Goods by Sea (2): Multimodal Transport, Container Transport and Freight

Anders Maersk, The [1986] 1 Lloyd's Rep 483 High Court of Hong Kong (Mayo J)

• *Transhipment*

Facts

The defendants shipped two boilers from Baltimore, USA, to Hong Kong on a through bill of lading which incorporated the provisions of the US Carriage of Goods by Sea Act 1936 and, therefore the Hague Rules, and conferred a liberty to tranship which was exercised in Hong Kong by the defendants. The goods were damaged on this transhipment leg of the voyage which was to Shanghai.

The plaintiff cargo owners sued the original carrier who had issued the bill of lading in Baltimore, but contended that since transhipment was in Hong Kong the final leg of the voyage in which the damage to the goods occurred was subject to the Hague-Visby Rules as enacted in Hong Kong and therefore to their appropriately modified enactment of the UK Carriage of Goods by Sea Act 1971. On the basis of this reasoning, the plaintiffs claimed the package limit contained in the Hague-Visby Rules applied and not the lower limit contained in the US Carriage of Goods by Sea Act 1936.

Held

The plaintiffs' claim failed. The through bill of lading issued in Baltimore was intended to govern the contract of carriage throughout. The defendants had simply exercised their right to tranship as conferred by that bill of lading. The provision relevant to that bill of lading was that contained in the US Carriage of Goods by Sea Act 1936. The words 'Shipment in Hong Kong' in s1(3) of the modified Carriage of Goods by Sea Act for Hong Kong was not intended to and did not embrace 'transhipment'. The reference to the bill of lading in s1(4) of that same Act must refer back to the original voyage contemplated by the parties. Since it gave the right to tranship, and there was no reference to Hong Kong made in it, the voyage contemplated by the parties must be taken as a voyage from Baltimore to Shanghai.

The defendant was therefore entitled to a limitation of liability based on the lower package limit contained in the US Carriage of Goods by Sea Act 1936.

Booth Steamship Ltd v *Cargo Fleet Iron Co Ltd* [1916] 2 KB 570 Court of Appeal (Lord Reading CJ, Warrington LJ and Scrutton J)

• *Vendor who stops goods in transit liable for return flight*

Facts

The defendants sold goods to S Co. The goods were carried on the plaintiff's ship. On learning that S Co was in financial difficulties, the defendants gave notice to the plaintiff to stop the goods in transit. The plaintiff claimed the freight from the defendants.

Held

If a vendor stops goods in transit and therefore

prevents them from being carried on to their ultimate destination, he/she is liable for the freight not only in respect of the whole voyage to the place at which the goods are in fact landed but also to the ultimate destination.

The carrier is bound to act upon notice from an unpaid vendor to stop the goods in transit and if he/she fails to do so he/she is liable to an action by the vendor for wrongful conversion.

Lord Reading CJ:

'This cases raises a novel and interesting point of law, ...whether an unpaid vendor who has stopped goods in transit can be made liable for the freight on the goods, or for damages for having prevented the carrier from earning the freight.

The plaintiff's claim to recover freight or damages from the defendants, the unpaid vendors of ... goods carried by the plaintiffs and consigned to the purchasers.'

Dakin v *Oxley* (1864) 10 LT 268
Court of Common Pleas (Willes CJ)

• *Freight payable even though goods damaged*

Facts
A cargo of coal was carried from Newport to Nassau. The cargo was damaged upon arrival, allegedly due to the unskilful navigation of the vessel and the damage was such that it was worth less than the freight paid to transport it. The question which fell to be answered was whether a charterer whose cargo is damaged by the fault of the master is entitled to abandon it to the shipowner and be excused from paying freight.

Held
Judgment given for the shipowner who was entitled to the freight despite deliver of the goods in a damaged condition.

Willes CJ:

'It would be unjust, and almost absurd that without regard to the comparative value of

the freight and cargo when uninjured, the risk of a mercantile adventure should be thrown upon the shipowner by the accident of the value of the cargo being a little more than the freight, so that a trifling damage, much less than the freight would reduce the value to less than the freight whilst if the cargo had been much more valuable and the damage greater, or the cargo worth a little less than the freight and the damage the same so as to bear a greater proportion to the whole, the freight would have been payable ... Yet this is the conclusion we are called on by the defendant to affirm in his favour, involving no less than that damage, however trifling, if culpable, may work a forfeiture of the entire freight ... It is evident that there is neither authority nor sound reason for upholding the proposed "defence" ...'

Comment
See *Asfar* v *Blundell* [1896] 1 QB 123 where it was held that if goods had been so damaged that they were no longer merchantable and could be considered a total loss, freight was not payable. See also *The Metula* [1978] 2 Lloyd's Rep 5 where the carrier was entitled to freight where goods were damaged but not to the extent of being unmerchantable.

Kulmerland, The [1973] 2 Lloyd's Rep 428 US Court of Appeals (Second Circuit) (Chief Judge Kaufman and Circuit Judges Anderton and Oakes)

• *Applying the financial limits to containers – a common sense test of 'functional' packages*

Facts
The plaintiffs were owners and shippers of cartons containing 350 adding machines bound for New York from Hamburg. The bill of lading issued for the containers was governed by the US Carriage of Goods by Sea Act

1936. The bill of lading noted the goods as 'said to contain machinery'.

Upon arrival at New York the container was broken into and its contents lost. The defendants claimed that their liability under the Carriage of Goods by Sea Act was $500 per package and that as the container constituted one package, the limit was not to be applied to each of the adding machines contained therein.

Held

Oakes J:

' … where the shipper's own packing units are functional a presumption is created that a container is not a "package", which must be overcome be evidence supplied by the carrier that the parties intended to treat it as such … when as here, the shipper's own individual units are not functional or usable for overseas shipment, the burden shifts to the shipper to show why the container should not be treated as the package (to which the limit in the Rules apply).

The "functional package unit" test we propound today is designed to provide in a case where the shipper has chosen the container, a "common sense" test under which all the parties concerned can allocate their responsibility for loss at the time of contract, purchase additional insurance if necessary, and thus "avoid the pains of litigation".'

Comment

See also *Owners of Cargo Lately Laden on Board the Ship River Gurara v Nigerian National Shipping Line Ltd* [1997] 4 All ER 498 (below).

Marbig Rexel Pty Ltd v ABC Container Line NV, The TNT Express [1992] 2 Lloyd's Rep 636 Australian Supreme Court of New South Wales (Admiralty Division) (Carruthers J)

• *Parties may rely on description of container in the bill of lading*

Facts

The plaintiffs claimed damages against the defendant owners of The TNT Express in respect of damage allegedly caused to the plaintiffs' cargo which had been carried in a container supplied by the defendant. It was found that the container had defective seals on the doors. The bill of lading issued by the defendants stated that the container had been received in apparently good condition.

Held

Judgment for the plaintiffs.

On the evidence the goods were in apparently good condition when loaded. The onus of establishing that the defective condition of the container would have been apparent on reasonable inspection by the defendant was on the plaintiff. 'Reasonable inspection' could not be defined but it did not require that the inspector had to be a skilled person such as a marine surveyor.

The defendants had failed to establish that the defective condition of the container was reasonably apparent and the plaintiffs were entitled to rely on the clean bill of lading. The fact that the condition was not reasonably obvious weighed heavily in favour of the plaintiffs.

Mayhew Foods Ltd v Overseas Containers Ltd [1984] 1 Lloyd's Rep 317 Queen's Bench Division (Commercial Court) (Bingham J)

• *Carrier remains fully responsible for the goods under art III Hague-Visby Rules for the safety of the goods during transhipment period*

Facts

In 1981 Mayhew entered into an oral contract with OCL for the carriage of frozen uncooked and partly cooked chickens and turkeys to Jeddah in Saudi Arabia. The cargo consisted of some 1,100 cartons carried by refrigerated container and, to remain in good condition, it was necessary that the goods be at all times kept deep frozen at minus 18° C.

At the time of contract, it was envisaged that the container would be shipped on board the defendants' vessel, The Benalder, from Southampton, England. This vessel and port were shown as the 'intended vessel' and 'intended port of loading' on the bill of lading, a combined transport shipment bill, issued by the defendants as carrier and made out showing Mayhew as the shipper and consignee to order. Clause 21 gave the carrier liberty at any time and without notice to the merchant to use any means of transport or storage and to tranship and the defendants took advantage of this liberty when The Benalder was instead scheduled to sail from Le Havre, France. The goods were collected from Mayhew's premises in Uckfield, Sussex, and stuffed into their refrigerated container on 3 December and then carried by road to Shoreham for shipment to Le Havre on the vessel Voline. The container was discharged at Le Havre early on 6 December and remained there until loaded on 11 or 12 December on The Benalder for carriage to Jeddah.

The Benalder arrived in Jeddah on 21 December but permission to discharge the container was refused because the contents had decayed and offensive juices were reported to be dripping from it. It was found that the temperature control on the container had been set at plus 2° C to plus 4° C and that far from being deep frozen, the poultry had been subject to heating while in the container. The container was set to deep frozen and remained aboard The Benalder as it continued on its journey to the Far East and was eventually returned to Mayhew Foods on 25 February 1982. The contents were declared unfit for human consumption and sold for animal feed at 2p per pound.

The evidence suggested that the damage had occurred while the cargo was lying ashore at Le Havre awaiting transhipment. OCL admitted breach of contract in failing properly to refrigerate the goods in the container

but contended that, on the basis of *Captain* v *Far Eastern Steamship Co* [1979] 1 Lloyd's Rep 595, the Hague-Visby Rules did not apply to this on-shore storage period but only to the transhipment from Le Havre to Jeddah and possibly also during the shipment from Shoreham to Le Havre. They therefore claimed that at any time that the Rules did not apply they were entitled to rely on cl 7 in the bill of lading which specified how any compensation recoverable should be calculated and specified an upper limit of:

' ... US \$2 per kilo of gross weight of the Goods lost or damaged.'

The effect of cl 8 on the reverse of the bill was to make cl 7 subject to the Hague-Visby Rules or any national law or international convention having mandatory effect in respect of the relevant damage. Clause 6 on the reverse of the bill stated:

'Carrier's Responsibility – Combined Transport 1 / The carrier shall be liable for loss or damage to the Goods occurring between the time when he receives the Goods for transportation and the time of delivery.'

Held

Judgment for Mayhew.

The parties intended and expected that a bill of lading should be issued and the bill issued provided for shipment from the United Kingdom. That port in the event was Shoreham by reason of the carrier exercising his liberty to tranship and to substitute vessels. From the time of shipment of the goods at Shoreham therefore, the Carriage of Goods By Sea Act 1971 and the Hague-Visby Rules did apply. It mattered not that the bill of lading was first issued once the goods had reached Le Havre and that it stated shipment on board Benalder from Southampton. The intention of the parties was plainly that shipment was to be on a vessel sailing from a UK port and that is what was done.

Bingham J distinguished *Captain* v *Far Eastern Steamship Co* on the grounds that:

'... the shipper there was told that there would be transhipment and there were separate bills of lading for the two legs of the journey.'

In the instant case the shipper had no knowledge that the carrier had invoked his liberty to tranship and had been issued with a bill of lading which had to be taken as covering the entire journey from Shoreham to Jeddah. Bingham J agreed with the decision of Devlin J in *Pyrene Co Ltd* v *Scindia Navigation Co Ltd* [1954] 2 QB 402 that the rights and liabilities under the Hague-Visby Rules attach to a contract or part of a contract and said:

'The contract here was for carriage of these goods from Uckfield to the numbered berth at Jeddah. The rules did not apply to inland transport prior to shipment on board a vessel, because under s1(3) of the 1971 Act, they are to have force of law only in relation to and in connection with the carriage of goods by sea in ships. But the contract here clearly provided for shipment at a United Kingdom port, intended to be Southampton but in the event Shoreham, and from the time of that shipment, the Act and the rules plainly applied. It does not matter that the vessel on which the container left this country was not Benalder, because OCL had liberty to substitute vessels or tranship and Benalder was only the intended vessel. Nor does it matter that the bill of lading was issued some days after the goods had arrived in Le Havre showing Benalder and Southampton as the intended vessel and port of shipment. The parties clearly expected and intended a bill of lading to be issued and when issued it duly evidenced the parties' earlier contract. Since this bill was issued in a contracting state and provided for carriage from a port in a contracting state, I think it plain that the rules applied once the goods were loaded on board the vessel at Shoreham.'

Moreover, the Rules continued to apply while the goods were lying ashore awaiting loading onto The Benalder. This was an interval between ports during the period of sea carriage. It was not the same as the period prior to any shipment and the period after discharge of the goods at the port of destination, both of which are governed by inland carriage. There is no inland carriage whilst the goods are lying on quay or otherwise waiting at port to be loaded and for this period no other rules can apply other than those for the carriage of the goods by sea for which this period is merely but a part. Bingham J continued:

'[The rules] do not apply to carriage or storage before the port of shipment or after the port of discharge, because that would be inland and not sea carriage. But between those ports the contract was ... for carriage by sea. If, during that carriage, OCL chose to avail themselves of their contractual right to discharge, store and tranship, those were, in my judgment, operations "in relation to and in connection with carriage of goods by sea in ships", to use the language of the Act, or were "within the contractual carriage", to use the language of cl 21(2) of the bill of lading conditions. It would, I think, be surprising if OCL could, by carrying the goods to Le Havre and there storing the goods before transhipment, rid themselves of liabilities to which they would have been subject had they, as contemplated, shipped the goods at Southampton and carried them direct to Jeddah, the more so since Mayhew had no knowledge of any voyage to Le Havre. My conclusion is that the rules, having applied on shipment from Shoreham, remained continuously in force until discharge at Jeddah. ....

If my foregoing conclusions are right, it does not matter whether the damage to the cargo occurred before or after the container was loaded on board Benalder, provided only that it occurred only after shipment at Shoreham, as it must have done since, on any showing, the goods needed some time to thaw out and deteriorate ...'

Owners of Cargo Lately Laden on Board the Ship River Gurara v *Nigerian National Shipping Line Ltd* [1997] 4 All ER 498 Court of Appeal (Hirst, Phillips and Mummery LJJ)

- *Hague Rules – definition of 'package' for the purposes of limitation of liability under art IV r5 Hague-Visby Rules*

Facts
In February 1989 while on a laden voyage from West Africa to Europe, the vessel, The River Gurara, was stranded off the coast of Portugal and subsequently broke up with loss of lives and a total loss of cargo. The plaintiff owners issued proceedings against the defendant shipowners on the bills of lading. Much of the cargo on board the vessel had been containerised and the various bills of lading issued by the defendants stated that the containers were 'said to contain' a specified number of items such as bales, parcels, bags, bundles, crates, cartons or pallets. The bills of lading were subject to the provisions of the Hague Rules and the defendants contended that art IV r5 of the Hague Rules limited their liability to '£100 per package or unit', and that for those purposes the containers constituted the package or unit. The plaintiffs contended that it was the items within the containers that constituted the relevant packages or units.

At the trial of the preliminary issues, Colman J had held that for the purposes of limitation, the number of items described by the bills of lading as being inside the container should apply, rather than the number of containers themselves. The defendants appealed, contending that the parties' agreement to the 'said to contain' qualification was an agreement to a bill of lading that merely enumerated the containers so that it was the number of containers which formed the basis for computing the limit of liability, and that for this calculation the description of the goods in the bills of lading was definitive.

Held
The appeal was dismissed and the decision of Colman J affirmed, although their Lordships reached this decision for different reasons.

Phillips LJ

'The principal issue to be resolved is whether, in the circumstances of this case, the packages on which the limit is to be calculated are the containers, or the individual items within them. Such an issue has been the subject of judicial decision in many other jurisdictions, but this is the first time that it has arisen for determination in this country.

I propose to consider the following questions. (1) Where packages are shipped in containers does the Hague Rules limit, on its true construction, fall to be calculated on the number of packages or the number of containers? (2) What is the effect of the description in the bill of lading on the basis for calculating the Hague Rules limit? In particular, (3) What is the effect of qualifying the description of the contents of a container by the words "said to contain".'

On the first question the court held that, for the purposes of art IV r5 of the Hague Rules, where parcels of cargo were loaded in containers, it was the parcels and not the containers which constituted the relevant 'packages'. Their Lordships expressed different opinions on the matters raised by the second and third questions. However, it was held that the defendants' limit of liability under the Hague Rules fell to be calculated on the number of packages that were proved to have been loaded within the containers rather than by reference to the description in the bills of lading. Phillips LJ:

'When I turn to consider decisions on the point in other jurisdictions, they reinforce my conclusion. They attach significance to the manner in which the bill of lading describes the cargo ... but where the bill of lading describes the cargo by reference to a specified number of packages loaded inside a specified number of containers, the courts have calculated the Hague Rules limit on the basis of the packages and not the containers. ...

The preference for the packages, rather than the containers in which they are stuffed, at least where the bill of lading states the number of each, has been shown, not merely by the courts of the United States, but by those of Canada, Australia, France, Holland, Italy and Sweden. The weight of this international authority, coupled with my provisional conclusion formed independently of it, leaves me in no doubt that in the present case the shipowners' limit of liability should be calculated on the basis of the number of packages carried in the containers rather than the number of containers, unless the manner in which the cargo has been described in the bills of lading requires a contrary approach.'

On whether a container could be described as a 'package', Phillips LJ said:

'[It was] ... submitted that to describe a container as a package was to strain the natural meaning of that word. With this also I agree. In *Bekol BV* v *Terracina Shipping Corp* (13 July 1988, unreported), which seems to be the only recorded case in which the English court has considered the meaning of "package" in the Hague Rules, Leggatt J referred to the definition of that word in the Oxford English Dictionary: "A bundle of things packed up, whether in a box or other receptacle, or merely compactly tied up ...". A huge metal container stuffed with goods which will normally themselves be made up in individual packages is not naturally described as a package.'

The description of the goods in a bill of lading is prima facie evidence of the nature of the cargo and statements made in it do not constitute an agreement between the parties as to the identity of that cargo. However, it remains

The judgment of Phillips LJ is interesting for the views expressed concerning statements in bills of lading generally, and particularly in connection with the qualification 'said to contain'. He was of the opinion that:

'Statements in a bill of lading describing the cargo shipped do not constitute an agreement between the parties as to the identity of that cargo. ... '

... under the Hague Rules, an unqualified description of the goods in the bill of lading does not constitute a binding agreement between the shipper and the carrier that the goods have been shipped as stated, but merely prima facie evidence of that fact. Furthermore, even before the initiation of container carriage, the rules catered for the possibility that the carrier would have no reasonable means of checking the 'number of packages or pieces, or the quantity, or weight', in which case he was under no obligation to record these matters on the bill of lading.'

It of course remains open to either party to prove, by reference to extrinsic evidence, that the bill of lading did not accurately state the nature of the cargo shipped and, in the event of either party successfully doing so, the limit of liability will fall to be calculated by reference to the number of packages proved to have been carried rather than the number stated in the bill of lading. This is wholly different to the argument put forward by counsel for the defendants who had argued that the descriptions of the goods in the bill of lading (ie the number of packages or number of containers) should provide the basis for calculating the limit of liability as this is what was agreed by the parties as constituting a package. Colman J himself had accepted that it was the intention of the parties expressed in the bill of lading which would determine what was to be treated as a package. Phillips LJ rejected this view and said:

'While I appreciate the desirability of international uniformity, I am unable to accept that the basis of limitation under the unamended Hague Rules depends upon the agreement of the parties as to what constitute the relevant "packages", as represented by the description of the cargo on the face of the bill of lading. ...

The Hague Rules limitation provisions were designed to prevent shipowners imposing on shippers unrealistically low limits of liability. If the parties are permitted to agree their own definition of "packages", shipowners will, by applying that definition to containers, succeed in evading the minimum limit of liability that the Hague Rules aimed to secure.'

His Lordship agreed that where the cargo claimant proved his loss and relied on the bill of lading as prima facie evidence of what was shipped, then in such circumstances, the description of the goods in the bill of lading would indeed form the basis of the Hague Rules limit of liability. However, Phillips LJ envisaged circumstances where the statements on the bill of lading would play no part in limitation - for example, where the cargo claimant proved his loss with evidence extrinsic to the bill of lading, then, according to Phillips LJ, the limit of liability should be calculated not by reference to what was actually shipped. He provided the example of a cargo claimant who proves he has lost a container containing three packages – the liability of the carrier will be based on those three packages, even though they were not enumerated in the bill of lading.

Hirst LJ agreed with the reasoning of Colman J and, for the sake of international uniformity, followed the approach of the American, Canadian, Australian, French and Dutch courts in treating the Hague Rules as having the same effect as the Hague-Visby Rules. However, he dissented on the point that the agreement of the parties as embodied in their bill of lading had no bearing on what should constitute a package.

6 Carriage of Goods by Sea (3): Rights of Suit, Carriage of Goods by Sea Act 1992

Aegean Sea Traders Corporation v Repsol Petroleo SA & Another, The Aegean Sea [1998] 2 Lloyd's Rep 39 Queen's Bench Division (Admiralty Court) (Thomas J)

•*Carriage of Goods by Sea Act 1992, ss2, 3 and 5 – bill endorsed in error does not make endorsee a lawful holder in good faith*

Facts

In December 1992, whilst proceeding to berth at La Coruna in Spain in heavy weather, The Aegean Sea grounded on rocks, broke in two, caught fire and exploded. She was carrying a cargo of crude oil, most of which was lost, and claims were brought against the plaintiff shipowners for the resultant extensive environmental pollution and damage to private property. The plaintiffs sought to recover these losses together with the value of the vessel, the bunkers on board and the freight (in total about US $65 million) from the first defendants, Repsol, an oil refinery company owned at the time by the state of Spain, on the basis of one of the bills of lading for the cargo of oil. The oil had been purchased fob under two bills of lading by the second defendants, ROIL, the charterers of the vessel and a trading subsidiary of Repsol. ROIL sold the cargo under both bills of lading to Repsol on 'ex ship La Coruna' delivery terms. One of these bills of lading stayed in the possession of ROIL alone and was not in issue. The plain-

tiffs were contending that Repsol had become liable to them under the terms of the other bill of lading which had been erroneously endorsed by the holder, Louis Dreyfus Energy Ltd, to Repsol instead of to ROIL.

The plaintiffs contention relied on three claims:

1. that Repsol became subject to the liabilities under that bill of lading by reason of the provision in the Carriage of Goods by Sea Act 1992;
2. that Repsol were liable to indemnify them through the terms of a letter of indemnity which they had been provided, as is usual for a short haul voyage, in anticipation that the cargo would be delivered without production of bills of lading;
3. that terms should be implied into the bill of lading as to nomination of a port and its safety and as to indemnity.

Repsol denied that they had become lawful holders of the bill of lading. The bills of lading in respect of both cargoes of oil had been forwarded to them by ROIL who had received them from Louis Dreyfus together with an invoice against which ROIL had paid. The error had then been noticed and Repsol had immediately arranged for the bills to be returned to Louis Dreyfus who voided the endorsement and re-endorsed the bills to ROIL. Repsol contended that the title in the cargo remained at all times with ROIL and that it had never been their intention that they would obtain possession of the bill of lading as endorsees.

Held

Thomas J:

'The claims under the bills of lading against Repsol can not in my view succeed because Repsol never became subject to the liabilities under the bills of lading; even if they had, the bills of lading did not contain the implied terms on which the Owners' claim is based.'

Repsol did not become lawful holders of the bill of lading and thereby acquire rights under that bill under s2(1) of the Carriage of Goods by Sea Act 1992. Thomas J found it to be unlikely that the 1992 Act intended such a result where the bill of lading had been endorsed in error and this error had been rectified. He rejected the shipowners' claim that Repsol must have first taken possession of the bill within the meaning of s5 in order to return it for re-endorsement:

'It cannot have been intended by the craftsman of the Act that a person to whom a bill of lading is endorsed and sent in error has then to act as if he was a person entitled to endorse the bill of lading as a precondition of the person who made the mistake being enabled to rectify his error by re-endorsing and delivering it to the correct party; the person to whom it was sent was not the lawful holder and not therefore entitled to endorse it.'

Repsol could not be said to be 'a person with possession of the bill as a result of the completion, by delivery of the bill, of any endorsement of the bill' as required by s5(2)(b). The mere delivery of an endorsed bill to them did not give them possession of it as holder. Whilst the definition of a holder of a bill of lading given in s5 might be said to be primarily relevant to the obtaining of rights under s2 and not to the imposition of liabilities under s3, this did not support the claim made by the plaintiffs' that it was irrelevant that Repsol did not want the bills as endorsees and that mere delivery should suffice. Possession as a result of the completion by delivery of an endorsement under s5(2)(b) obviously

required a consensual element on the part of the endorsee or transferee. Repsol had not intended to become endorsees of the bill and when they received the bill they had set about rectifying the error. They could not therefore be said to have become a holder of the bill merely by reason of it having being sent to them. Thomas J:

'I do not consider that a person satisfies the requirements under s5(2)(b) and becomes the holder of a bill of lading if that person obtains the bill of lading merely in consequence of someone endorsing it and sending it to him. The section requires him to have possession as a result of the completion of an endorsement by delivery. Although the sending and receipt of a document through the post often constitutes service of a document, the sending of a bill of lading through the post does not without more constitute delivery; the person receiving it has to receive it into his possession and accept the delivery before he becomes the holder.'

Furthermore, the bill of lading had not been delivered to Repsol. ROIL requested early delivery of the documents to expedite claims for the loss of the vessel and her cargo and were sent these by Louis Dreyfus, under cover of a letter addressed to ROIL. Thomas J was of the opinion that the facts bore the interpretation that Louis Dreyfus intended ROIL to receive all documents as principals, not as agents for Repsol. Accordingly, in forwarding the bills of lading to Repsol, ROIL were not acting as agents for Louis Dreyfus. The bills were forwarded by ROIL as a principal to enable Repsol to act as ROIL's agents for the purposes of making a claim against the cargo underwriters. On the basis of these findings Thomas J held:

'In my view Repsol therefore never obtained possession of the bill of lading as the result of completion by delivery of the bill by endorsement. There was never any delivery of the bill of lading by Louis Dreyfus to Repsol to complete the endorsement. Even if Repsol had obtained possession of the bill of lading from Louis

Dreyfus, they never accepted delivery of it as the endorsee or transferee. As soon as they saw the endorsement to them, they sent it back to be endorsed to the rightful endorsee and transferee.'

The plaintiffs had also argued that property had passed to Repsol on endorsement and Thomas J firmly dismissed the notion that the 1992 Act meant there to be any link between the passing of property and rights under a bill of lading:

'A point was raised as to the passing of property. I must therefore make it clear that in my view the endorsement required did not have to be an endorsement that was intended to pass the property; it was, in my view, irrelevant that, on the facts, it was clear that the endorsement by Louis Dreyfus to Repsol was never intended to pass property to Repsol. The provisions of COGSA 1992 do not depend on the passing of property; it would be impermissible, in my view, to re-introduce the link between the passing of property and rights under the bill of lading that existed under the Bills of Lading Act 1855 by interpreting the word endorsement in such a way as to link it with the passing of property.'

Thomas J also took the view that there was no argument that Repsol had become a lawful holder of the bill 'in good faith' under s5 and said:

'In the commercial context of bills of lading, the meaning of the term good faith should be clear, capable of unambiguous application and be consistent with the usage in other contexts and countries. In my view, it therefore connotes honest conduct and not a broader concept of good faith such as "the observance of reasonable commercial standards of fair dealing in the conclusion and performance of the transaction concerned".
...
There can be no question but that the circumstances in which Repsol acquired the bill of lading were honest, and therefore if they were holders, then they became holders in good faith. However when the requirements of s5 are read together, the require-

ment of good faith in the sense in which I consider it must be interpreted reinforces the view to which I have come that Repsol did not obtain possession of the bill as a result of the completion, by delivery, of the endorsement. Repsol knew that the bill of lading should have been endorsed to ROIL and not to them, because it was ROIL and not Repsol who had purchased the cargo from Louis Dreyfus; they therefore never accepted the delivery or endorsement of the bill of lading to them. If the requirement of good faith is limited to honest conduct, then it is a further pointer that the requirements of possession as a result of the completion by delivery of an endorsement must have the consensual elements on the part of the endorsee or transferee which I have concluded are necessary.'

The plaintiffs' second route for establishing the liability of Repsol was based on the terms of the letter of indemnity. Thomas J was not willing to accept that the letter of indemnity amounted to the obligations claimed by the plaintiffs:

'In the first place, ... the letter of indemnity did not oblige the Owners to deliver the cargo to Repsol. The obligation under the letter of indemnity was limited to circumstances where delivery was made to Repsol or to their order. If the Owners did deliver the cargo, then and only then did the indemnity and the obligation to produce duly endorsed bills of lading arise.

Next, I do not consider that the duly endorsed bills of lading required under the letter of indemnity had to be endorsed to Repsol or their order. ... The letter of indemnity required duly endorsed bills of lading; this meant, in my view, duly endorsed to the person who had in fact taken delivery. That might or might not have been Repsol. On the facts, as they appear to me, it would have been ROIL not Repsol who would have taken delivery under the bills of lading.'

Repsol had not received the bill of lading and title to the goods remained in ROIL. In any case, even if they had become holders of the bill of lading, they did not demand delivery of the oil under s3(1). Repsol had received the oil wastes and other salvaged oil on the instruction of the Spanish government and Thomas J considered that receipt under compulsion was not intended by the legislators when drafting s3:

> 'The imposition of liabilities under COGSA 1992 on the lawful holder, when he took delivery or made a demand for delivery from the carrier under the bill of lading or make a claim against the carrier, was a reflection of the principle that it was only fair to impose liabilities on the lawful holder (or a person who subsequently became the lawful holder) if he took or demanded delivery or made a claim; it was that voluntary act of making the demand or taking delivery or making a claim that made it appropriate to impose liabilities. On the other hand, if he did not demand delivery or take delivery or make a claim against the carrier, the liabilities were not to be imposed on him. It would be contrary to that clear intention that liabilities should be imposed in consequence of the involuntary act of being compelled by a civil governmental authority to accept the cargo, particularly in circumstances where the recipient was the only person with the facilities to take it.'

It was further arguable the salvaged oil would in any case not be treated as crude oil for trading on the oil market and was therefore not as a matter of business the same oil that was shipped under the bills of lading: *Asfar* v *Blundell* [1895] 1 QB 123.

The letter of indemnity was not in terms a demand for delivery. Repsol did not demand delivery of the oil under s3(1) of the 1992 Act and the obligation to deliver duly endorsed bills of lading did not arise.

> '... Repsol never requested delivery. The small quantity that was received at their refinery was not pursuant to a request, but pursuant to the order of the civil government. The cargo was not in any event delivered by the Owners. It was taken from the vessel by the salvors employed by the Owners through a pipeline over the rocks and sent to the refinery in a fleet of tankers

where it was received only on the order of the civil government. That did not amount to delivery. The fact that the Owners failed to deliver the cargo meant that the condition precedent to the obligation to deliver duly endorsed bills of lading did not arise.'

The plaintiffs' third contention was that the bill of lading contained an implied term giving the other party to the bill of lading a right to nominate the port of discharge, an implied term as to the safety of the port so nominated and an implied indemnity. They claimed that La Coruna was nominated by Repsol (as the other party to the bill of lading or on that party's behalf) and was unsafe, and that Repsol thereby became liable under the implied term as to safety or the implied indemnity for the losses occasioned by the stranding of the Aegean Sea at that port.

Thomas J found that neither on the business efficacy nor officious bystander test was it necessary to imply a term that the other party to the bill of lading had a right to nominate the port. This was a short-haul trade. The express terms of the bill of lading did not give the right to nominate the port to anyone since it would be highly unlikely that those who were the other parties to the bill of lading before the vessel arrived would have any interest in nominating a port of discharge, and no one would have contemplated giving that right to such a person. Nor would it make sense that the ultimate receiver have the right as he would never have had rights under the bill of lading at the time a nomination was required.

It was only if there was a right to nominate that an implied term as to safety might arise. Even if the right to nominate could be implied, there was no general rule that a term as to safety would always be implied into voyage charterparties where there was an unspecified range of ports. The law was more certain as regards time charters where a warranty of safety would often be implied but some standard forms of voyage charterparty do not contain an express warranty of safety. The authorities have only implied such a term into a voyage charter where there was good reason to do so on the basis of the other terms of the charter and no case has implied the same term into the bill of lading. Even if the right to nominate the port were to be implied into the bill of lading, it would not follow that a term as to safety should also be implied since that would pass an onerous liability to the lawful holder of the bill and, as such, would fail the officious bystander test. If it had been intended to impose obligations as to safety, the bill of lading would have made that express. Thomas J expressed this as follows:

'Although it would be necessary to imply a term that the port nominated be one at which it was possible for the vessel to discharge the cargo she had loaded, the implication of a term as to safety of that port would create a very onerous liability on those who became subjected to the liabilities under the bill of lading. The bill of lading does not specify that the port is to be safe and given the potentially onerous liabilities, it is difficult to see how an officious bystander would say "of course" if the term were proposed. The position of the charterer is very different as he is in direct contractual relationship with the shipowner and will often insure his liabilities under a charterer's liability policy. In the case of a bill of lading that liability as to safety will be passed to the lawful holder who takes or demands delivery at the end of the chain; it would not necessarily be certain that in the case of this bill of lading that would be Repsol and it would be unlikely that they would ever contemplate insurance against such liabilities as the holders of a bill of lading, assuming such insurance was available. In my view if it had been intended that the onerous obligations as to safety were imposed under the bill of lading, the bill of lading would have made this express.'

If the right to nominate the port was implied this did not carry with it a tacit offer to indemnify. If a term as to safety was implied, the need for an implied indemnity would not arise at all. In any event, no term as to indemnity should be implied and certainly not one of the width proposed by the plaintiffs which read: 'the Owners would be entitled to an indemnity in respect of any costs or losses incurred as a result of complying with the orders of the other party to the bill of lading contract'. Thomas J thought that such a term would introduce an unacceptable uncertainty into the bill of lading.

'It was suggested by Owners, however, that this term was necessary as it would encompass bad weather; however, in considering whether it is necessary to imply a term, it must be necessary to consider the scope of the term contended for. The language of the term contended for is very similar to that in the common form of employment and indemnity clause to be found in charterparties; the exact scope of such a clause is not settled – see in particular: *Larinnaga SS Co v R* [1945] AC 246 and *The Ann Stathatos* (1950) 83 Ll LR 228 at 233 and the cases cited in Scrutton at p367. However, it is clear that the ordinary incidents of navigation are not within the scope of such a clause.

It is difficult therefore to see precisely what the clause would cover given the relationship between the holder of a bill of lading and the shipowner, as it would not cover the ordinary incidents of navigation. In the circumstances, I do not consider it would, in any event, be right to imply an indemnity of uncertain scope into the bill of lading; if there is an implied term that the port nominated be safe, then the Owners have the benefit of that and it would provide the Owners with what they contend that they require. If, for the reasons I have given, such a clause is not to be implied, it would also be unnecessary to imply a term for indemnity of an uncertain scope for which Owners contend.'

Thomas J considered the decision in *Naviera Mogor SA* v *Société Metallurgique de Normandie, The Nogar Marin* [1988] 1 Lloyd's Rep 412 in which Mustill LJ had distinguished two groups of cases, the right of indemnity arising from an act done at the request of another and those concerned with indemnities and other rights arising from carriage under bills of lading, such as *Krüger & Co Ltd* v *Moel Tryvan Ship Co Ltd* [1907] AC 272, and concluded:

'Owners contended that the correct analysis, based on the judgment of Mustill LJ, was that if there was a request by the other party to the bill of lading to go to a port, then as the shipowner was obliged to act or in fact acted on that request, a right of indemnity should be implied. However, the implication of this indemnity must depend on the particular circumstances. For very much the same reasons as I have given in respect of the term as to safety, I do not consider that a term should be implied. If such an onerous obligation was to be contained in the bill of lading, it would have had to have been expressly agreed.'

Comment

Thomas J thought, obiter, that once liability had been imposed under s3, it was not divested by later re-indorsement of the bills of lading. Thus, if Repsol had requested delivery, a later indorsement would not have divested them of it. The Court of Appeal later took a different view in *Borealis AB* v *Stargas Ltd and Another, The Berge Sisar* [2000] 1 WLR 209 (see below).

Aramis, The [1989] 1 Lloyd's Rep 213 Court of Appeal (O'Connor, Bingham and Stuart-Smith LJJ)

• *The facts of the presentation of shipping documents by the receivor of goods to the carrier at the port of discharge determines whether there is an implied contract*

Facts

In May 1980 the Aramis loaded 3,209 tonnes of linseed expellers at Necochea in Argentina. Two parcels of this bulk were bound for Rotterdam: one of 204 tonnes carried under bill of lading No 5, and another of 255 tonnes carried under bill of lading No 6. Both bills of lading were signed on behalf of the master and recorded that freight had been paid. Among the many clauses in the bills were clauses providing for the payment of demurrage and extra handling charges by 'the merchant' which expression was defined as

including the shipper, consignee, the holder of the bill of lading and the owner of the goods. Other clauses required the merchant to take delivery of the goods by day or by night, on to quay or into lighters, midstream or in the roads and provided that if he failed to do so the ship should be at liberty to deposit the goods into warehouses etc, at the risk and expense of the merchant.

The shippers duly endorsed the bills each of which thereafter reached the hands of one of the two plaintiffs who were buyers under contracts governed by English law. On arrival of the ship at Rotterdam the plaintiffs' agents presented the two bills of lading to the defendant shipowners' agents. It soon became clear that there was a substantial shortage of cargo, perhaps because of over-delivery at Rouen, the intermediate discharge port. In the event, nothing was delivered under bill No 5 and only 11.5 tonnes were delivered under bill No 6.

If the bills had not related to goods which were part of a larger bulk, the plaintiffs' course of action would have been straightforward: they would have sued the shipowners for breach of the bill of lading contract, relying for their entitlement to do so on s1 of the Bills of Lading Act 1855. However, their position was not straightforward. Following the decision in *Leigh & Sillivan* v *Aliakamon Shipping Co, The Aliakamon* [1986] AC 785 (see below) the plaintiffs had no claim in tort as the buyers because they were not owners of the goods when the loss or misdelivery took place. In order to bring a claim against the shipowners, therefore, it was necessary to show a breach of contractual relationship on which they could sue and their problem, in the face of s16 Sale of Goods Act 1979 and s1 Bills of Lading Act 1855, was being able to show such a relationship.

Held

The appeal from the judgment of Evans J was allowed.

First, the plaintiffs were not entitled to sue under s1 Bills of Lading Act 1855. When property in the goods passed upon or by reason of an endorsement, contractual rights or suit and liabilities were transferred to the endorsee, but here the goods formed part of a single undivided bulk cargo and therefore no property in the goods passed.

O'Connor LJ:

'In *Sewell* v *Burdick* (1884) 10 App Cas 74 shipowners brought an action against the endorsee of the bills of lading for unpaid freight. The shipper of specific goods consigned to himself endorsed the bills of lading in blank and deposited them with bankers as security for a loan. The House of Lords held that the bankers were pledgees and as such although "a" property could be said to have passed, "the" property had not. The result was that shipowners could not rely on s1 of the Bills of Lading Act 1855 and this claim failed.

The problem where there is a sale of a quantity of bulk cargo is quite different. Section 16 of the Sale of Goods Act 1979 makes it clear that property does not pass until the contract quantity is separated from the bulk. Normally this will happen at the time when delivery is made be it from ship or silo to the person presenting the bill of lading. In the present case the endorsees of bill 6 were agents for buyers who had paid the purchase price, so the question is whether when the 11 tonnes were delivered the property passed to them "upon reason of the endorsement": s1 Bills of Lading Act 1855. Obviously, no property passed "upon" the endorsement for I do not think that concept has any application where the bill of lading is endorsed in blank because I think that "upon" means "at the time when the bill is endorsed".

Can it be said that property passed "by reason of the endorsement" at the time of delivery? There is authority for the proposition that, despite the wording of s1 Bills of Lading Act 1855 "every endorsee of a bill of lading", intermediate endorsees drop out and the transfer of rights and liabilities are to the endorsee who can take delivery: *Smurthwaite* v *Wilkins* (1862) 11 CB (NS) 847 cited by Lord Selbourne with approval in *Sewell* at 87.

Ordinarily for property to pass "by reason

of endorsement" I think that this must be at the time when the bill of lading is handed over against payment of the purchase price. That is not this case. I have no doubt that that is the sense I which these words have been understood. I do not think that the passage in Lord Selbourne's speech can alter the situation. ...'

Second, it was impossible to imply a contract between the plaintiffs and the defendants on the bare facts for either bill of lading. The presentation of the bill of lading No 6 coupled with part delivery was entirely consistent with the performance of obligations and rights of the parties under their existing contractual arrangements with others. There was no evidence of the performance of any act which was explicable only on the basis that the terms of the bill of lading governed their relationship inter se. In the case of bill of lading No 5 where there was no delivery there was no basis for implying a contract. Bingham LJ stated:

'Most contracts are of course made expressly whether orally or in writing. But here on the evidence nothing was said, nothing was written. So regard must be paid to the conduct of the parties alone. The questions to be answered are I think twofold: (1) Whether the conduct of the bill of lading holder in presenting the bill of lading to the ship's agent would be reasonably understood by the agents (or the shipowner) as an offer to enter into a contract on the bill of lading terms; (2) Whether the conduct of the ship's agent in accepting the bill of lading or the conduct of the master in agreeing to deliver or in giving delivery would be reasonably understood by the bill of lading holder as an acceptance of his offer.

... It must be necessary to identify conduct referable to the contract contended for or at the very least conduct inconsistent with there being no contract made between the parties to the effect contended for. Put another way I think it must be fatal to the implication of a contract if the parties would or might have acted exactly as they did in the absence of a contract.

If this approach is correct I think it is impossible to imply a contract on the bare facts of this case. Nothing that the shipowners or the bill of lading holders did need have been different had their intention been not to make a contract on the terms of the bill of lading. Their business relationship was entirely efficacious without implication of any contract between them. Although the bill of lading holders had no title to any part of the undivided bulk cargo they has a perfectly good right to demand delivery and the shipowners had no right to refuse or to impose conditions.'

Bingham LJ noted the shortcomings s1 of the 1855 Act and the hope for amendment to the law when he said:

'… Mr Justice Evans below attributed to the bill of lading holders an offer to take delivery "of the cargo specified in the bill of lading and on its terms", but there is nothing to show that they offered to take the cargo on those terms. He treated the acts of the crew and other agents on behalf of the shipowners as enough to constitute acceptance, but those acts were in no way referable to the bill of lading terms. If the Judge's approach is correct there is in truth no need for the 1855 Act because it is almost impossible to imagine circumstances in which a bill of lading holder could obtain goods without becoming a party to the bill of lading contract. It may, of course, be said, and with truth, that the draftsman of the 1855 Act was not concerned to legislate for undivided bulk cargoes consigned or assigned to a number of different consignees or assignees. On that account it may fairly be said that the modern prevalence of undivided bulk cargoes calls for a new, commercially workable solution. I agree. But the solution is in my view to be found in an amendment to the 1855 Act along the lines now under consideration by the Law Commission rather than in an implication of a contract where the grounds for such implication do not exist.'

Comment

The reform to which Bingham LJ referred culminated in the passing of the Carriage of Goods by Sea Act 1992. This case was one of a series of decisions which demonstrated the inadequacies of using s1 of the 1855 Act to avoid privity of contract as between a transferee of the bill of lading and the carrier. For the position since the passing of the 1992 Act and the way in which cases like Sewell and Aramis have been discussed, see *Borealis* v *Stargas Ltd, The Berge Sisar* [1998] 2 Lloyd's Rep 475 (CA) and *Effort Shipping Co Ltd* v *Linden Management SA, The Giannis K* [1998] 1 Lloyd's Rep 337.

Borealis AB v Stargas Ltd and Another, The Berge Sisar [2000] 1 WLR 209 House of Lords (Lords Brown-Wilkinson, Steyn and Clyde)

• *Transfer of rights and liabilities under a bill of lading: s3 COGSA 1992*

Facts

Stargas, the first defendant, purchased a quantity of propane from the Saudi Arabian Oil Co, the second defendant, and in turn sold the goods to Borealis, the plaintiffs. Stargas took a charter on The Berge Sisar from Begensen, the owner of the vessel, and the goods were loaded on board ship by the second defendant in Saudi Arabia for shipment to the plaintiffs. The five bills of lading issued for the shipment named the Saudi Arabian Oil Co as the shipper.

The contract of sale between Borealis and Stargas contained an express term that the propane should not contain corrosive compounds beyond a defined limit and on arrival at the port of discharge the propane was tested and failed this corrosion test. Borealis then sold the goods to Dow Europe on cif terms, endorsing the bills of lading to them, and brought an action against Stargas claiming damages for breach of contract on the grounds that the propane was not of contractual quality or, in the alternative, that Stargas was in breach of the charterparty and s3 of the US Carriage of Goods by Sea Act 1936.

Stargas claimed an indemnity from Begensen, the shipowner, who in turn counterclaimed for alleged damage caused to the vessel due to the corrosive propane. Pursuant to s3(1)(c) of the UK Carriage of Goods by Sea Act 1992, Begensen claimed against the Saudi Arabian Oil Co as shipper of the cargo and against Borealis as a holder of the bill of lading which had requested delivery of the cargo.

Held

The plaintiffs' liability under the bills of lading ceased when they indorsed the bills to the sub-buyer, Dow Europe.

The class of persons who were subject to liability under a contract of carriage was limited by s3 of the Carriage of Goods by Sea Act 1992 in that a lawful holder of a bill of lading was only liable under s3 until the bill was indorsed to someone who fulfilled the conditions of liability specified in s3(1). Thus, when rights under the bill of lading are transferred to the transferee, the transferor's rights are extinguished. A holder was not meant to be liable indefinitely and the intention of s3 was that once the holder indorsed the bill to someone else, the original holder was no longer liable under the contract of carriage. Those who should be liable on the contract of carriage are those holders of the bill of lading who took steps to enforce rights under the contract of carriage.

Comment

The holding in this case makes it clear that as to holders of bills of lading, when one right commences another right terminates.

Glyn Mills Currie & Co v The East and West India Dock Company VII

(1882) 7 App Cas 591 House of Lords (Lord Selborne LC, Lords Cairns, O'Hagan, Blackburn, Watson and Fitzgerald)

• *Bills of lading issued in several counterparts*

Facts

A cargo of sugar had been shipped for London and was consigned to C. The ship's master signed a set of three bills of lading marked respectively 'First', 'Second' and 'Third', making the sugar deliverable to C or their assigns, freight payable in London. Each bill of lading contained the provision: 'In witness whereof the master or purser of the said ship hath affirmed the three bills of lading, all of this tenor and date, the one of which bills being accomplished, the others to stand void.'

During the voyage, on 15 May 1878, C endorsed in blank the bill marked 'First' to the appellants, London bankers, in consideration for a loan. The ship arrived at London on 27 May 1878 and, on the 28th, the master landed the sugar and deposited it with the respondents in their docks. On 29 May, the master lodged with the respondents a notice to detain the sugar until payment of the freight. On 31 May, C brought the bill marked 'Second' to the respondents who entered C in their books as owners of the sugar.

On 7 June, the freight having been paid by C, the stop for freight was removed. In July the respondents, bona fide and without notice or knowledge of any claim by the appellants, delivered the sugar to W, who held delivery orders signed by C.

C had gone into liquidation in August and the appellants demanded the sugar from the respondents, producing the bill of lading marked 'First'. The respondents were not able to deliver and the appellants brought this action against them claiming damages for the value of the sugar.

Held

The respondents were not guilty of a conversion and, therefore, the appellant bankers could not maintain any action against them. Lord Blackburn (at p613):

'I think ... that where the master has notice that there has been an assignment of another part of the bill of lading, the master must interplead or deliver to the one who he thinks has the better right, at his peril if he is wrong. And I think it would probably be the same if he had knowledge that there had been an assignment, though no one had given notice of it or as yet claimed under it.'

Comment

This case highlights the dangers in issuing bills of lading in several counterparts notwithstanding the provision to the effect that if one counterpart be acted upon, the others are thereby rendered void.

Leigh & Sillivan v Aliakmon Shipping Co, The Aliakmon [1986] AC 785 House of Lords (Lords Brandon of Oakbrook, Keith of Kinkel, Brightman, Griffiths and Ackner)

- *Cif buyer's rights in tort*

Facts

The plaintiffs contracted to buy a quantity of steel coils c & f Immingham. The sellers were to draw a bill of exchange for the price payable after 180 days and, if presented together with a bill of lading, this was to be indorsed by the buyers. The buyers had intended to pay for the steel by reselling it before the price was due but the market price fell dramatically and they were unable to do so. Consequently the bank refused to back the bill of exchange. However, the buyer and seller agreed to make joint efforts to sell the steel. A letter was appended to the bill of lading in the possession of the buyers the effect of which was to retain the seller's right of disposal of the goods, which could only be sold with their consent. Since all the costs of discharging and warehousing the goods were to be bourne by the sellers, the only liability to be assumed by the buyers was that of agent of the seller.

When the steel arrived at Immingham the buyers acting under the instruction of the sellers, warehoused them and paid the appropriate discharging fees. It was then discovered that the steel was damaged as a result of negligent stowage and the buyers sued the shipowners.

The Court of Appeal ([1985] QB 350) found that the shipowners were not liable to the buyers either in contract or in tort. The bill of lading, although delivered to the buyers, did not confer on them any right to sue in contract under s1 of the Bills of Lading Act 1855 because the buyers had assumed no right under that section and had instead reserved the right of disposal of property in the goods under s19(1) of the Sale of Goods Act 1979. The transfer of the bill of lading, therefore, did not transfer property by reason of the consignment or indorsement of it as required under s1 of the Bills of Lading Act 1855. There was no implied contract upon which the buyer could sue without having property in the goods because of the effect of the letter appended to the bill of lading. The buyers had not agreed to pay the discharging costs and the freight on arrival and so could not show an implied contract between themselves and the shipowners by which they agreed to pay charges in consideration for the damaged goods: *Brandt v Liverpool Steam Navigation* [1924] 1 KB 575 applied. Further, the shipowners were not liable in tort. The buyers were claiming the right to impose on the shipowners a higher duty of care than the shipowners owed to the seller under the bill of lading. In reaching this part of their decision, their Lordships differed in their views (see **Comment** below).

Held

The House of Lords dismissed an appeal brought by the buyers.

In respect of the buyers' right to sue the shipowners in contract, the House of Lords agreed with the decision reached by the Court of Appeal. Although a cif or c & f buyer will ordinarily get property in the cargo assigned to him when the bill of lading is endorsed to him against payment of the price, and, therefore, a right to sue in contract under s1 Bills of Lading Act 1855, the sellers' reservation of the right of disposal of property did not pass on endorsement of the bill. Accordingly, at the time the damage was done to the cargo, the appellants had a risk in that cargo but no legal property.

As to the buyers' claim in tort, the House took the view that the consignee can claim in tort only if he can show that he had a possessory title or that he had legal ownership at the time that the loss or damage took place. It is not sufficient that at that time he had a contractual right affecting such property: *Candlewood* v *Mitsui* [1986] AC 1. The decision in *Margarine Union* v *Gambay Prince, The Wear Breeze* [1969] 1 QB 219 remains good law to the extent that it states that the buyer must have a proprietary or possessory right at the time of damage. In that case, lack of either of these had prevented a bulk buyer of copra from being able to sue on the bill of lading.

It had been argued by the buyers that since a cif and a c & f contract intended that ownership should pass, a distinction should be drawn between these and other contracts when determining whether a duty of care was owed. The House of Lords rejected this argument as a spurious ground of distinction and also rejected the argument that the buyer under such a contract acquired in any event an equitable ownership on shipment. Sections 16–19 of the Sale of Goods Act is clearly meant to constitute a complete code to regulate passing of property which leaves no room for a residual distinction between equitable and legal property, and this applies equally to all contracts including those on cif or c & f terms.

The decision in *The Nea Tyhi* [1982] 1 Lloyd's Rep 606 was disapproved and the decision in *Schiffhart & Kohlen GmbH* v *Chelsea Maritime, The Irene's Success* [1982] QB 481 was overruled. The latter case had held that cif buyers of a cargo of coal damaged due to an incursion of sea water caused by the shipowners' negligence were entitled to claim in tort even though they never became holders of the bill of lading and were not the owners of the goods, because it ought reasonably to have been in the contemplation of the carriers that failure to deliver the goods in the condition in which they were shipped would cause damage to the person who bore the risk of damage at the time of shipment. Lloyd J had taken the view that public policy considerations should not operate to exclude the duty altogether, but only to limit its scope, and that there was no floodgates argument to be considered. The House in the instant case rejected this, holding that an exception to the rule for carriage by sea to allow someone to sue without proprietary or possessory rights would eventually be sought to be extended to other areas of the law and it would create uncertainty. As a matter of public policy, the scope of a duty owed by a carrier in a relationship of sufficient proximity to justify the existence of a duty between himself and the consignee fell to be determined in the light of the terms of the bill of lading under which the goods were originally carried. In this case no duty of care existed and it was therefore unnecessary to go further and consider to what extent the duty would have been qualified by the terms of the bill of lading.

Where the buyer has the risk in the goods but no property in them, and the seller has the property in those goods and has received the price for them, in the event of those goods being damaged or lost in transit it is for the seller to claim full damages from the carrier, even though risk has passed to the buyer. The bar to the buyer's claim is avoided by the buyer requiring the seller to sue on his behalf whether under a term in the contract of sale or otherwise.

Comment

In the Court of Appeal, Goff LJ thought there was no objection in principle to the buyer having a claim in tort against the shipowner but considered that on the facts of the case the claim had to fail. He thought that whilst *The Wear Breeze* had established that liability in tort was limited to the owner of the goods or someone who was in possession of them at the time of the commission of the tort, following the decision in *Anns* v *London Borough of Merton* [1978] AC 728, the *The Irene's Success* had instead found that the shipowner could be liable to the buyer in tort. Donaldson and Oliver LJJ both found that the plaintiffs had no right to sue in tort, although they reached this conclusion on different grounds. Donaldson LJ thought that, by applying the second strand of the test in *Anns* v *London Borough of Merton*, there were policy reasons for holding that a duty of care should not be owed by the shipowners to the plaintiffs. He considered that the Hague-Visby Rules recognises as a matter of international domestic public policy that carriers should be able to rely on exemptions in respect of obligations owed to cargo owners and that, accordingly, the carrier cannot be deprived of the right to rely on those exemptions and limitations by reason of being found to owe an obligation to a party that would deprive him of that right. He said:

> 'I have of course considered whether any duty of care owed in tort to the buyer could in some way be equated to the contractual duty of care owed to the shipper, but I do not see how this could be done. The commonest form of contract of carriage is one on the terms of the Hague-Visby Rules. But this is an intricate blend of responsibilities and liabilities (Art III), rights and immunities (Art IV), I am quite unable to see how this can be synthesised into a standard of care.'

Oliver LJ agreed that *The Irene's Success* was wrongly decided but thought it to be a misguided approach to assume that Lord Wilberforce was, in his *Anns* v *London Borough of Merton* formulation, advocating a two-tier test which had to be always rigorously applied. He did however agree that it would be unreasonable to impose upon the shipowner a duty of care to those other than the cargo owner where the effect of doing so would be to deprive the shipowner of the benefit of the exemptions and limitations in the Hague-Visby Rules. It was not clear whether he saw this as preventing a duty from arising in the first place or simply operating as a policy reason to exclude the duty once it had arisen, but he seemed to prefer the former.

Lickbarrow and Another v *Mason and Others* (1787) 2 Term Rep 63; 100 ER 35 King's Bench (Askhurst J)

- *The bill of lading and third parties*

Facts

The plaintiffs presented evidence that Turing and Son, Merchants, shipped corn on board The Endeavour for Liverpool on the instructions of Freeman of Rotterdam. Holmes, the master of the ship, signed four bills of lading to order or assigns. Turing endorsed two of the bills in blank and sent them to Freeman together with an invoice. Freeman received the documents. One bill of lading was retained by Turing, and the fourth was kept by Holmes, the master. Turing drew four bills of exchange on Freeman in respect of the price of the goods and they were accepted by Freeman. Freeman sent to the plaintiffs the two bills of lading, together with the invoice he had received from Turing in order that the goods might be taken possession of and sold on Freeman's account. The same day Freeman drew three sets of bills of exchange on the plaintiffs, who accepted them and paid on them.

The plaintiffs were creditors of Freeman. Before the four bills of exchange by Turing on Freeman became due, Freeman was declared bankrupt. The bills were protested and Turing, hearing of Freeman's bankruptcy, endorsed to the defendants the bill of lading retained by them. An invoice was also sent to the defendants. On arrival of the ship, the defendants applied to the master for the goods, producing the bill of lading. The master delivered the goods and the defendants sold them on the account of Turing. Before the bringing of this action, the plaintiffs demanded the goods from the defendants, tendering to them the freight and charges, but did not offer to pay the defendants for the goods.

Held (inter alia):

Askhurst J (at p39):

'... where the delivery is to be at a distant place, as between the vendor and vendee, the contract is ambulatory until delivery; and therefore, in case of the insolvency of the vendee in the meantime, the vendor can stop the goods in transit. But, as between the vendor and third persons, the delivery of a bill of lading is a delivery of the goods themselves; if not, it would enable the consignee to make the bill of lading an instrument of fraud.'

Comment

This is a frequently cited case as to the status of the bill of lading as a document of title and the relationship between parties to commercial documents who put them into circulation, and those who have been injured by such circulation through no participation of their own. As Askhurst J stated (at p39), 'Whenever one of two innocent persons must suffer by the acts of a third, he who has enabled such third person to occasion the loss must sustain it.'

Sewell (J) and Nephew v James Burdick and Others (1884) 10 App Cas 74 House of Lords (Earl of Selborne LC, Lords Blackburn, Bramwell and Fitzgerald)

• *Effect of endorsement of a bill of lading as pledge for a loan*

Facts

In September 1880 Mercessiantz shipped some machinery on the respondent's ship to be carried from London to Poti in the Black Sea. Under the bills of lading the goods were made deliverable to the shipper or assigns, freight and disbursements to be paid at destination, in default of which the carriers were to have an absolute lien on the goods and liberty to sell by auction and retain the freight and all charges.

The bills of lading were endorsed in blank and in November 1880 deposited by Mercessiantz with the appellant bankers as security for a loan of £300. In the meanwhile, the goods had landed at Poti and were warehoused at the Russian customs house.

Mercessiantz disappeared and after a year, in accordance with Russian law, the goods were sold to pay the customs duties and charges. In the meantime the appellants had endorsed the bills of lading to their agents in Tiflis, instructing the agents to protect their interests and inform the carriers that if the goods were sold to pay freight, that the appellants claimed all proceeds over and above the amount due to the carriers for freight etc.

The respondents, Burdick, brought an action for freight and charges against Sewell as endorsee of the bills of lading.

Held

Judgment for the appellants.

The mere endorsement of a bill of lading by way of pledge for a loan does not pass the property in the goods to the endorsee so as to transfer to him all liabilities in respect of the goods within the meaning of the Bills of Lading Act 1855, s1. Here, the main issue, which was answered in the negative, was, in the words of the Earl of Selborne LC (at pp77–78):

'... whether under the Bills of Lading Act 1855 ... every holder of a bill of lading, endorsed in blank, who has taken it by security for an advance of money (and has not afterwards parted with it) is liable, by reason of such endorsement only, to an action for freight by the shipowner; although he may not have obtained delivery of the goods or derived any other benefit from his security.'

The authorities from *Lickbarrow* v *Mason* (1787) 2 Term Rep 63 up to the date of this judgment were examined and discussed and the conclusion reached was that under the facts at hand, the endorsement and deposit of a bill of lading passes only a 'special property' in the goods, leaving the 'general property' in the shipper. As expressed by the Earl of Selborne, LC (at p83):

'It would be strange if the Bills of Lading Act has made a person whose name has never appeared on the bill of lading, and who (as between himself and the shipowner) has never acted upon it, is liable to an action by the shipowners upon a contract to which he was not a party.'

Comment
This case consolidates the law under previous cases in reversing the judgment of the Court of Appeal and placing emphasis on the difference for purposes of the Bills of Lading Act 1855 between 'the' property to which the Act applied and 'a' property. The latter imputes a lower nexus with the goods, as arose here in the endorsement for the limited purpose of securing a loan, to which the Bills of Lading Act does not apply.

Sucre Export SA v *Northern Shipping Ltd, The Sormovskiy 3068*
(1994) The Times 13 May Queen's Bench Division (Clarke J)

• *Reasonable explanation required for the absence of the original bill of lading.*

Facts
The defendants (Northern Shipping Ltd) delivered cargo at the port of discharge without the production of an original bill of lading. The plaintiff charterers sought damages for breach of contract.

Held
The defendants wee liable to pay damages for breach of contract.

In the absence of the original bill of lading, goods should not be delivered unless it was proved to the master's reasonable satisfaction that the person seeking possession of the goods was entitled to do so and that there was some reasonable explanation for the absence of the original bill of lading. Where the master or shipowner delivered the cargo in breach of contract otherwise than in return for an original bill of lading, the person entitled to possession would be able to recover substantial damages if he had suffered loss and damage as a result.

In dealing with the defendants' submission that they would not be in breach of contract if they delivered the cargo in accordance with the law, the custom and the practice of the port of discharge.

Clarke J was of the opinion that a distinction should be drawn between the three concepts:

1. If it had been a requirement of the law of the place of discharge that the cargo should be delivered to the port authority as the plaintiffs' agent without the presentation of an original bill of lading the defendants would not have been in breach of contract.
2. Custom meant custom in its strict sense, that is it had to be reasonable, certain, consistent with the contract, universally accepted and not contrary to law. If it was the custom to deliver goods to the port authority without the presentation of an original bill of lading, the defendants would not be in breach of contract.
3. Practice was different from custom. It would not be good performance of the contract if it had merely been the practice for vessels to deliver goods to the port authority without the bill of lading being presented, where neither the law nor custom required it.

Comment

Sometimes a buyer who does not have the bill of lading will be able to arrange for an indemnity for the carrier and will therefore be allowed to collect the cargo: see *Sze Hai Tong Bank Ltd* v *Rambler Cycle Co Ltd* [1959] AC 576.

7 Carriage of Goods by Sea (4): Seaworthiness, Carriage of Goods by Sea Act 1971

AICCO SA* v *Forggensee Navigation Co, The Polar [1993] 2 Lloyd's Rep 478 Queen's Bench Division (Clarke J)

• *Stowage*

Facts

The Polar was chartered to a third party to carry potatoes from Egypt to Dover, UK. Congenbills of lading were issued which incorporated the charterparty and were subject to the Hague-Visby Rules. The claimants were the buyers of the potatoes.

The shipowners failed to reduce temperatures to the necessary figures within 48 hours of the closing of hatches, as required by cooling instructions of the shippers that they were obliged to comply with as part of their duty to 'stow carefully'.

When the potatoes were discharged at Dover they were found to be infected with rot. The buyers sued the defendants, claiming a failure to obey carriage instructions and improper stowage.

Held

The rot was an anaerobic rot caused by cargo sweat and cool conditions when the vessel had arrived at Dover and which had resulted in condensation. There was not improper stowage of the cargo on board ship for the voyage. Although use of a tight stow had impeded ventilation and caused some increase in temperature, the condensation levels on the voyage were not significant. Accordingly, the defendants failure to comply with the cooling instructions was not the cause of the damage to the potatoes and they were not liable to the buyers.

Albacora SRL* v *Westcott & Laurence Line Ltd [1966] 2 Lloyd's Rep 53 House of Lords (Lords Reid, Guest, Pearce, Upjohn and Pearson)

• *The carrier's duty to 'properly' look after cargo*

Facts

A cargo of 1,200 cases of wet salted fish was shipped under clean bills of lading in the defendants' ship for carriage from Glasgow to Genoa. The fish arrived in a damaged condition due to a 'reddening'. The plaintiffs, endorsees of the bills of lading, claimed for the damage on either the basis that the defendants were in breach of contract or were negligent, or both.

The plaintiffs alleged that the defendants were in breach of art III r2 of the Hague Rules which provides that the carrier 'shall properly load, handle, stow, carry, keep, care for and discharge the goods carried.' The plaintiffs also alleged that the defendants were negligent in stowage and ventilation of the cargo. The carriers claimed exemption under the contract of carriage in that the damage was due to the inherent vice or latent defect within the meaning of art IV r2 (m), (p).

Evidence was admitted for the plaintiffs that the 'reddening' always occurs from bacterial action when fish which are dead are carried in a salt solution of 20 per cent to 30 per cent, with access to oxygen in holds which are warmer than 41 F, which the holds were in this case.

Held

'Properly' within the meaning of art III r2 meant in accordance with a sound system, and that the obligation under that rule was to adopt a system in light of all the knowledge which the carrier had or ought to have had about the nature of the goods. Here, the carriers had no reason to know that the fish required any different treatment from what they received and, therefore, the carriers were not liable for breach of contract.

Second, inherent vice is a variable concept which depends on the carriage required by the contract. In this case, there was inherent vice as the contract did not call for refrigeration and the fish could not withstand the carriage authorised by the contract. As expressed by Lord Guest (at p59):

'It follows that whether there is an inherent defect or vice must depend on the kind of transit required by the contract. If this contract had required refrigeration there would have been no inherent vice.

But as it did not there was inherent vice because the goods could not stand the treatment which the contract authorised or required.'

Comment

This frequently cited case gives useful guidance both on the standard of care required of carriers in dealing with goods, and as to the somewhat variable nature of the concept of inherent vice.

Athanasia Comninos, The [1990] 1 Lloyd's Rep 277 Queen's Bench Division (Commercial Court) (Mustill J)

• *Dangerous cargo – no single test for shipper's duties*

Facts

Two ships carrying coal suffered fire and explosions by reason of the ignition of a combination of oxygen and the methane gas emitted by the coal. In both cases it was established that the coal was not adequately ventilated so as to prevent the emission of the gas. Shipowners in both cases sued the cargo owners in contract, making various allegations.

Held

Mustill J expressly did not decide whether the shipper's duties as to the nature of the cargo and his contractual obligations relating to the suitability of the cargo for transit were absolute or limited to that which he ought to have known. However, his Lordship expressed preference for an absolute duty.

He also held that dangerousness was not an absolute quality but a question of the risks expressly or impliedly accepted by the carrier regarding the cargo: see *Bamfield* v *Goole* [1910] 2 KB 94. First, therefore, the contract must be construed to assess whether the carrier had contracted to bear the actual risks involved: see for instance *Brass* v *Maitland* (1856) 26 LJQB 49. Second, the court must consider the knowledge, skill and equipment of the carrier to find any implied acceptance of risks, unless expressly excluded by the contract.

Mustill J thought that no single test was adequate. He thought it would be helpful in most cases to refer to the proper method of carriage of the goods. A carrier who consents to carry goods of a particular description contracts to perform carriage in a manner appropriate to those goods. He thereby assumes all the risks of accident if caused by failure to proceed in that manner. His Lordship recognised that this did not resolve problem cases where the nature of goods is such that even strict compliance with accepted methods of carriage would not suffice to eliminate the possibility of accident. There is in such cases a gap between safe carriage and acceptable carriage.

Mustill J thought risk should fall on the carrier since he had contracted to carry goods of that description, and had therefore assented to their presence on board. The degree of acceptability would vary from goods to goods, and would have to be found as a fact in each case. The standard of care required in carriage would vary with the state of the art.

Comment

Although it was suggested that the duties of a carrier may be absolute as to the careful carriage of goods, what that duty required was determined by the particular characteristics of the goods in question.

Derby Resources AG v *Blue Corinth Marine Co Ltd* [1998] 2 Lloyd's Rep 410 Queen's Bench Division (Colman J)

• *Cargo contamination caused by shipowner's breach of duty – recoverable loss and materiality of available market for cargo, sound and damaged*

Facts

The plaintiffs purchased a cargo of jet kerosene shipped on board the defendants' vessel. On arrival the cargo was found to be contaminated by fuel oil, and specifically asphaltene. This reduced its colour rating to being well below that specified in the receivers' purchase contract and well below that to be expected of jet kerosene.

The contamination was found to have occurred after the cargo was shipped on board and after title to the cargo had passed to the third plaintiff, National Iranian Oil Company (NIOC), under the terms of its purchase contract. Title remained with NIOC throughout the time the cargo was on board the vessel. Their agreement with Derby Resources, the first plaintiffs, provided for quality analysis samples to be taken during the loading of the cargo. The master and the chief officer incorrectly informed the surveyors about the previous cargoes carried by the vessel and the procedures for washing the tanks. The last but one cargo had been fuel oil, whereas it is good practice to carry no less than two intermediate cargoes of gas oil before loading a kerosene cargo. The washing of the tanks had been for much less than the time considered as good practice for a carriage that was to follow two gas oil cargoes and a carriage of a fuel oil cargo. Acting on this misinformation, the surveyor passed the vessel as fit to load the kerosene. Loading was not halted, as requested, whilst the quality analysis samples were being taken. By the time loading was complete, composite samples indicated that the entire cargo had a colour rating well below the contract specification.

In September 1987 there was no available market for jet kerosene in Iran due to the command economy in operation in that country during the Iran-Iraq war. In accordance with their contract, NIOC used the cargo as a blending agent to improve the properties of gas oil. The price paid by Derby was reduced down to that of gas oil. NIOC sought to recover against the defendant shipowners in tort. The defendants conceded that they were in breach of their duty of care in failing to provide a ship whose lines and tanks were fit to receive the cargo, but argued that NIOC's loss was not caused by that breach of duty. They further argued that because there was no market either for kerosene or off specification kerosene in Iran at the relevant time, there was no evidence of any reduction in value and that NIOC had therefore used the cargo as a blending agent in just the same way as it would have used sound kerosene.

Held

Judgment for the plaintiffs. They were entitled to damages in respect of the total quantity of kerosene delivered off specification, together with interest.

The defendants were not liable for the contamination of the kerosene. The surveyors, Caleb Brett, and the shippers did not cause the damage by allowing the cargo to be loaded.

Nor were they contributorily negligent. The surveyors had been deceived by the defendants' employees as to the previous cargoes carried and the washing of the tanks. The contamination damage was caused exclusively by the negligence of the shipowners who were in breach of their duty of care in relation to the cargo. There was an unbroken chain of causation from the defendants' breach to the entire damage to the cargo. The plaintiffs' loss was in consequence of that damage.

Colman J considered the evidence in respect of the taking of samples and said:

'On the basis of these findings, I conclude that the contamination of the kerosene was caused exclusively by the defendants' breach of their duty of care in respect of the cargo. It was not caused wholly or partly by the conduct of the Caleb Brett inspectors and their conduct cannot be relied upon to found an allegation that NIOC failed to mitigate its loss. There was an unbroken chain of causation from the breach of duty by the defendants to the entire damage to the cargo. Moreover, Caleb Brett were not agents employed by NIOC but by Phibro. For the purposes of failure to mitigate loss, the inspectors' conduct was not NIOC's conduct. The fact that independent inspectors were required to be appointed under the Derby-NIOC Agreement does not lead to a position where the defendants, who were strangers to that contract, are entitled in defence to a claim in tort to impute to NIOC the decisions of the inspectors. Unless therefore they can establish that the cause of some or all of the cargo damage was the conduct of the inspectors, as distinct from the dirty condition of the cargo lines and spaces, the defendants must be liable for that damage. This, in my judgment, they have failed to do ...'

The surveyors conduct could not be relied on to found an allegation that NIOC had failed to mitigate its loss. They were the agents of the second plaintiff not of NIOC.

NIOC had suffered recoverable loss. NIOC was entitled to be given the financial means of providing itself with goods in as sound condition as the goods carried should have had if the defendant had exercised reasonable care. The carrier wrongfully caused the goods to be damaged in the course of carriage and transferred possession at the place of delivery of damaged goods instead of sound goods. In tort, goods that cannot be replaced or re-instated entitle the owner to be restored to 'the same position' and this is achieved by calculating the difference in monetary value between the damaged property delivered to him and the sound property which ought to have been delivered to him. Colman J distinguished between contractual and non-contractual loss as follows:

'If the measure of damages in the case of the non-delivery or total loss of the goods in breach of contract cases is defined by reference to the monetary value of the lost goods entirely abstracted from the "circumstances" or contracts of the receiver, there can be no conceptual basis for any different approach where the claim is for damage to the goods and is tort-based as distinct from contract-based.'

There were two distinct and fundamental questions as to the basis upon which negligent damage to goods is to be compensated in damages: (i) what function in this exercise is played by an available market and (ii) how damages are to be measured if there is no such market.

Colman J held that the relevance of an available market in this exercise is simply to provide evidence of the monetary value of the goods, both in their sound condition and in their damaged condition. If there was no available market, because there was a command economy, the value of the goods still had to be ascertained on the available evidence. He cited two authorities for this proposition:

'The circumstances which confronted Staughton J in *The Good Friend* [1984] 2 Lloyd's Rep 586 illustrate the evidential problems encountered in such cases in arriving at the measure of diminution in value of the goods. Evidence of the market price for such goods at a different place and even at a different time may be the only available means of quantification of loss. It is thus only if the evidence is of market prices at different places and at different times which are so remote from the place and time of delivery as to be of no probative value in arriving at the sound and damaged value of the goods that it can be said that market prices do not help and that there is thus no available market. Even if, however, there is no available market in this sense, the value of the goods must still be "ascertained as best it can on the available evidence", per Lord Goff of Chieveley in *The Texaco Melbourne* [1994] 1 Lloyd's Rep 473. There may be cases where the probative value of market prices at different place or at different dates is weak but where the monetary value of the goods indicated by that evidence can be corroborated by other evidence from the place of delivery at the time of delivery with the result that on the whole of the evidence the court can reach a conclusion. It is, however, important to keep in mind that the purpose of the exercise is to ascertain the objective monetary value of the goods and not their utility to the receiver in the circumstances peculiar to him.'

The price at which the damaged goods were sold was evidence of their value in damaged condition, but the particular circumstances of the delivery and hence the utility of the goods to NIOC were irrelevant to an objective assessment of any reduction in value:

'Whereas I have said that there may be cases where the only evidence of the market value in their damaged condition is the price at which the receiver resells the goods in that condition, that is because the price results from an objective valuation of those goods. Where, however, the receiver uses the goods in their damaged condition for a particular purpose his doing so will in general be incapable of providing evidence of the damaged value of the goods unless the purpose involves some objectively-assessed valuation of the goods.'

Considerable evidence was submitted to show that there were a number of uses for the cargo as delivered other than the one which NIOC had put it to, but Colman J was satisfied that the spectrum of usefulness in Iran of this off-specification kerosene was so wide that it was of substantially the same value as sound kerosene. He held:

'... I am satisfied that it would be entirely unrealistic to approach the quantification of the plaintiffs' loss on the basis of reinstatement costs. The correct approach is to ascertain the disposal value in monetary terms of the cargo in its off-specification condition and to calculate from that the extent of reduction in the sound arrived value. The weight of the evidence points to the gas oil price as the appropriate and normal benchmark.'

The court accepted NIOC's evidence, based on market rates sufficiently closely related to the time and place of delivery, that the value of sound kerosene at Hormuz at the relevant time was US $184.50 per metric ton.

Comment
The case raises a point of some importance on the method of calculating loss attributable to negligent damage to goods by a carrier.

Elder, Dempster & Co Ltd v *Paterson, Zochonis & Co Ltd* [1924] AC 522; [1924] All ER 135 House of Lords (Viscounts Cave and Finlay, Lords Dunedin, Sumner and Carson)

* *When bad stowage amounts to unseaworthiness*

Facts
A cargo of casks of palm oil were stowed at the bottom of holds in a ship and a heavier cargo of palm kernels were placed on top of the casks. The ship did not have 'tween decks which were designed to relieve cargo stored in the lower part of the holds from the weight of cargo store in the upper part of the holds. The weight of the palm kernels crushed the casks of palm oil. The shippers of the palm oil

brought an action against the charterers and shipowners for damages for breach of the contract of carriage or, alternatively, for negligence.

Held

The ship was structurally sound to carry the cargo of palm oil and therefore the damage to the oil was not due to the ship being unseaworthy. The damage was the result of bad stowage. The charterers and shipowners were entitled to rely on the exceptions in the bills of lading.

Comment

This case should be compared with *Kopitoff* v *Wilson* (1876) 1 QBD 377 where a cargo of armour plates was badly stowed and the ship was damaged when an armour plate shifted during a storm. It was held that the bad stowage meant that the ship was unseaworthy. In *Elder* v *Dempster* the bad stowage caused damage to cargo but not to the ship.

Empressa Cubana Importadora v *Iasmos Shipping Co SA, The Good Friend* [1984] 2 Lloyd's Rep 586 High Court (Day J)

• *Seaworthiness under art III r1 Hague Rules includes cargoworthiness to destination and the carrier cannot rely on the 'restraint of princes' indemnity where it is lack of cargo-worthiness that results in a prohibition on unloading imposed by a port authority*

Facts

The plaintiffs were the purchasers and indorsees of the bill of lading covering a cargo of soya bean meal shipped on the defendants' vessel at Ontario for carriage to Havana. On arrival it became clear that the cargo had become infested and as a result it could not be discharged in Cuba and was carried to salvage buyers in Las Palmas.

The plaintiffs claimed that the defendants

had failed to exercise due diligence to provide a seaworthy ship before and at the beginning of the voyage under art II of the Hague Rules. The defendants claimed that they had exercised due diligence and said the damage was due to latent defect or inherent vice.

Held

On the balance of probabilities. the infestation did not come from within the cargo itself but from an live infestation of trogoderma on board the vessel as a result of a previously carried cargo. Accordingly, it was present before and at the start of the voyage in question and rendered the vessel unfit to receive and carry the cargo of soya bean meal: *Tattersall* v *National Steamship Co Ltd* (1884) 12 QBD 297 applied.

Day J:

'... where there is a contract to carry goods in a ship there is, in the absence of any stipulation to the contrary, an implied engagement on the part of the person so undertaking to carry that the ship is reasonably fit for the purposes of such carriage ...

This obligation may be referred to as cargoworthiness. art III r1 Hague Rules makes no mention of it but it is without doubt included in the use of the word 'seaworthiness'. It would otherwise be pointless to insist upon the ship being fit to receive the cargo at the start of the journey if she did not have to carry this cargo to its destination.

This vessel was not seaworthy.'

Day J also considered the decision in *The Aquacharm* [1982] 1 Lloyd's Rep 7, in which the Court of Appeal held that a vessel was not unseaworthy merely because she was overloaded, and opined that:

'... merely overloading a vessel as in that case or providing some kind of temporary impediment is completely different from failing to provide a vessel which is fit to carry the goods. The Aquacharm was fit to carry her cargo but the vessel in the instant case was not and her condition was not a temporary one, rather it was a major obstacle to the completion of the contractual voyage. Therefore no analogy can be drawn.'

There was no indemnity on the basis of 'restraint of princes or rulers or people or seizure under legal process'. This immunity covers cases of government action such as import bans, quarantine, embargoes and so on and is not applicable to obligations imposed on the carrier to exercise due diligence. The unseaworthiness was the cause of the loss not the action of the port authorities at Havana in prohibiting the unloading of the vessel.

The plaintiffs had suffered loss as a result of the non-delivery of the soya meal in July and they had reasonably deferred in purchasing a replacement cargo until September. Their measure of damage was what the soya beans would have been worth if delivered with the market value assessed at September rates.

Comment

See also *Ciampa* v *British India Steam Navigation Co* [1915] 2 KB 774.

Europa, The [1908] P 84 Probate Division (Divisional Court) (Bucknill J)

• *Unseaworthiness does not affect the carrier's liability unless it causes the loss*

Facts

The Europa was chartered to carry sugar in bags from Stettin to Liverpool. Whilst entering the docks at Liverpool the vessel collided with the dock wall and the impact caused a water pipe to fracture and burst. Water escaping from this pipe ran into the 'tween decks (upper decks where cargo can be stowed) and damaged bags of sugar stowed there. Prior to loading, old scupper holes in the 'tween decks had not been properly plugged after the pipes to the bilges pumps were detached and water from the burst water pipe flowed through these scupper holes and entered the lower holds, damaging bags of sugar stowed there.

The charterparty included an exception for 'collision'. The shipowners admitted that the damage to the sugar stowed in the lower holds was caused by unseaworthiness. However, they denied liability in respect of the sugar stowed in the upper decks on the grounds that their liability was excluded by the exception for collision.

The county court judge found in favour of the cargo-owners' holding that the carriers' breach of the obligation of seaworthiness deprived the shipowner of the benefit of all exceptions.

The shipowners appealed to the Divisional Court.

Held

The appeal was allowed. Unseaworthiness does not affect the carrier's liability unless it causes the loss. Unseaworthiness was not the cause of the loss of the sugar in the upper holds. The collision with the dock wall was a peril of the sea and the carrier was entitled to be able to rely on the exclusion for collision in the charterparty.

Bucknill J:

'We have to decide whether "seaworthiness" is to be classed with non-deviation as a condition precedent, the non-performance of which voids the contract of affreightment, so that in the case of the *Europa*, she being unseaworthy, even though she had carried all the cargo specified in the bill of lading to the proper destination, yet could not claim exemption from liability for damage caused, not by the unseaworthiness, but by a peril of the seas or other exception in the bill of lading.

Except so far as appears in the judgment of the Court of Appeal in *The Orchis* [1907] 1 KB 660, we have not found any case where such a proposition has been enunciated, if it was, which we doubt. ...

In our opinion there must be a time when the charterer or cargo owner has no longer a right to treat the promise or warranty of the shipowner as a condition precedent, but must rely on his breach of warranty, and must then prove that the damage sued for has been caused by the unseaworthiness of the ship at the material time.'

It had been submitted that the decision in *The Orchis* was authority for the proposition that a warranty of seaworthiness in a charterparty was to be treated the same as in a policy of marine insurance, where such warranty may be made expressly or by implication. Bucknill J disagreed, saying that in his opinion Lord Collins in that case had in his mind an analogy between a deviation and the warranty of seaworthiness in an insurance policy and on the basis of this reasoning he said:

'For these reasons we are of the opinion that *The Orchis* is not a case that can properly be relied on as an authority justifying the judgment of the county court judge from whose decision this appeal comes, and in our judgment the plaintiffs are only entitled to recover from the defendants such damages as directly resulted from the want of seaworthiness and not for the damage caused by the water that got into the 'tween decks through the collision between the ship and the dock wall, which was covered by the excepted perils in the charterparty, and to the protection of which the shipowner was still entitled, notwithstanding the unseaworthiness of the vessel ...'

Comment

The decision in this case was approved by the House of Lords in *J & E Kish* v *Charles Taylor, Sons and Co* [1912] AC 604, see especially Lord Atkinson at p616, with whom the other Lords agreed.

Two things that should be noted are:

1. it is sufficient for the cargo owner to prove on a balance of probabilities, that the loss has been caused by one of a number of competing causes; the burden of proof under Hague-Visby Rules art III r1 does not require the cargo owner to show that unseaworthiness is the sole cause of the loss, and see also the decision in *Smith Hogg & Co Ltd* v *Black Sea and Baltic General Insurance Co Ltd* [1940] AC 997 for the application of this to the policy of marine insurance; and

2. following the decision in *Hong Kong Fir Shipping Co* v *Kawasaki Kisen Kaisha* [1962] 2 QB 26 (see below), the obligation to provide a seaworthy vessel is not a condition of the contract but is an 'innominate' or 'intermediate' term.

Hain Steamship Co Ltd v *Tate & Lyle Ltd* [1936] 2 All ER 597 House of Lords (Lord Wright MR, Lords Atkin, Thankerton, Macmillian and Maugham)

• *An unjustified deviation goes to the root of the contract*

Facts

A steamer was chartered to load sugar at Cuba and at San Domingo. After loading at Cuba the master did not receive loading instructions for the port in San Domingo and, therefore, headed for home. The steamer was recalled and ordered to go a port in San Domingo where cargo was loaded. On leaving San Domingo the steamer was badly damaged when she stranded and some of the cargo was lost. The indorsees of the bill of lading brought an action against the owners of the steamer on the ground, inter alia, that there had been an unjustified deviation from the charterparty voyage.

Held (inter alia)

There was an unjustified deviation which was waived by the charterers.

Lord Atkin:

'... the departure from the voyage contracted to be made is a breach by the shipowner of his contract, but a breach of such a serious character that however slight the deviation the other party to the contract is entitled to treat it as going to the root of the contract.'

Lord Wright expressed the opinion that if there is a slight deviation, but the goods arrive safely, the carriers may claim freight on a quantum meruit basis as the cargo owner has received the benefit of the contract.

Hong Kong Fir Shipping Co v *Kawasaki Kisen Kaisha* [1962] 2 QB 26 Court of Appeal (Sellers, Upjohn and Diplock LJJ)

• *Unseaworthiness – innominate terms*

Facts
The shipowners chartered their vessel mv Hong Kong Fir to the charterers for a period of 24 months. It was a term of the charter that the vessel be '... in every way fitted for service'.

The age of the vessel was such that she required maintenance by a competent and adequate staff. In fact the crew were insufficient on sailing, the master was drunk and in consequence there were many breakdowns so that her journey from Liverpool to Osaka took longer than it should have done and the vessel was off-hire for five-and-a-half weeks undergoing repairs. She spent further time at Osaka being repaired at substantial expense, so that repair time totalled approximately 20 weeks.

The charterers repudiated the charter and claimed damages for breach of contract regarding the unseaworthiness of the vessel. The shipowners claimed damages for wrongful repudiation. Alternatively, the charterers claimed that the charter was frustrated.

Held
The unseaworthiness of the vessel was not a condition of the charter, breach of which automatically allowed the charterer to repudiate.

The delay was insufficient to amount to frustration. Two questions therefore fell to be answered:

1. Is the obligation of seaworthiness a term which will, if broken, allow the charterers to treat the contract as repudiated?
2. When there is a delay in the performance of a contract by what standard is that delay to be measured in order to determine

whether it amounts to repudiation of the contract?

Unseaworthiness may manifest itself in a variety of ways. Many of them are trivial. It would therefore be quire wrong to allow them to be treated as either conditions of the contract or conditions precedent to a charterer's liability and thereby justifying cancellation by the charterer.

Sellers LJ:

'If what is done or not done in breach of the contractual obligation does not make the performance a totally different performance of the contract from that intended by the parties, it is not so fundamental as to undermine the whole contract. Many existing conditions of unseaworthiness can be remedied by attention or repairs so that the vessel becomes seaworthy ...'

Where the charterers are aware in advance of the seaworthiness of the vessel they should point this fact out to the shipowner. The time of delivery of the vessel is a condition of the contract. If the shipowner then fails to ensure that the vessel is seaworthy he is in breach of contract when the delay in remedying the breach is so long in fact or likely to be so long in reasonable anticipation that the commercial object of the contract is frustrated.

There is substantial authority for the fact that unseaworthiness is not a condition of the contract: *Kish* v *Taylor* [1912] AC 604.

As a concept, seaworthiness can be broken by even the slightest failure to be fitted 'in every way for service', and it would be contrary to common sense to treat all these terms as repudiatory.

Terms of a contract are historically divided into conditions and warranties. It is for the parties to the contract to make it clear that a stipulation goes to the root of the contract so that any breach constitutes repudiation. If they do not expressly state this, it is a matter of construction of the contract. It would however be dangerous to assume that simply because the parties had not specifically stated that a term was a condition, damages for breach of warranty are an adequate remedy. Upjohn LJ stated:

> 'The remedies open to the innocent party for breach of a stipulation which is not a condition strictly so called, depend entirely upon the nature of the breach and its foreseeable consequences. Breaches of stipulation fall naturally into two classes. First there is the case where the owner by his conduct indicates that he considers himself no longer bound to perform ... the charterer may accept the repudiation and treat the contract as at an end ... second ... due to misfortune such as perils of the sea, engine failures, incompetence of the crew and so on, the owner is unable to perform a particular stipulation precisely in accordance with the terms of the contract ... in that case ... does the breach of the stipulation go so much to the rot of the contract that it makes further commercial performance of the contract impossible, or ... the whole contract is frustrated?'

In this case the unseaworthiness did not go to the root of the contract.

Diplock LJ criticised the dual classification of contract terms into conditions and warranties:

> 'Clearly there are breaches of certain terms of which it can always be predicated that the breach will deprive the party not in default of substantially the whole benefit he should have obtained under the contract. That is a condition. Equally there will be breaches of which it can safely be predicated that no breach will ever deprive the party in default of substantially the whole benefit. This is a breach of warranty.
>
> There are, however, many contractual undertakings of a more complex character which cannot be categorised as being conditions or warranties ... Of such undertakings, all that can be predicated is that some breaches will and others will not, give rise to an event which will deprive the party not in default of substantially the whole benefit which it was intended that he should obtain from the contract; and the legal consequences of a breach of such an undertaking,

unless provided for expressly in the contract, depend on the nature of the event to which the breach gives rise, and do not follow automatically from a prior classification of the undertaking as a condition or a warranty ...

> Such is the undertaking of seaworthiness. It may if broken, relieve the charterer of the need for further performance or allow him only monetary compensation. It is neither condition nor warranty but one of a large class which may be tantamount to either according to the consequences of the breach.'

Comment
With regard to innominate terms: see also *Cehave NV v Bremer Handelsgesellschaft mbH, The Hansa Nord* [1976] QB 44 where 'shipped in good condition' was held to be an intermediate stipulation and in the circumstances was to be treated as a warranty.

Leesh River Tea v British India Steam Navigation [1967] 2 QB 250
Court of Appeal (Sellers, Danckwerts and Salmon LJJ)

• *'Seaworthy ship' under the Hague-Visby Rules is an obligation which exists at the start of the journey not subsequent stages.*

Facts
The plaintiffs shipped chests of tea from Calcutta to London. The route taken was via Colombo and Port Sudan. After the commencement of the voyage the ship called at Port Sudan where it loaded a cargo of cotton-seed.

The loading of this cargo was undertaken by a firm of stevedores based at Port Sudan and appointed by the defendants.

The vessel completed her loading and continued her voyage. During a storm it was discovered that water was entering the hold which contained the tea, because a storm valve cover plate had been stolen by a stevedore at

Port Sudan. The absence of the cover plate could not reasonably have been detected by the crew.

The bills of lading were subject to rules identical to those in the Carriage of Goods by Sea Act 1924.

Held

That the defendants were not allowed to rely upon the exemption contained in art IV r2(1) of the Schedule to the Act of 1924, as clearly the removal of the cover plate could not be termed as 'act of neglect or default' in the management of the ship.

The defendants were allowed to rely upon art IV r2(q). This exempted them from loss or damage from 'any other cause'.

Danckwerts LJ:

'… It seems to me the vital point in the case is whether the theft of the brass plate was made by the stevedore at Port Sudan, in the course of his employment by the shipowners. He was to be regarded as agent of the shipowners for the purpose of loading and unloading the cargo. There is no doubt that this gave him the opportunity to effect the theft of the plate … When he stole the plate he was acting in a way that was deliberately outside the scope of his employment on behalf of the shipowners. The theft could not have been prevented by any reasonable diligence of the shipowners through officers and crew of the ship.'

Therefore, since the theft was outside the course of his employment and was not incidental to discharge and loading, the defendants were not liable.

The obligation under the Rules was to provide a seaworthy ship 'before and at the beginning of the voyage'. The defendants complied with this obligation by exercising due diligence to ensure that the ship was seaworthy when she left Calcutta.

Comment

Compare *Hourani v Harrison* 32 Com Cas 305, where a stevedore employed by the carrier to load and unload cargo stole some of the cargo. In this case the stevedore was seen as an agent of the carrier when dealing with the cargo, albeit acting in an unauthorised manner, and therefore the loss to the cargo owner had been the result of fault of servants and agents and the carrier was liable for the loss.

McFadden v *Blue Star Line* [1905] 1 KB 697 King's Bench Division (Channell J)

• *Implied warranty of seaworthiness*

Facts

Cotton was shipped from Wilmington to Bremen aboard The Tolosa, a vessel of the defendants, under bills of lading which provided, inter alia, that the shipowners would not be liable for perils of the sea or accidents of navigation even when caused by negligence. During loading, a ballast tank was filled with water and the sea cock appeared to have been closed, but it was faulty and had not. As a result, water continued to flow until the pressure build up was sufficient to force a valve chest that was also defective. This allowed water to pour through a sluice door which had not been properly screwed down and into the cargo hold where the plaintiffs' cotton was stowed. The plaintiffs claimed that the defendants were in breach of implied warranty of seaworthiness on the grounds that there was an implied warranty that the vessel be fit for reception of the goods and for carrying them upon the voyage in question.

Held

The warranty claimed by the plaintiffs was an absolute warranty; if the ship is unfit at the time when the warranty begins, it does not matter that its unfitness is due to some latent defect which the shipowner does not know of. Best endeavours to make the ship good is no defence. The warranty arises at the time of sailing and does not continue throughout the voyage, but there is a breach of warranty of seaworthiness to put to sea with defects that are a source of danger to the vessel and her cargo. The defect in the valve chest, unlike those in the sea cock and the sluice door, existed before the plaintiffs' goods were loaded and was a substantial defect that amounted to a breach of the implied warranty of seaworthiness. The same would be true for the sluice gate if it could be shown that it was in that condition before the goods were loaded. The sea cock was intended to be closed and was apparently closed, and was consequently in a dangerous condition, but it was brought about after the goods were loaded and consequently was not a breach of warranty.

Comment

The breach of warranty of seaworthiness is now provided for by the Hague-Visby Rules for voyages that incorporate these Rules. This case is an early decision based on the view of seaworthiness that now pertains, though, under Hague-Visby Rules, the warranty of seaworthiness now continues as from loading to sailing: see above *Empresa Cubana Importadora* v *Iasmos Shipping Co SA, The Good Friend* [1984] 2 Lloyd's Rep 586, *Hong Kong Fir Shipping Co* v *Kawasaki Kisen Kaisha* [1962] 2 QB 26, and *Leesh River Tea* v *British India Steam Navigation* [1967] 2 QB 250.

Owners of Cargo Lately Laden on Board Subro Valour v *Owners of Subro Vega, The Subro Valour and The Subro Vega* [1995] 1 Lloyd's Rep 509 Queen's Bench Division (Admiralty Court) (Clarke J)

• *Seaworthiness at commencement of voyage*

Facts

There was a fire in engine room of The Subro Vega. This probably occurred as a result of mechanical damage to wiring caused by shelv-

ing having rubbed against it before the voyage commenced. An alternative cause was that inflammable material had been left too close to a hot exhaust prior to the commencement of the voyage. The smoke alarm was defective and it was impossible to shut off the ventilation. The fire occurred in the ordinary weather expected for the voyage and spread quickly.

The plaintiffs' cargo had to be salvaged and, as a result, it arrived too late for them to receive an EC subsidy as contemplated. The plaintiffs also incurred salvage expenses. They claimed these expenses and damages for the delayed arrival of the cargo from the defendants on the grounds that, in breach of art III r1 of the Hague-Visby Rules 1968, the vessel was unseaworthy at the commencement of the voyage, and that this caused the fire and contributed to its spread.

Held

The defendants had not exercised due diligence in making the vessel seaworthy at the commencement of the voyage. The unseaworthiness was the conditions that allowed a fire to occur in the ordinary weather expected for the voyage and which arose either by reason of the condition of the wiring or shelving at the commencement of the voyage, or by reason of inflammable material left in close proximity to a hot exhaust prior to the commencement of the voyage.

The defective smoke alarm and inability to shut off the ventilation did not cause the loss. They were particular defects in fire-fighting capability and in any case were not relevant as the fire would have spread too quickly even if they had been working properly.

The plaintiffs' right to sue the defendants lay either with endorsement of the bill of lading passing the property to them and thereby giving them rights of suit under the s1 of the Bills of Lading Act 1855, or on the basis of an implied contract.

The plaintiffs were entitled to recover the costs of the salvage service because they had been incurred by or on behalf of the plaintiffs. They were also entitled to damages for the delayed arrival of the cargo. That loss was not too remote because it was within the reasonable contemplation of the defendants that the price and value of goods may be affected by EC subsidies, which vary from time to time. Accordingly, it was not necessary for them to have special knowledge of the particular relief levy since it was reasonably foreseeable that any delay may affect the net amount payable by buyers for goods.

Renton (G H) & Co Ltd v Palmyra Trading Corporation of Panama, The Caspiana [1957] AC 149 House of Lords (Viscount Kilmuir LC, Lords Morton of Henryton, Tucker, Cohen and Somerwell of Harrow)

• *Alternative carriage where contract for route fails.*

Facts
Timber was shipped at Canadian ports under bills of lading for carriage to London and Hull 'or so near thereunto as the vessel may safely get'. The bills of lading incorporated the Hague Rules as enacted in Canada and provided by cl 14(c) that 'should it appear that ... strike ... would prevent the vessel from ... entering the port of discharge or there discharging and leaving again ... safely and without delay, the master may discharge the cargo at port of loading or any other safe and convenient Port'. Clause 14(f) provided that 'The discharge of cargo under the provisions of this clause shall be deemed due fulfilment of the contract'.

While the ship was en route a strike broke out in the port of London followed by a strike at Hull. The shipowners redirected the ship to Hamburg and there they discharged the timber. They took no steps to forward it to England at their own expense but made it available at Hamburg to the endorsees and holders of the bills of lading upon payment of the full freight.

Held
In an action by the holders and endorsees of the bills of lading against the shipowners, that cl 14(c) coupled with cl 14(f) was not repugnant to, or inconsistent with, the main intention of the contract. They made provision for the rights and obligations of the parties in the event of obstacles arising to prevent or impede the performance of the contract in accordance with its primary terms.

Additionally, it was held that the diversion to Hamburg was not, under the circumstances, an improper deviation.

Comment
This case shows that with regard to contracts of carriage, it is open to the parties to contractually include alternative methods of performance in the event that the originally anticipated method fails for some defined reason.

Riverstone Meat Co Pty Ltd v Lancashire Shipping Co Ltd [1961] AC 807 House of Lords (Viscount Simonds, Lords Merriman, Radcliffe, Keith of Avonholm and Hodson)

• *'Due diligence' means diligence by whomsoever the act may be done*

Facts
A cargo of tinned meat was subject to the Carriage of Goods by Sea Act 1924 and the Hague Rules.

Article IV r1 required the carrier to exercise due diligence to make the ship seaworthy, and fit for the reception, carriage and preservation of the cargo.

On arrival of the goods at their destination, it was found that they had been damaged by the sea water. This had entered the holds as a result of the negligence of the fitter, who removed the storm valve covers for inspection, to re-secure them so that they could withstand the ordinary incidents of the voyage.

The question to be determined by the

House of Lords was whether or not the carriers have satisfied the obligation imposed on them by the Rules to exercise due diligence, since the only person who was negligent, was the fitter.

Held

The carriers had not discharged the burden of proving that they had exercised due diligence to make the ship seaworthy.

Viscount Simonds:

'... no other solution is possible than to say that the shipowner's obligation of due diligence demands due diligence in the work of repair by whomsoever it may be done ...'

In the course of his judgment, the following authority was cited:

'In *Smith Hogg* v *Black Sea and Baltic General Insurance* (1939) TLR 766, MacKinnon LJ said:

"... the exercise of due diligence involves not merely that the shipowner personally shall exercise due diligence, but that all his servants and agents shall exercise due diligence ..."

Lord Wright said in the same case:

"The unseaworthiness, constituted as it was by loading an excessive deck cargo, was obviously only consistent with want of due diligence on the part of the shipowner to make her seaworthy. Hence the qualified exception of unseaworthiness does not protect the shipowner ... such an exception can only excuse against latent defects ..."

In *Australia Newsprint Mills Ltd* v *Canadian Union Line* (1952) 1 DLR 850, Cody J said:

"... It seems to me that due diligence imposed by the statute and as interpreted by the authorities, is not made out by evidence that someone else was engaged to perform this duty on behalf of the defendants – someone on whom the defendants relied and in whom the defendants had confidence. The duty of the defendants was to exercise due diligence and this applies to their servants and their agents and that duty is absolute except as to latent defects not discernible by the exercise of due diligence ...'''

Comment

At common law the duty of the shipowner in providing a seaworthy ship is an absolute duty. The duty to exercise due diligence under the Hague-Visby Rules may therefore at first seem a less onerous duty, but under the Rules a carrier/shipowner may not use the excepted perils if due diligence has not in fact been exercised.

Stag Line Ltd v *Foscolo Mango*
[1932] AC 328 House of Lords
(Lords Buckmaster, Warrington of Klyffe, Atkin, Russell of Killowen and Macmillan)

• *Meaning of 'reasonable' deviation in art IV r4 Hague-Visby Rules*

Facts

The owners of the vessel Ixia chartered her to carry a cargo of coal from Swansea to Constantinople. The charterparty contained a clause which gave the vessel liberty 'to call at any ports in order for bunkering or other purposes or to make trial trips after notice'.

This clause was incorporated into the bills of lading. The vessel carried two engineers who remained on board in order to observe whether or not the heating machinery was operating correctly.

The engineers were dropped off at St Ives. After landing them the vessel and cargo were totally lost through being too close to the Cornish coast.

The charterers, Foscolo Mango contended that the deviation was unlawful.

Held

The clause in the bill of lading which allowed deviation for 'other purposes' meant deviation for 'business purposes'.

Lord Atkin:

'I think … that the purposes intended are business purposes which would be contemplated by the parties as arising in carrying out the contemplated voyage of the ship. This might include in a contract other than a contract to carry a full and complete cargo, a right to call at port or ports on the geographical course to load and discharge cargo for other shippers. It would probably include a right to call for orders. But I cannot think that it would include a right such as was sought to be exercised in the present case, to land servants of the shipowners or others who were on board at the start to adjust machinery, and were landed for their own and their owner's convenience because they could not be transferred to any ingoing vessel. I think therefore that the shipowner is not excused by this clause …'

In considering whether the deviation was 'reasonable' within the meaning of art IV r4 of Schedule to the Carriage of Goods by Sea Act 1924 Lord Atkin stated:

'A deviation may, and often will, be caused by fortuitous circumstances never contemplated by the original parties to the contract; and may be reasonable though it is made solely in the interests of the ship or solely in the interests of the cargo, or indeed in the direct interests of neither; as for instance where the presence of a passenger or of a member of the ship or crew was urgently required after the voyage had begun on a matter of national importance. … The true test seems to be, what departure from the contract might a prudent person controlling the voyage at the time, make and maintain, having in mind all the relevant circumstances existing at the time, including the terms of the contract and the interests of all parties concerned, but without obligation to consider the interests of any one as conclusive …'

Lord Macmillan:

'… the reasonableness of an act must be judged in relation to the circumstances existing at the time of its commission and not by an abstract standard. The act too must be considered as a whole in the light of all the attendant circumstances.'

Comment

Sometimes a buyer who does not have the bill of lading will be able to arrange for an indemnity for the carrier and will therefore be allowed to collect the cargo: see *Sze Hai Tong Bank Ltd* v *Rambler Cycle Co Ltd* [1959] AC 576.

Standard Oil Co of New York v *Clan Line Steamers Ltd* [1924] AC 100
House of Lords (Earl of Birkenhead, Viscount Haldane, Lords Atkinson and Parmoor)

- *Competence of crew*

Facts

Clan Line Steamers owned ships built for them to a special design by Doxfords, a firm of shipbuilders in Sunderland. One of these vessels, The Clan Gordon, was chartered to Standard Oil. However, another of the vessels, The Clan Ranald, had capsized in 1909 and investigations into the causes revealed that the ship's design was one which, contrary to usual practice, required the water ballast tanks to be kept full when the vessel was fully loaded. Clan Line had received special instructions on this from Doxfords following those investigations, but Clan Line had failed to pass these instructions on to the master of The Clan Gordon. On a fully laden voyage from New York under the defendant's charter, and whilst still in calm seas shortly after leaving port, the master ordered her ballast tanks to be emptied and she keeled over and sank.

Held

The vessel was unseaworthy at the time the voyage began because the master was unaware of how to run the ship. In not properly informing the master of the special instructions for the ballasting of the vessel, the shipowner had failed to exercise due diligence.

Lord Atkinson:

'It is not disputed, I think, that a ship may be rendered unseaworthy by the inefficiency of the master who commands her. Does not that principle apply where the master's inefficiency consists, whatever his general efficiency may be, in his ignorance as to how his ship may, owing to the peculiarities of her structure, behave in circumstances likely to be met with an ordinary ocean voyage? There cannot be any difference in principle, I think, between disabling want of skill and disabling want of knowledge. Each equally renders the master unfit and unqualified to command, and therefore makes the ship he commands unseaworthy. And the owner who withholds from the master the necessary information should, in all reason, be as responsible for the result of the master's ignorance as if he deprived the latter of the general skill and efficiency he presumably possessed.'

Lord Parmoor:

'... I am unable to come to any other conclusion than that a vessel, which requires special precautions of an unusual character to be taken in the maintenance of sufficient water ballast to ensure conditions of stability which would not be known to a captain of ordinary skill and experience, and which have not been brought to his notice, although they had been specifically indicated to the shipowners in instructions sent to them from the shipbuilders, is not manned so as to be seaworthy, and that there was a duty on the respondents to have brought such instructions to the notice of the captain ...'

Comment

Article III r1(2) Hague-Visby Rules states that 'The carrier shall be bound before and at the beginning of the voyage to exercise due diligence to: ... (2) Properly man, equip and supply the ship.' This obligation of due diligence likewise places an obligation on the

shipowner to ensure that the ship has a competent and sufficient crew which includes a ship's master who is aware of how to run the ship and knows of its idiosyncrasies. See also *Hong Kong Fir Shipping Co* v *Kawasaki Kisen Kaisha* [1962] 2 QB 26 (above).

Svenska Tractor Aktiebolaget v *Maritime Agencies (Southampton) Ltd* [1953] 2 QB 295 Queen's Bench Division (Pilcher J)

• *Deck cargo – Hague Rules and whether there can be an exception of 'perils of the sea'*

Facts

The plaintiffs were the consignees for 50 tractors carried on board the Glory, a vessel chartered by the defendants. It was agreed that the defendants were to be treated as the carrier and that references in the bill of lading to shipowner were references to them. The bill of lading incorporated the Carriage of Goods by Sea Act 1924. That Act required a bill of lading to state that goods were actually being carried on deck in order to remove them from the definition of 'goods'. The bill of lading issued contained a clause that stated:

'... steamer has liberty to carry goods on deck and owners will not be responsible for any loss, damage or claim arising therefrom.'

During the voyage a tractor that had been stowed on deck was washed overboard. The plaintiffs brought an action against the defendants on the grounds that the defendants were in breach of their obligation under art III r2 of the Hague Rules to 'properly and carefully load, handle, stow, carry, keep, care for and discharge the goods carried.'

The defendants sought to rely on the liberty clause in the bill of lading. They alternatively sought to rely on the defence of 'perils or accident of the sea' under art IV r2 of the Hague Rules.

Held

Judgment for the plaintiffs.

The liberty clause in the bill of lading was ineffective to exclude the carriers' liability: a general liberty to carry goods on deck is not a statement that the goods will in fact be carried on deck for the purposes of art I of the Hague Rules.

Pilcher J:

'The intention of the Act and Schedule in relation to deck cargo appears to me to be reasonably clear. At common law a shipowner is only authorised to stow goods on deck in certain circumstances: the principle is set out accurately in *Scrutton on Charter Parties*, 15th ed, at p57, as follows:

The shipowner or master will only be authorised to stow goods on deck; (1) by a custom binding in the trade, or port of loading, to stow on deck goods of that class on such a voyage; or (2) by express agreement with the shipper of the particular goods so to stow them. The effect of deck stowage not so authorised will be to set aside the exceptions of the charter or bill of lading and to render the shipowner liable under his contract of carriage for damage happening to such goods.'

Pilcher J then examined the reason for the exclusion of deck cargo from the definition of 'goods' in the Carriage of Goods by Sea Act 1924:

'The policy of the Carriage of Goods by Sea Act 1924, was to regulate the relationship between the shipowner and the owner of goods along the well-known lines. In excluding from the definition of "goods", the carriage of which was subject to the Act, cargo carried on deck and stated to be so carried, the intention of the Act was, in my view, to leave the shipowner free to carry deck cargo on his own conditions, and unaffected by the obligations imposed upon him by the Act in any case in which he would, apart from the Act, have been entitled to carry such cargo on deck, provided that the cargo in question was in fact carried on deck and that the bill of lading covering it contained on its face a statement that the par-

ticular cargo was being so carried. Such a statement on the face of the bill of lading would serve as a notification and a warning to consignees and indorsees of the bill of lading to whom the property in the goods passed under the terms of s1 of the Bill of Lading Act 1855, that the goods which they were to take were being shipped as deck cargo. They would thus have full knowledge of the facts when accepting the documents and would know that the carriage of the goods on deck was not subject to the Act. If, on the other had, there was no specific agreement between the parties as to the carriage on deck, and no statement on the face of the bill of lading that the goods carried on deck had in fact been so carried, the consignees or indorsees of the bill of lading would be entitled to assume that the goods were goods the carriage of which could only be performed by the shipowner subject to the obligations imposed on him by the Act.'

The Carriage of Goods by Sea Act 1924 applied to the cargo and the carriers' liberty to ship cargo on deck was subject to their obligations under art III r2 'properly and carefully to load, handle, stow, carry, keep and care for' the goods in question:

'A mere general liberty to carry goods on deck is not in my view a statement in the contract of carriage that the goods are in fact being carried on deck. To hold otherwise would in my view do violence to the ordinary meaning of the words of art I(c). I hold, accordingly, that the plaintiffs' tractors were being carried by the shipowners subject to the obligations imposed upon them by art III, r2, of the Act.'

The tractors should not have come loose under normal weather conditions and therefore there was a breach of art III r2. The carrier could not bring itself into the exception of 'perils of the sea'. For this exception to avail the carrier, something unusual or unexpected had to have happened at sea. As expressed by Pilcher J:

'One does not need to know a great deal about the sea to appreciate that a little coaster like the Glory, in the conditions of wind and sea which she is likely to encounter in October in the North Sea, may easily have her foredeck covered by the seas as she rolls according to the direction of the wind in relation to her course. It is quite clear that that is what happened to the Glory, and it is exactly what the master expected.'

Comment

This case shows the reasoning behind the section of the Hague Rules which normally requires that when goods are to be carried on deck that the bill of lading states that they are actually so carried.

Under art I(c) of the Hague Rules and Hague-Visby Rules deck cargo is outside the definition of 'goods'. Deck cargo for the purpose of the Rules is cargo which is carried on deck and which in the bill of lading is stated will be carried on deck. This case shows that a mere liberty to carry on deck is not sufficient to make cargo which is carried on deck come within the definition of deck cargo.

Tattersall v *National Steamship Co Ltd* (1884) 12 QB 297 High Court (Day and Smith JJ)

• *A vessel which was not disinfected was not fit to receive and carry cargo*

Facts

Cattle belonging to the plaintiff were shipped on board a vessel owned by the defendants for a voyage from London to New York.

The bill of lading contained a clause excluding liability on the part of the shipowners for 'accident, disease or mortality and that under no circumstances shall they be held liable for more than a fixed sum for each of the animals'.

Some of the cattle contracted foot and mouth disease because the vessel had previously carried infected cattle and had not been disinfected before taking on board the plaintiff's cattle.

Held

The defendants could not rely on the limitation of liability clause.

Day J:

'... where there is a contract to carry goods in a ship there is, in the absence of any stipulation to the contrary, an implied engagement on the part of the person so undertaking to carry, that the ship is reasonably fit for the purposes of such carriage. ... In this case it is clear that the ship was not reasonably fit for the carriage of these cattle. There is, therefore, a breach of their implied engagement ...

It is argued that the plaintiff's damages cannot exceed a fixed sum per animal ... therefore we have to consider whether there are any ... stipulations in the bill of lading restricting or qualifying the liability of the defendants by reason of their not having provided a reasonably fit vessel, for ... reception and carriage of the animals.'

Whilst the provision in the bill of lading would apply to any damaged occasioned in the course of the voyage where the ship was originally fit for the carriage and reception of cargo, it did not exempt or restrict the liability of the shipowners as regards damage resulting from their failure to provide a ship that was fit to receive and carry the goods.

Thus, the plaintiff was entitled to damages for loss of his cattle and those damages were not limited by provisions in the bill of lading.

8 Carriage of Goods by Sea (5): Indemnities and Excluded Liabilities

Brown Jenkinson & Co v *Percy Dalton (London)* [1957] 2 QB 621
Court of Appeal (Lord Evershed MR, Morris and Pearce LJJ)

• *Indemnities given in return for clean bill of lading in circumstances where the consignee would be entitled to reject the goods would be illegal and unenforceable*

Facts
The defendants shipped orange juice to Hamburg. Some of the barrels were old and some were leaking. The defendants requested the plaintiffs to issue them with a clean bill of lading on an undertaking that they would provide the plaintiffs with an indemnity in which they agreed to indemnify the master and the owners of the vessel against all losses which they incurred as a result of a clean bill of lading being issued. The plaintiffs were accordingly liable for the lost barrels to the consignees of the cargo. They then sued the defendants under the indemnity.

Held
The Court criticised the offering of such indemnities as follows:

'... the shipowners made in the bill of lading a representation of fact that they knew to be false, and which they intended should be relied upon by persons who received the bill of lading. They were committing the tort of deceit and the defendants' promise to indemnify the shipowners against loss resulting from the making of that representation was accordingly unenforceable ... the promise upon which the plaintiffs rely is

this: if you will make a false representation, which will deceive indorsees or bankers, we will indemnify you against any loss that may result to you. I cannot think that a court should lend it aid to enforce such a bargain.'

Comment
Where the Hague-Visby Rules apply to the contract of carriage, a carrier will have an indemnity from the shipper if the information supplied by the shipper is incorrect resulting in a claim by the cargo owner against the carrier. However, a carrier should not include information on the bill of lading of which s/he is suspicious and has no reasonable opportunity of checking.

Browner International v *Monarch Shipping, The European Enterprise* [1989] 2 Lloyd's Rep 185 QB High Court (Steyn J)

• *Incorporation of the Hague-Visby Rules – the method of incorporation will determine whether the Rules have statutory effect precluding alteration or contractual effect*

Facts
Contract for carriage of meat in a refrigerated container from Dover to Calais. The contract was contained in or evidenced by a waybill. There was no statement that the waybill was to have effect as a bill of lading. The waybill incorporated the Hague-Visby Rules but altered the limitation of liability clause (art IV r5) with a substantially less generous provision. Goods were loaded on the upper deck.

The vessel entered Calais during heavy weather. The goods overturned and were damaged. Carrier admitted liability under art III r2 of the Rules. The question was the limit on his liability. This depended on whether the contract fell within s1(6)(b) of COGSA 1971:

'... the Rules shall have the force of law in relation to ...

(b) any receipt which is a non-negotiable document marked as such if the contract contained in or evidenced by it is a contract for the carriage of goods by sea which expressly provides that the Rules are to govern the contract as if the receipt were a bill of lading.'

Held

Steyn J disagreed with Lloyd J in *The Vechstroon* [1982] 1 Lloyd's Rep 301, where it had been held that the receipt under s1(6)(b) of COGSA 1971 did not require the words 'as if a bill of lading' to give the Rules statutory force and not merely contractual force. His Lordship did so on the grounds that he had had the benefit of fuller argument from counsel, particularly citing articles and texts by Mustill, Diamond and Scrutton. Parliament's intention behind the section was for two formal requirements: a non-negotiable document marked as such and a statement that the document is to take effect 'as if a bill of lading'. In their absence the Hague-Visby Rules would have only contractual force and could be altered by agreement. On the facts this was so. The contractual limits on liability applied.

Ciampa v *British India Steam Navigation Co Ltd* [1915] 2 KB 774 King's Bench Division (Rowlatt J)

• *Unseaworthiness by failure to obtain a clean bill of health displaces any defence under 'restraint of princes'*

Facts

The plaintiffs shipped lemons on the defen-dants' vessel, The Matiana, from Naples to London. Prior to arriving at Naples, The Matiana had called at Mombassa where there was an outbreak of plague and had sailed from there with a foul bill of health. On the voyage from Naples to London the ship called at Marseilles where her cargo was subjected to dératisation by sulphur fumigation as a result of having sailed from a plague-affected area and being still without a clean bill of health. The fumigation process damaged the skins of the lemons and the plaintiffs claimed damages for the loss.

The defendants argued that since the fumi-gation was done by an order under a decree of the French Ministry of the Interior, they were entitled to rely on the immunity give under 'restraint of princes' (ie circumstances beyond the shipowners control) as a defence to the plaintiffs claim.

Held

It was well known that the fumigation process would cause the damage it had done to a cargo such as lemons, and the decree issued by the French government requiring dératisation had been in force since 1906. The carriers there-fore knew when they sailed from Naples that the fumigation at Marseilles would be inevitable in the circumstances and that the process would damage the cargo. The carriers' knowledge of both these matters and their failure to obtain a clean bill of health at Naples meant that they had, in effect, deliberately subjected the cargo to a damaging fumigation treatment. This rendered the vessel unseawor-thy at Marseilles in that she was not fit to carry the cargo of lemons safely, and the carriers were liable to the plaintiffs for their loss. They were not entitled to rely on the defence of 'restraint of princes' because in the words of Rowlatt J:

'When facts exist which show conclusively that the ship was inevitably doomed before the commencement of the voyage to become subject to a restraint, I do not think that there is a "restraint of princes".'

Effort Shipping Co Ltd v *Linden Management SA and Another, The Giannis NK* [1998] 1 All ER 495; [1998] 1 Lloyd's Rep 337 House of Lords (Lords Goff of Chieveley, Lloyd of Berwick, Steyn, Cooke of Thorndon and Clyde)

• *The carrier's rights in respect of dangerous cargo under art IV r6 Hague Rules are not qualified by the art IV r3 exoneration of liability where there is no fault or neglect on the part of the shipper*

Facts

In November 1990 the second defendants shipped a cargo of groundnuts from Dakar, Senegal, to Rio Haina in the Dominican Republic on board the plaintiff shipowner's vessel, The Giannis NK. A bill of lading was issued which incorporated the Hague Rules. Property in the goods was passed to the first defendants, the receivers, by endorsement of the bill of lading.

The cargo was loaded in number 4 hold. Unknown to both parties, at the time of shipment the hold was infested with khapra beetle. The vessel sailed to San Juan, Puerto Rico, where she discharged part of a previously loaded cargo of wheat pellets. She then sailed to Rio Haina to discharge the remainder of the wheat cargo and the groundnut cargo and it was then that the beetle infestation in number 4 hold was first discovered. The vessel was placed in quarantine and unsuccessfully fumigated twice before being ordered to leave port with all her remaining cargo. However, she had by then been arrested by the receivers and this arrest was lifted by an undertaking given by the vessel's P & I Club which required her to return to San Juan in an attempt to find a purchaser for the cargo.

At San Juan further inspection revealed the presence of dead khapra beetles and khapra beetle larvae in number 4 hold, and the vessel was served with a notice by the US authorities to return the cargo to its country of origin or dump it at sea. As it was the only practical alternative, the carriers dumped the groundnuts and the wheat at sea and then returned to San Juan for final inspection. However, live khapra beetles and khapra beetle larvae were again found in number 4 hold and she was retained for further fumigation. After a delay of two-and-a-half months in total, the vessel was eventually cleared to load under her next charter, at Wilmington, North Carolina.

The plaintiff shipowners sought to recover damages for the delay to the vessel and the cost of the fumigations from the shippers under art IV r6 of the Hague Rules, which provides that the carrier may discharge or destroy goods 'of an inflammable, explosive or dangerous nature to the shipment' that he has not consented to carry with knowledge of their nature, and further provides that the shipper is liable for 'damages and expenses directly or indirectly arising out of or resulting from such shipment'.

The shippers argued that art IV r6 was qualified by art IV r3 and that they were therefore not responsible for loss or damage which occurred without fault or neglect on their part. They alternatively contended that s1 of the Bills of Lading Act 1855 divested them of liability to the owner.

The trial judge and the Court of Appeal found in favour of the plaintiff shipowners. The defendants appealed.

Held

The appeal was dismissed.

The infested cargo was goods of a 'dangerous nature' within art IV r6 of the Hague Rules. It was not necessary to show that the goods would cause direct physical damage to other goods nor was it correct to imply that damage be 'directly' caused by the dangerous nature of the goods. Although the infestation presented no physical danger to the ship and was unlikely to spread to the other holds, it rendered the vessel and all its cargo subject to exclusion from the countries where the cargo was to be discharged. The carriers were left with no choice other than to dump all of the vessel's cargo at sea. The infested cargo therefore clearly presented a danger to the other jettisoned goods and fell within art IV r6.

Steyn LJ:

'What made the cargo dangerous was the fact that the shipment and voyage was to countries where the imposition of a quarantine and an order for the dumping of the entire cargo was to be expected. In that sense the khapra-infested cargo posed a physical danger to the other cargo. On that factual basis the judge ruled that as a matter of law the cargo was "of a dangerous nature" within art IV r6. I agree.

Given the somewhat philosophical debate at the Bar about the meaning of "goods of ... [a] dangerous nature" in the context of notions such as attributes, properties and substance, I would mention only two practical matters. First, it would be wrong to apply the ejusdem generis rule to the words "goods of an inflammable, explosive or dangerous nature." These are disparate categories of goods. Each word must be given its natural meaning, and "dangerous" ought not to be restrictively interpreted by reason of the preceding words. Secondly, it would be wrong to detract from the generality and width of the expression "goods of... [a] dangerous nature" by importing the suggested restriction that the goods must by themselves, or by reason of their inherent properties, pose a danger to the ship or other cargo. For my part I would resist any temptation to substitute for the ordinary and non technical expression "goods ... of a dangerous nature" any other formulation.'

The shipper could not rely on the requirement for fault or neglect on the part of the shipper found in art IV r3 to exonerate his liability under art IV r6. That requirement neither expressly nor impliedly qualified art IV r6 which was a wholly separate provision intended to deal with dangerous goods and for which it imposed a strict liability on the shipper of those goods. Article IV r6 therefore applied irrespective of whether there was any fault or neglect on the part of the appellants.

Lord Lloyd of Berwick stated:

'Turning to the English cases, Mustill J in *The Athanasia Comninos* [1990] 1 Lloyd's Rep 277 expressed the view, obiter, that art IV r.6 is not qualified by art IV r3. In *Mediterranean Freight Services Ltd v BP Oil International Ltd, The Fiona* [1993] 1 Lloyd's Rep 257 Judge Diamond QC, sitting as a deputy Commercial Court judge, with all his great experience of this branch of the law, expressed the same view. I agree with those views ... art IV r6 is a free standing provision dealing with a specific subject matter. It is neither expressly, nor by implication, subject to art IV r3. It imposes strict liability on shippers in relation to the shipment of dangerous goods, irrespective of fault or neglect on their part.'

Lord Steyn:

'In the present case my view is that the contrast between the generality of art IV r3 and the specificity of art IV r6 goes some way to supporting the proposition that the latter ought be construed as free-standing. But I am not saying that on its own this is a decisive factor in favour of the interpretation put forward by the owners. The second point of substance is the argument that art IV r6 in its three different parts points in a similar direction. The right given in the first and third parts to the carrier to land, etc, dangerous cargo cannot sensibly depend on whether the shippers knew or ought to have known of the dangerous nature of the cargo. That would be impractical: the carrier must be able to land, etc, dangerous cargo irrespective of his shippers actual or constructive knowledge. Counsel for the shippers did not dispute this proposition. But he said that this liberty to land dangerous cargo already existed under the common law. That is no answer: pro tanto the Hague Rules upon their enactment displaced the common law. It follows that the liberty to land dangerous cargo under the first and third parts derives exclusively from art IV r6. And in respect of the first and third parts it exists irrespective of the actual or constructive knowledge of the shippers. If one were now to accept the shippers' argument there would be this difference between the first and third parts as contrasted with the second part: only in respect of the second part would the rights of the owners be conditional upon the actual or constructive knowledge, or due diligence, of the shippers. But this is prima facie implausible because the rights to land, etc, dangerous cargo, and to claim damages seem to arise in the same circumstances. Indeed the second part in imposing liability for damage resulting from "such shipment" refers back the "shipment" of dangerous cargo, etc, in the first part. The natural construction is therefore that in neither the first nor the second parts (or for that matter the third part) are the rights of owners conditional upon the actual or constructive knowledge, or due diligence, of shippers. This is a point of some weight.'

Although it was not necessary to the decision of the court, consideration was given to whether the shipper's liability for shipping dangerous goods at common law depended on his knowledge or means of knowledge that the goods were dangerous. Lord Lloyd of Berwick:

'The dispute between the shippers and the carriers on this point is a dispute which has been rumbling on for well over a century. It is time for your Lordships to make a decision one way or the other. In the end that decision depends mainly on whether the majority decision in *Brass* v *Maitland* (1856) 26 LJQB 49, which has stood for 140 years, should now be overruled. I am of the opinion that it should not. I agree with the majority in that case and would hold that the liability of a shipper for shipping dangerous goods at common law, when it arises, does not depend on his knowledge or means of knowledge that the goods are dangerous.

An incidental advantage of that conclusion is that the liability of the shipper will be the same whether it arises by virtue of an implied term at common law, or under art IV r6 of the Hague Rules.'

The shipper could not rely on s1 of the Bills of Lading Act 1855 to exonerate liability for the shipment of dangerous goods. The second appellants were liable to the respondents for shipping a dangerous cargo and this liability was not divested when property in the ground nuts passed to the receivors by endorsement of the bill of lading. Lord Lloyd of Berwick stated:

'The Act of 1855 has been repealed and replaced by the Carriage of Goods by Sea Act 1992. The point at issue is now expressly covered by section 3(3) of the Act of 1992. But we were told that there were a number of outstanding cases which are still governed by the Act of 1855.

The mischief to which the Act of 1855 was directed appears clearly enough from the preamble. ... Whereas property in the goods will pass by virtue of the consignment or endorsement of the bill of lading, rights under the contract of carriage could not be enforced by the receiver of the goods by reason of the peculiar rule of English law that prohibits jus quaesitum tertio. Cases in the early part of the 19th century illustrate the inconvenience of the rule and the efforts of the courts to get round it. In the end it proved necessary for Parliament to take a hand.

It will be noticed that whereas the preamble refers, as one would expect, to the passing of rights under the contract, it says nothing about the passing of liabilities. One finds the same contrast in section 1. It provides for all rights of suit to be "transferred to and vested in" the holder of the bill of lading; it does not provide for the transfer of liabilities. Instead it provides for the holder of the bill of lading to be subject to the same liabilities as the shipper. It seems clear that this difference of language was intentional. Whereas a statutory assignment of rights under the bill of lading contract would represent but a modest step forward in pursuit of commercial convenience, a statutory novation, depriving the carriers of their rights against the shippers, and substituting rights against an unknown receiver, would have represented a much more radical change in the established course of business.

The legislative solution was ingenious. Whereas the rights under the contract of carriage were to be transferred, the liabilities were not. The shippers were to remain liable, but the holder of the bill of lading was to come under the same liability as the shippers. His liability was to be by way of addition, not substitution.'

Comment

See *Mediterranean Freight Services Ltd v BP Oil International Ltd, The Fiona* [1993] 1 Lloyd's Rep 257 for the position under the Hague-Visby Rules and *The Athanasia Comninos* [1990] 1 Lloyd's Rep 227 where the nature of dangerousness was discussed.

Gosse Millerd Ltd v Canadian Government Merchant Marine Ltd, The Canadian Highlander [1929] AC 223 House of Lords (Lord Hailsham LC and Viscount Sumner)

• *The scope of 'management of the ship' within the meaning of art IV r2(a) Hague Rules*

Facts

A steamship carrying a cargo of tinplates collided with the dock wall on entry into a port of call and was damaged sufficient to be kept in dock for some weeks while undergoing repairs. Whilst the repairs were being carried out the hatches to the holds were left open to enable the workmen to get in and out of the holds and, as a result, rain got into the holds and damaged the tinplates. There was probably also carelessness as regards the replacing of tarpaulins intended to protect the openings of the holds but too many different persons had entered the holds during the period of repairs to decide who were the persons responsible for that negligence.

The owners of the tinplates brought a claim against the shipowners based on a breach of art III r2 of the Rules and the respondents relied on art IV r2(a):

'Neither the carrier nor the ship shall be responsible for loss or damage arising from – (a) Act, neglect, or default of the master, mariner, pilot, or the servants of the carrier in the navigation or in the management of the ship.'

Wright J ([1927] 2 KB 432) at first instance found that:

'The words "properly discharge" in art III, r2, mean, I think, "deliver from the ship's tackle in the same apparent order and condition as on shipment", unless the carrier can excuse himself under art IV ...'

He commented on the new regime introduced by the Hague Rules as having 'radically changed the legal status of sea carriers under bills of lading' and went on to say:

'According to the previous law, shipowners were generally common carriers, or were liable to the obligations of common carriers, but they were entitled to the utmost freedom to restrict and limit their liabilities, which they did by elaborate and mostly illegible exceptions and conditions. Under the Act and the Rules, which cannot be varied in favour of the carrier by any bill of lading, their liabilities are precisely determined, and so also are their rights and immunities ...'

Held

The shipowners failed 'properly and carefully' to carry, keep and care for the tinplates as required by art III r2 and the onus was on them to prove that they were protected from liability by art IV r2(a). The shipowners could not rely on that protection since failure correctly to secure the tarpaulin covers over the hatches, even if carried out by members of the crew, did not amount to negligence 'in the management of the ship' as stipulated by art IV r2(a) but instead to negligence in the care of the cargo.

Lord Hailsham LC:

'The argument at the bar turned mainly upon the meaning to be placed upon the expression "management of the ship" ... I am unable to find any reason for supposing that the words as used by the legislature in the Act of 1924 leave any different meaning to that which has been judicially assigned to them when used in contracts for the carriage of goods by sea before that date ...

It is clear that the tinplates were not safely and properly cared for or carried; and it is for the respondents then to prove that they are protected by the provisions of art IV, and that the damage was occasioned through the neglect or default of their servants in the management of the ship. In my judgment they have not even shown that the persons who were negligent were their servants; but even if it can be assumed that the negligence in dealing with the tarpaulins was by members of the crew, such negligence was not negligence in the management of the ship, and therefore is not negligence with regard to which art IV r2 (a) affords any protection ...'

Viscount Sumner:

'By forebearing to define "management of the ship" ... the legislature has, in my opinion, shown a clear intention to continue and enforce the old clause as it was previously understood and regularly construed by the courts.'

Comment

The finding of Wright J at first instance in this case was agreed with by Scrutton LJ in *Silver v Ocean Steamship Company Limited* [1930] 1 KB 416 (CA), but was later disagreed with by Lord Reid in *Albacora SRL v Westcott & Laurance Line* [1966] 2 Lloyd's Rep 53 (see Chapter 7 above). See also *International Packers London Ltd v Ocean Steam Ship Co Ltd* [1955] 2 Lloyd's Rep 218 (below) where the shipowners could rely on the protection of art IV r2(a).

International Packers London Ltd v *Ocean Steam Ship Company Ltd*
[1955] 2 Lloyd's Rep 218 Queen's Bench Division (McNair J)

• *Management of the ship under art IV r2(a) Hague Rules*

Facts

At Brisbane and Melbourne 4,400 cartons of tinned meat were shipped on the defendants' ship, The Hector, for delivery to the plaintiffs at Glasgow. In the course of the voyage, tarpaulins were stripped from hatch covers covering the holds in which the mast had been stowed. Sea water entered.

On arrival at Freemantle the master sought the advice of a surveyor. Part of the cargo was discharged and sold damaged. The rest was carried to Glasgow. Further damage was caused by heating of wet damaged canary seed stowed above the plaintiffs' cargo.

The plaintiffs claimed that the defendants, in breach of art III r1, failed to exercise due diligence to make the vessel seaworthy on leaving Melbourne in that:

1. the wedges securing the tarpaulins were not tightly or securely driven home; and
2. the tarpaulins were not held in place by locking bars or secured by lashings or nets. Alternatively, the carriers were in breach of art III r2 in that they had failed in their duty of care of cargo.

Held

The weather experienced on the voyage to Freemantle was such as to require added precautions to be taken to secure the hatches, such as the use of locking bars, and the defendants in their failure to take such steps were in breach of their duty of care of cargo under art III r2. But that failure was negligence in the management of the ship and was excused under art IV r2(a).

A carrier's duty of care of cargo under art III r2 was non-delegable and the defendants were liable if they acted on what turned out to be wrong advice given by their surveyor, and accordingly the defendants were liable for the increased damage caused by the on-carriage from Freemantle.

Comment

This case gives useful guidance on the meaning of the exception of 'management of the ship'. It also makes it clear that the carrier's duty of care of cargo is a non-delegable duty which is not displaced by such opinions as a surveyor may give.

Lennard's Carrying Company Ltd v Asiatic Petroleum Co Ltd [1915] AC 705 House of Lords (Viscount Haldane LC, Lords Dunedin, Atkinson, Parker of Waddington and Parmoor)

• *The meaning of 'actual fault and privity'*

Facts

Under s502 of the Merchant Shipping Act 1894 the owner of a British ship shall not be liable to any extent for 'any loss or damage happening without his actual fault or privity' where any goods put on board his ship are lost or damaged by reason of fire on board the ship.

Here, a cargo of benzine being carried on board the defendants' ship was lost by a fire caused by the unseaworthiness of the ship due to defective boilers. The carriers were a limited company and the managing owners were another limited company. The managing director of the latter company was the registered managing owner and took an active part in the management of the ship. He knew, or at least had the means of knowing, the defective condition of the boilers, but gave no special instructions to the captain or the chief engineer and took no steps to prevent the ship from putting to sea with her boilers in an unseaworthy condition.

Held

The owners had failed to satisfy the burden of proving that the loss happened without their actual fault or privity. It is to be noted that the ship in question had been re-certified for another year but only on the condition that the boiler pressure be reduced from 160 lbs (its usual pressure) to 130 lbs. This made a great deal of difference in the energy-developing capacity of the engines of the ship. Due to this reduced capacity, the ship grounded on several occasions and finally came to rest in the Scheldt on her way to Rotterdam where she burst a tube. The deck then bulged allowing the benzine to escape. The benzine got into the furnace and caused a fire.

As expressed by Viscount Haldane LC (at p713):

> 'For if Mr Lennard was the directing mind of the company, then his action must, unless a corporation is not to be liable at all, have been an action which was the action of the company itself within the meaning of s502.'

Comment

This case usefully focuses on the fine line which distinguishes one who may be considered the alter ego of a company from one who is a mere servant or agent. This case is often cited when looking at the excepted peril in art IV r2(b) of the Hague-Visby Rules.

Mediterranean Freight Services Ltd v BP Oil International Ltd, The Fiona [1993] 1 Lloyd's Rep 257 Queen's Bench Division (Judge Diamond QC)

• *Dangerous cargo – shipowners' indemnity under Hague-Visby Rules and common law*

Facts

The defendants shipped fuel oil on board the plaintiffs' tanker. There was an explosion during discharge of the cargo and the tanker was damaged. The fuel was contaminated by residual condensate carried on a previous voyage. The plaintiffs contended that the defendants had shipped a dangerous cargo and that they had not been warned of the possibility that an explosive mixture could be formed. They claimed damages at common law on the basis of an implied undertaking not to ship dangerous cargo and, alternatively, an indemnity under art IV r6 of the Hague-Visby Rules.

Held

The claim was dismissed. It was not open to the carrier to rely on any implied undertaking at common law. The Hague-Visby Rules provide an exclusive remedy.

The exception in art IV r6 relates to damage caused 'directly' or 'indirectly' and the carrier is obliged to show that the damage has resulted either directly or indirectly from the shipment. Under the exception this includes, but is not limited to, cases where the carrier has landed dangerous goods or rendered the goods innocuous. On the evidence, the fuel oil as shipped was inflammable, explosive and dangerous and the dominant cause of the explosion was the contamination of the fuel oil with condensate. The exception provided by art IV r6 is qualified by, and always remains subject to, the carriers' overriding obligation to make the ship seaworthy under art III r1. That obligation cannot be displaced by the claim that the shipper has not commenced a suit for unseaworthiness within the Hague-Visby Rules art III r6 one-year time-bar. The carrier is not entitled to an indemnity where the damage is caused by a non-excepted peril such as the unseaworthiness or by the concurrent effects of a peril specified in the Rule. The presence of the condensate was a breach of the duty to make the ship seaworthy under art III r1 and, in any event, was certainly a contributory cause of the explosion.

It is relevant to ask if the risks were of a totally different kind from those expected of the cargo described. The carrier had not been warned of the possibility of any danger but there was an awareness amongst oil companies that fuel oil can produce an explosive mixture, though there had been no recorded explosions and carriers generally did not consider it to be an explosive cargo. Under the Rules the carrier is deemed to have knowledge which it ought to have. It is not relevant that the shipper knew of the dangerous nature of the goods or was at fault. Article IV r3 does not qualify art IV r6. When the carriers consented to the shipment they were ignorant of the nature and characteristics of the cargo and did not take precautions that they might have done.

Meredith Jones and Co Ltd v *Vangemar Shipping Co Ltd, The Apostolis* [1997] 2 Lloyd's Rep 241 Court of Appeal (Leggatt, Morritt and Phillips LJJ)

• *Hague-Visby Rules art III r1 – whether the carrier has exercised due diligence to make the vessel seaworth – the entitlement of the defendant to rely on the exclusion contained in art IV r2(b)*

Facts

In December 1992, the defendant owners of the vessel, The Apostolis, concluded a contract with the plaintiff charterers for the carriage of bales of raw cotton from Salonika to various South American ports. The contract for carriage included a term that the owners' 'rights, immunities, liabilities and responsibilities' were to be 'as defined in the Hague-Visby Rules'. During loading at Thessalonika, a fire occurred on board the vessel which resulted in the cargo in holds 4 and 5 being badly damaged. The plaintiffs argued that the fire was caused by a spark from welding which was going on above the hold during the loading and that this was a breach by the defendants of art III r1 Hague-Visby Rules which provides that:

'The carrier shall be bound, before and at the beginning of the voyage, to exercise due diligence to:
(a) make the ship seaworthy ...
(c) make the holds ... and all other parts of the ship in which goods are carried, fit and safe for their reception, carriage and preservation.'

The plaintiffs contended that, in these circumstances, the defendants were not entitled to rely on the exclusion contained in art IV r2(b) which provides that 'Neither the carrier nor the ship shall be responsible for loss or damage arising or resulting from ... (b) fire unless caused by the actual fault or privity of the carrier.' The defendants argued that the most probable cause for the fire was a discarded cigarette and that, accordingly, they were not liable for the loss.

At trial, the evidence was that a spark had gained access to the hold through a gap between the hatch cover and the coaming. On these facts, the trial judge found the vessel was unseaworthy on the ground that the cargo was exposed to the risk of fire caused by a spark from the welding getting into the hold, and held that the defendants were in breach of art III r1 of the Rules. Moreover, they were found to be privy to the fault by which the fire was caused and so in breach of art III r2.

The shipowners appealed.

Held
Appeal allowed.

The decision is interesting for the Court of Appeal's interpretation of the requirements of art III r1 of the Hague Visby Rules. The facts of the case are similar to those of *Maxine Footwear Co* v *Canadian Government Merchant Marine* [1959] AC 589 but with one important difference: in *Maxine* it was the cork lining of the hold, ie the ship itself, that was on fire, not the cargo. The defendants in that case were held to be in breach of art III r1 because it was this that rendered the ship unseaworthy. By contrast, in the present case, the fact that the cargo was on fire did not, in itself, render the vessel unseaworthy, and the defendants were not in breach of art III r1.

The plaintiffs had further argued that with sparks around them from the welding on deck, the shipowners exposed the cargo to danger and that this made the ship unseaworthy in the sense of being uncargoworthy. While this submission had been accepted by Tuckey J at first instance, it was rejected by the Court of Appeal. A ship will not be unseaworthy simply because the cargo will be endangered by an activity which is taking place on board. The defendants were entitled to rely on art IV r2(b) because, on the facts, the fire was not caused by the defendants fault or privity.

Leggatt LJ:

'To show breach of art III r1 the plaintiffs must show that the carriers failed to make the ship seaworthy and that their loss or damage was caused by the breach, or in other words that the fire was caused by unseaworthiness. The plaintiffs have to contend that the unseaworthiness consisted in exposure of the cargo to the risk of fire from a spark entering the hold. But even if that is what occurred, it was not unseaworthiness which caused the fire, but the fire which rendered the vessel unseaworthy. The judge found that "the fire was caused as a direct result of welding carried out to the cylindrical pulley", so that "because the forward hatch covers had not been dropped there was a risk ... that sparks from the welding ... would enter the hold through the gap between the underside of the hatch cover and the coaming" ... The welding was not done directly above an open or partly open hold, and it may have occupied no more than a short time. The judge's conclusion that the carrier "was carrying out welding work above the hold which resulted in sparks raining into it" was therefore an ill-judged hyperbole. Nothing about the state of the ship rendered her unseaworthy. The owners were not in breach of art III r1 merely because welding exposed the cargo to an ephemeral risk of ignition. The holds themselves were not intrinsically unsafe. In *Maxine* the House of Lords found it unnecessary to decide whether the vessel was on fire before the cargo was loaded. It was fire in the fabric of the vessel, namely the cork lining of the hold, which rendered her unseaworthy. Here the ship only became so on account of the fire in the cargo. It cannot even be said that the welding was taking place in order to render the ship seaworthy. The fire might as well have been caused by a discarded cigarette, which, as the judge accepted, could not be a breach of art III r1.

In my judgment, therefore, the judge's resolution of this point, which he did not find easy, was wrong. Even if the fire was caused as he found, there was no breach of art III r1, and the owners were not liable on that ground.'

Phillips LJ:

'For a ship to be unseaworthy, or more strictly uncargoworthy, there must be some attribute of the ship itself which threatens the safety of the cargo. If a hold is dirty, that is properly considered as an attribute of the ship. But the fact that a hold contains cargo which threatens damage to other cargo stowed in proximity is not an attribute of the ship and does not render the ship unseaworthy. ...

A ship will be unseaworthy if she is not in such a state as will preserve the cargo from the risk of damage from the necessary incidents of a ship's existence, whether at sea or in harbour. But a ship will not be unseaworthy simply because she or her cargo will be endangered if an act or activity occurs on board her which it is not necessary to perform while she is in that condition and which reasonable care requires shall not be performed while she is in that condition. If a repairer shoots a Cox gun bolt into a gas filled tank, so that the tank explodes, he does not thereby demonstrate that the ship is unseaworthy. Hatches have to be off while cargo is being loaded, and it will at that point be possible to envisage various activities capable of damaging the cargo while that condition prevails, but if such an activity is indulged in and the cargo is damaged, it does not follow that the vessel is unseaworthy or that the condition of the vessel is the cause of the damage. The cause of the damage in such a case is the activity.

Were the judge correct to have found that welding was taking place near a gap in the hatch cover that enabled sparks to gain access to the cargo, and that a spark from the welding gained access and ignited the cargo, the conclusion should have been that the cause of the damage to the cargo was fire caused by the act of welding and not unseaworthiness.'

Midland Silicones Ltd v *Scruttons Ltd* [1962] AC 446 House of Lords (Viscount Simonds, Lords Reid, Keith of Avonholme, Denning and Morris of Borth-y-Gest)

• *Stevedores are not privy to contracts of carriage between shipper and carrier and cannot rely on the exemptions therein.*

Facts
There was a contract for the carriage of goods from the USA to England. The bill of lading contained a clause which limited the liability of the carrier in the event of the goods being damaged as a result of the negligence of the shipowner. During unloading the cargo was damaged as a result of the negligence of the stevedores.

When sued, they contended that they could rely upon any limitation clause which would have been available to the carrier.

Held
The stevedores could not rely on the exemption in the contract between the shipper and carrier, because they were not privy to that contract.

The cargo owners could not be affected by the terms of a separate contract between the carrier and the stevedores, which provided that the stevedores should be able to avail themselves of the same protection as that which was afforded to the carrier, because they were unaware of such a contract and, therefore, since no agency was alleged, the stevedores were responsible for the damage.

Lord Reid foresaw the possibility of an agency contract. He said:

'I can see a possibility of success of the agency assignment if (first) the bill of lading makes it clear that the stevedore is intended to be protected by the provisions in it which limit liability, (secondly) the bill of lading makes it clear that the carrier, in addition to contracting for these provisions on his own behalf, is also contracting as agent for the stevedore, (thirdly) the carrier has authority from the stevedore to do that, or perhaps later ratification from the stevedore would suffice, and (fourthly) that any difficulties about consideration moving from the stevedore were overcome. And then, to affect the consignee, it would be necessary to show that the provisions of the Bills of Lading Act 1855, apply.'

Comment

A bill of lading which contains a Himalaya clause covering independent contractors would satisfy the agency requirement referred to in Lord Reid's judgment above.

The consideration element was dealt with in *New Zealand Shipping Co Ltd* v *Satterthwaite, The Eurymedon* [1975] AC 154 (below) where it was held that a pre-existing obligation to load and unload cargo could amount to consideration moving from the stevedore to the cargo owner.

Motis Exports Ltd v *Dampskibsselskabet AF 1912 Aktieselskab and Others* [2000] 1 Lloyd's Rep 211 Court of Appeal (Stuart-Smith, Mummery and Mance LJJ)

• *Delivery of goods against forged bill of lading – effect on exemption clause*

Facts

Various goods were shipped in containers by the plaintiffs and were carried from ports in China and Hong Kong to West Africa aboard the shippers' vessel. The seven bills of lading issued in respect of these shipments stated that consignees were to order and the 'Carrier's Responsibility' clause (cl 5.3) exempted the carrier from liability for any loss or damage to goods howsoever caused before loading or after discharge over the ship's rail.

The bills presented to the carrier were in fact forged. Both the owner of the goods and the shippers (who were also the carriers) were

ignorant of the forgery and the goods were discharged against the bills on arrival at ports in West Africa with the result that the goods were lost to the consignees. The consignees sued the carrier for failure to deliver the goods and the carrier relied on cl 5.3 as exonerating him from any liability.

Held

The carriers were liable for the misdelivery of the goods notwithstanding cl 5.3, by reason of implied limitations on the effect of the clause. A forged bill of lading is a nullity and the exemption clause did not cover loss due to delivering up goods against forged documents; it covered physical perils, not misdelivery.

In giving his judgment, Stuart-Smith LJ placed emphasis on the reasoning of Lord Denning in *Sze Hai Tong Bank Ltd* v *Rambler Cycle Co Ltd* [1959] 2 Lloyd's Rep 114. In that case, which also involved non-delivery and its relation to a similarly wide and absolute exemption clause, Lord Denning said:

'The exemption, on the face of it, could hardly have been more comprehensive, and it is contended that it is wide enough to absolve the shipping company from responsibility for ... the delivery of the goods to a person who, to their knowledge, was not entitled to receive them. If the exemption clause upon its true construction absolved the shipping company from an act such as that, it seems that by parity of reasoning they would have been absolved if they had given the goods away to some passer-by or had burnt them or thrown them into the sea. If it had been suggested to the parties that condition exempted the shipping company in such a case, they would both have said: "Of course not." There is, therefore, an implied limitation on the clause.'

Stuart-Smith applied this principle of implied limitations to absolute exemption clauses to the clause in question and found the carriers' obligation to be such that it would amount to the same result as that reached by Lord Denning. The counsel for the shippers had argued that what had happened was not mere misdelivery but in fact theft and, therefore, should be covered by the exemption clause. In rejecting this argument, the Court was of the opinion that the clause in the bill of lading should not be construed in such a way as to excuse the carrier 'from performing an obligation of such fundamental importance' (per Stuart-Smith LJ).

Comment

The case restates the important principle that a carrier will be liable for misdelivery of the goods, whether it is delivery in the absence of the bill of lading or delivery against a forged bill of lading. The breadth of implied limitations on exemption clauses is an area that has still to be fully tested in future cases.

New Zealand Shipping Co Ltd v A M Satterthwaite & Co Ltd, The Eurymedon [1974] 1 Lloyd's Rep 534 Privy Council (Viscount Dilhorne, Lords Wilberforce, Hodson, Simon of Glaisdale and Salmon)

• *Use of a 'Himalaya' clause extends carrier's exemptions to stevedores*

Facts

A drilling machine belonging to the plaintiffs was shipped on the vessel Eurymedon at Liverpool for carriage to New Zealand. The bill of lading contained a clause in the following terms:

'It is hereby expressly agreed that no servant or agent of the carrier (including every independent contractor from time to time employed (by him)) shall in any circumstances whatsoever be under any liability whatsoever to the shipper, consignee or owner of the goods or to any holder of this Bill of Lading, for any loss, damage or delay of whatsoever kind, arising or resulting directly or indirectly from any act, neglect or default on his part while acting in the course of or in connection with him employment and without prejudice to the foregoing provisions ... every exemption limitation condition and liability herein contained and every right, exemption from liability, defence and immunity of whatsoever nature applicable to the carrier ... shall also be available and extend to protect every such servant or agent of the carrier ... and for the purpose of all the foregoing provisions of this clause the carrier is or shall be deemed to be acting as agent or trustee on behalf of and for the benefit of all persons who are or might be his servants or agents from time to time.'

The bill then went on to stipulate:

1. that the carrier's liability would not exceed £100 per package or unit; and
2. that the contract of carriage was governed by the Carriage of Goods by Sea Act 1971.

When the machine arrive in New Zealand it was damaged during unloading by stevedores.

It was argued that cl 1 of the bill of lading was a 'Himalaya' clause which attempted to take advantage of the vicarious immunity theory suggested by Lord Denning in *Adler v Dickson* [1955] 1 QB 158. It was further argued that the stevedores could not rely on cl 1 in the bill of lading because the Bills of Lading Act 1855 operated to transfer the rights and obligations in the bill to the consignee; or, the exemptions in the bill could not be transferred by the Act as the bill could only operate to transfer rights and obligations, not exemptions.

Held

The bill of lading brought into existence a unilateral bargain which became a full contract when the stevedores discharged the goods.

The discharge of the goods for the benefit of the shipper was the consideration by the shipper that the stevedores should have benefit of the exemptions and limitations in the bill of lading.

Lord Wilberforce:

'In the opinion of their Lordships to give the

appellant the benefit of the exemptions and limitations contained in the bill of lading is to give effect to the clear intentions of a commercial document, and can be given within existing principles. They see no reason to strain the law or the facts in order to defeat these exemptions.

It should not be overlooked that the effect of denying validity to the clause would be to encourage actions against servants, agents and independent contractors in order to get round exemptions (which are almost invariable and often compulsory) accepted by shippers against carriers, the existence and presumed efficacy of which, is reflected in the rates of freight. They see no attraction in this consequences.'

Comment

See *Midland Silicones* v *Scrutton* [1962] AC 46 (above) where the agency and consideration requirements were discussed. In *The Eurymedon* there was a discussion centering on a unilateral contract becoming a bilateral contract once the stevedores provided consideration by loading or unloading cargo.

Port Jackson Stevedoring Pty Ltd v *Salmond & Spraggon (Australia) Pty Ltd, The New York Star* [1980] 3 All ER 257 Privy Council (Lords Wilberforce, Diplock, Fraser, Scarman and Roskill)

• *Bill of lading 'Himalaya' clause can extend benefit of defences and liabilities conferred on carrier to stevedore employed by carrier*

Facts

The respondents were the consignees for a consignment of razor blades carried by the Blue Star Line on board its vessel The New York Star for a voyage from Canada to Sydney, Australia. The appellant company was part-owned and commonly acted as stevedores for the Blue Star Line at the port of Sydney.

Clause 2 of the bill of lading was a 'Himalaya' clause extending the benefit of defences and immunities conferred by the bill on the carrier to independent contractors employed by the carrier. Clause 5 provided that the carrier's responsibility terminated as soon as the goods left the ship's tackle at the port of discharge and under cl 8 the consignee was to take delivery of the goods from the ship's rail immediately the ship was ready to discharge or else pay demurrage.

On their discharge from the ship at Sydney, the goods were placed by the stevedores, in accordance with the normal practice in the port, in a shed on the wharf under the control of the stevedore. When the consignee presented the bill of lading the goods were found to have been stolen from the wharf, having been delivered by servants of the stevedores to persons who had no right to receive them.

The Court of Appeal of New South Wales allowed an appeal by the consignee from the trial judge on the ground that there was no proof of consideration moving from the stevedores to entitle it to the defences in the bill of lading. The High Court of Australia dismissed the stevedores' appeal against that decision and the stevedores now appealed to the Judicial Committee of the Privy Council.

Held (inter alia)

The stevedores were entitled to rely on the Himalaya clause in the bill of lading to obtain all the exemptions which were available to the carrier. The precise relationship of carrier and stevedore and the practice at the port of discharge would act as evidence in the individual case, but in the normal situation commercial practice required that a stevedore in the employment of a carrier should enjoy the benefit of contractual provisions in the bill of lading. Shippers, carriers and stevedores knew that such immunity was intended and that the carrier would handle the goods both whilst they were on the vessel and whilst they were in storage.

Lord Wilberforce gave consideration to the

decision in *New Zealand Shipping Co Ltd v A M Satterthwaite & Co Ltd* [1974] 1 All ER 1015, where the bill of lading contained very similar provisions, and said:

'First, as to the Board's decision in *Satterthwaite*'s case. This was a decision, in principle, that the Himalaya clause is capable of conferring on a third person falling within the description "servant or agent of the Carrier (including every independent contractor from time to time employed by the Carrier)" defences and immunities conferred by the bill of lading on the carrier as if such persons were parties to the contract contained in or evidenced by the bill of lading. But the decision was not merely a decision on this principle, for it was made clear that in fact stevedores employed by the carrier may come within it, and moreover that they normally and typically will do so. It may indeed be said that the significance of *Satterthwaite*'s case lay not so much in the establishment of any new legal principle as in the finding that, in the normal situation involving the employment of stevedores by carriers, accepted principles enable and require the stevedore to enjoy the benefit of contractual provisions in the bill of lading. In the words of Mason and Jacobs JJ in the High Court:

"When the circumstances described by Lord Reid in *Scruttons Ltd v Midland Silicones Ltd* [[1962] 1 All ER 1 at 10, [1962] AC 446 at 474] exist, the stevedore will on the generally accepted principles of the law of contract be entitled to his personal contractual immunity. The importance of [*Satterthwaite*'s case] is the manner in which on the bare facts of the case their Lordships were able to discern a contract between the shipper and the stevedore, and, we would add, to do so in a manner which limited the approach to those commercial contexts in which immunity of the stevedore was clearly intended in form and almost certainly known by both the shipper and the stevedore to be intended."

Although, in each case, there will be room for evidence as to the precise relationship of carrier and stevedore and as to the practice at the relevant port, the decision does not support, and their Lordships would not encourage, a search for fine distinctions which would diminish the general applicability, in the light of established commercial practice, of the principle. ...

... the factual situation in the present case in all respects typical of that which the Board, in *Satterthwaite*'s case, thought sufficient to confer [the] benefit [of the contract] ...'

The Court then considered the inter-relationship between cl 5 and cl 8 of the bill of lading, their effect within the contract as a whole, and the commercial expectations of the effect of such clauses. The clauses clearly contemplated that the carrier might continue to have some responsibility for the goods after discharge if the consignee failed to take delivery ex ship's rail. Since cl 5 attributed that responsibility to the carrier as bailee, a carrier acting as stevedore would be liable for the goods as bailee. Where the carrier instead employed a third party to carry out duties under the bill of lading that he would have had to perform, his immunity extended to that third party. The appellant stevedores were acting in the course of the carrier's employment and so were entitled to the same immunity as the carrier would have had. Lord Wilberforce:

'Their Lordships now deal with the "capacity" argument. This rather inapposite word has been used, for convenience, in order to indicate the general nature of the submission. More fully, this was that, at the time when the loss occurred, the goods had been discharged and were no longer in the custody of the carrier. Consequently, the stevedore was acting not as an independent contractor employed by the carrier to perform the carrier's obligations under the bill of lading, but as a bailee. His liability, in the capacity, was independent of and not governed by any of the clauses of the contract. This point enables a distinction to the made with Satterthwaite's case, for there, since the goods were damaged in the course of discharge, the capacity of the stevedore as a person acting on behalf of the carrier was not contested. ...

[Clause 5 and cl 8] must be interpreted in the light of the practice that consignees rarely take delivery of goods at the ship's rail but will normally collect them after some period of storage on or near the wharf. The parties must therefore have contemplated that the carrier, if it did not store the goods itself, would employ some other person to do so. Furthermore a document headed "Port Jackson Stevedoring Pty. Ltd. Basic Terms and Conditions for Stevedoring at Sydney, N.S.W." showed that it was contemplated that the stevedore would be so employed. ...

... since the carrier may not have insisted that the consignee take delivery [clause 5 recognises] that the carrier may continue to have some responsibility for the goods after discharge. He cannot after all dump them on the wharf and leave them there. So to suppose would be commercially unreal and is not contemplated by the bill of lading. Clause 5 in terms attributes responsibility to the carrier as bailee and defines the period in express terms as 'continuing after leaving the ship's tackle'. There is nothing in the latter part of cl 8 that is inconsistent with this. It merely provides that delivery ex ship's rail shall constitute due delivery and that the carrier's liability shall cease at that point. But this leaves open the option not to insist on delivery ex ship's rail, and leaves, to be governed by cl 5, his responsibility if he does not.

... what is the carrier's position if he acts as his own stevedore and himself stacks and stores the goods? ... in view of the provisions referred to above, their Lordships think that the answer is clear, namely that he would be liable for them, as bailee, under the contract. If that is so, it seems indisputable that if, instead, the carrier employs a third party to discharge, stack and store that person would be acting in the course of his employment, performing duties which otherwise the carrier would perform under the bill of lading, and so would be entitled to the same immunity as the carrier would have. ... It is made clear by cl 5 that, irrespective of the period of carriage defined by the contract, the immunity of the carrier is not coextensive with this period but extends both before and after it. The stevedore's immunity extends, by virtue of cl 2, over the same period.'

Comment

See *New Zealand Shipping Co Ltd* v *Satterthwaite, The Eurymedon* [1975] AC 154 (above), where it was held that a pre-existing obligation to load and unload cargo could amount to consideration moving from the stevedore to the cargo-owner, and the dictum of Lord Reid in *Midland Silicones Ltd* v *Scruttons Ltd* [1962] AC 446 (above).

9 Marine Insurance (1): Contract and Policy

Anglo-African Merchants Ltd and Another v Bayley and Others [1970] 1 QB 311 Queen's Bench Division (Megaw J)

• *Duty of disclosure*

Facts
The plaintiff companies sought to insure a number of unused 20 or more years old army leather jerkins against 'all risks' at Lloyd's. Insurance was put in place through two firms of brokers. The plaintiffs informed the first brokers that the goods were leather jerkins, that they were government surplus and that they were 'new', but the information conveyed to the second brokers, and hence to the underwriters, was that they were 'new men's clothes in bales for export'.

Following the loss of part of the consignment from warehouse storage, the plaintiffs claimed under the policy but the underwriters denied liability on the ground of non-disclosure of material facts, namely that the jerkins were 20 years old and army surplus.

Held
The use of the word 'new' did not amount to a mis-description of the clothing, but since it was not disclosed that it was 20 years old and army surplus, the underwriters were entitled to disclaim liability.

McGaw J (at p319):

'Having considered the whole of the evidence on this aspect, I am also satisfied that each of these matters – the fact that the goods were surplus and their age – was a fact which was material: it would have affected the mind of a prudent underwriter in deciding whether or not to underwrite the risk at all, in deciding what limitations he might wish to impose as to the risks to be covered, in deciding what premium to quote and in deciding whether or not to require an inspection of, and report on, the goods or the place where they were being stored, or both. In particular, in relation to the fact of war surplus, I am satisfied that underwriters, rightly or wrongly, but not unreasonably, regard war surplus goods, or at any rate war surplus clothing as "hot", that is involving an abnormally high risk of theft. In relation to the age of the goods, underwriters would normally and reasonably be concerned with the possibility of defects, such as staining ...'

Comment
This case well describes the factors commonly considered by underwriters in deciding whether to take a risk and, if so, what premium to set. The relevance of the non-disclosure to underwriters that the clothing was war surplus is that such jerkins are made by the millions, with no distinguishing marks except for size, and therefore easy to be sold by someone without title to them.

Bank of Nova Scotia v Hellenic Mutual War Risk Association (Bermuda) Ltd, The Good Luck
[1991] 3 All ER 1 House of Lords
(Lords Goff of Chieveley, Bridge of
Harwich, Brandon of Oakbrook,
Oliver of Aylmerton and Lowry)

• *Breach of promissory warranty automatically discharges the insurer from liability as from the date of the breach
because fulfilment of the warranty is a
condition precedent to the liability or
further liability of the insurer*

Facts
The Good Luck was one of a number of
vessels owned by the Good Faith Group
(GFG), a group of Greek shipowners, which
were mortgaged to the Bank of Nova Scotia
(the bank) as security for a loan, the terms of
which required GFG to insure the vessels
against, inter alia, war risks. The insurance
polices were taken out with the defendant P
& I Club (the club) and were absolutely
assigned to the bank. In undertaking 3 of their
letter of undertaking, the club undertook to
advise the bank 'promptly' if it ceased to
insure any vessel. Cessation of cover could
occur under rules 20 and 25 of the insurance
policy. The insurance was deemed to contain a
warranty by the shipowner to comply with the
prohibitions in the policy. A specified waiver
of prohibition was allowed by written arrangement.

Rule 20 was a 'held covered' provision
which permitted the club to specify zones or
areas as 'Additional Premium Areas' (APA),
ie the shipowner is required to pay an additional premium to hold the cover on the vessel
whilst in that area. Prior notification of intention to enter an APA was required and it was
stated that failure to give the club such notice
would result in the rejection of all claims.

Rule 25 permitted the club to impose prohibitions upon areas directly affected by
warfare where it would be unacceptable for it

to provide war risk cover. A proviso in 25(C)
stated that breach of warranty would not to
operate to invalidate the insurance if the
shipowners could prove that it occurred
without fault or want of due diligence on their
part or that it was to avoid loss by insured
risks.

All parties were aware that GFG traded
into the Arabian Gulf and that their vessels
were chartered to Iranian charterers with the
right to order her to Iranian ports. In 1982,
during the hostilities between Iran and Iraq,
the Gulf area was covered by rules 20 and 25
and in June 1982, while proceeding up the
Khor Musa channel to Bandar Khomeini, The
Good Luck was hit and sunk by an Iraqi
missile. GFG had known The Good Luck's
itinerary and progress but had not notified the
club of her entry into the area. When the
agents of the club had become aware of it they
had not taken steps to procure the appropriate
notifications and had not notified the bank that
The Good Luck was now uninsured. They also
learnt and failed to notify the bank that The
Good Ocean, another GFG vessel mortgaged
to the bank, was at Bandar Khomeini without
notification and therefore uninsured.

The casualty of The Good Luck occurred
shortly before GFG completed negotiations
with the bank for the rescheduling of their
loan facility on their mortgaged vessels. The
bank were aware of the loss of The Good Luck
but were not aware that she was uninsured at
the time of loss until notified of this by the
club on 5 August 1982. By this time the bank
had agreed the refinancing and in the second
half of July had permitted GFG to draw down
a substantial advance. Exclusion of The Good
Luck from the loan rescheduling would have
reduced the available security value and,
therefore, reduced the permitted advances.

The club denied an indemnity claimed by
the shipowners against their constructive total
loss of The Good Luck on the grounds that
GFG were not ignorant of the prohibited zone
and had not, as they had falsely pretended,
given an advance declaration of entry into the
additional premium area. Upon this rejection,

the bank sued the club for damages for failing to inform them that The Good Luck had become uninsured in breach of the express terms of the letter of undertaking given by the club to the bank and in breach of the promissory warranty in rule 25 of the club rules. They contended that the club had jeopardised their war risks insurance as assignees by failing to inform them that vessels regularly traded in a prohibited war zone and that further, or alternatively, the club were in breach of a duty of utmost good faith in failing to inform the bank of all material facts known to the club which affected the operation and validity of the war risks insurance, and in breach of duty and/or negligent in failing to take all proper and reasonable care to ensure that certain information given by them to the bank was accurate.

Hobhouse J at first instance ([1988] 1 Lloyd's Rep 514) held the club liable in damages for breach of the letter of undertaking but rejected the bank's argument based on a duty of utmost good faith. Since the insurers did not owe a duty of utmost good faith to the assured it followed that no duty was owed to the bank as assignee since assignees do not have any better rights than the assignor. The Court of Appeal ([1989] 3 All ER 628) agreed with the judge's findings in respect of the duty of utmost good faith but not with his findings on the letter of undertaking. It was the opinion of the Court that the rule in non-marine insurance applied equally to the provision contained in s33(3) of the Marine Insurance Act 1906 and that, accordingly, breach by an insured party of a promissory warranty did not automatically bring the contract to an end but instead gave the insurers an option to avoid the contract. Since in their opinion the entry of the shipowners' vessel into a prohibited zone in breach of warranty did not automatically cause the insurance to cease so as to require the insurers to inform the bank of that fact pursuant to its undertaking, it followed that the insurers were not in breach of any term of the contract contained in its letter of undertaking. The bank appealed to the House of Lords.

Held

On the issue of the letter of undertaking their Lordships restored the decision of the trial judge. Although the insurers were discharged from liability under the insurance by the owners' breach, they were in breach of their letter of undertaking to the bank. The failure by the club to comply with its obligations led to the bank making an advance which was inadequately secured and which it would not otherwise have made. Accordingly, the bank's loss was caused by the breach of the club's letter of undertaking and they were liable to the bank for their loss. Their Lordships required to hear no argument on the other two issues.

Point 1: the insurers were discharged from liability under the insurance by the owners' breach.

The duty to inform the bank arose only in the event of cessation of cover on the vessel. It was therefore necessary to establish that the insurers' liability had been discharged by the shipowners' breach of warranty. Lord Goff, whose speech was agreed with by all their Lordships, disagreed with the Court of Appeal's finding that breach of promissory warranty gave the insurer an option to avoid the contract. He instead found it to be settled law for policies of marine insurance that any statement of a fact bearing on the risk introduced into the written policy was to be construed as a warranty, compliance with which was a condition precedent to the attaching of the risk. For the loss claimed, the insurance risk was subject to the shipowners' warranty to comply with the prohibitions in the policy. This was a condition precedent to the attaching of that risk. Entry of the shipowners' vessel into a prohibited zone in breach of that warranty, therefore, caused the insurance to cease and discharged the insurers from liability as from the date of the breach which, in this case, was the date that they first became aware that The Good Luck was in a prohibited area and uninsured (see Point 2 below). Lord Goff of Chieveley stated:

'Section 33(3) of the 1906 Act reflects ...

the inveterate practice in marine insurance of using the term "warranty" as signifying a condition precedent. ...

Once this is appreciated, it becomes readily understandable that, if a promissory warranty is not complied with, the insurer is discharged from liability as from the date of the breach of warranty, for the simple reason that fulfilment of the warranty is a condition precedent to the liability or further liability of the insurer. This moreover reflects the fact that the rationale of warranties in insurance law is that the insurer only accepts the risk provided that the warranty is fulfilled. This is entirely understandable; and it follows that the immediate effect of a breach of a promissory warranty is to discharge the insurer from liability as from the date of the breach. ...

[I]t is laid down in s33(3) that, subject to any express provision in the policy, the insurer is discharged from liability as from the date of the breach of warranty. Those words are clear. They show that discharge of the insurer from liability is automatic and is not dependent upon any decision by the insurer to treat the contract or the insurance as at an end; though, under s34(3), the insurer may waive the breach of warranty.'

The use of the word 'automatic' is interesting and suggests that the immediate effect of a breach of a promissory warranty is to discharge the insurer, automatically and independently of any decision by him, from liability as from the date of the breach. It is only the insurer's liability or further liability that is terminated by the breach of promissory warranty. The contract itself is not brought to an end; the contract ab initio cannot be avoided since it is possible that certain obligations of the insured under the contract, such as a continuing liability to pay an additional premium, might survive the discharge. Lord Goff was at pains to make this point clear and said:

'Here, where we are concerned with a promissory warranty, ie a promissory condition precedent, contained in an existing contract of insurance, non-fulfilment of the condition does not prevent the contract from coming into existence. What it does (as s33(3) makes plain) is to discharge the insurer from liability as from the date of the breach. Certainly, it does not have the effect of avoiding the contract ab initio. Nor, strictly speaking, does it have the effect of bringing the contract to an end. It is possible that there may be obligations of the assured under the contract which will survive the discharge of the insurer from liability, as for example a continuing liability to pay a premium. Even if in the result no further obligations rest on either parties, it is not correct to speak of the contract being avoided; and it is, strictly speaking, more accurate to keep to the carefully chosen words in s33(3) of the Act, rather than to speak of the contract being brought to an end, though that may be the practical effect.'

When considering the effect of this on the scheme imposed by rule 25 of the insurance, Lord Goff agreed with the findings of Hobhouse J who had said (at 519):

'The scheme of r25 is also clear. It lays down an express warranty in the marine insurance sense. Therefore, by s33(3) of the Marine Insurance Act 1906, the warranty "is a condition which must be exactly complied with ... (and) if it be not so complied with then ... the insurer is discharged from liability as from the date of the breach of warranty ..." It is, of course, possible for the insurer to waive the breach of warranty but, unless and until the insurer so chooses, the warranty has the effect of excluding cover from the date of breach.'

The insurer may waive breach of warranty under s34(3). Waiver was also permitted by the insurance but GFG had not sought this in writing as required. GFG argued that the club had in any case waived any breach of warranty because they had not regarded themselves to be discharged of liability and had instead disputed GFG's claim on the basis that an insured peril occurring in the prohibited zone was not covered by the policy. Lord Goff rejected this submission:

'On the assumption that, despite the fact that

the vessel was a constructive total loss, there was a waiver by the club in respect of the future, there was in my opinion no waiver in respect of the period when the vessel was in the prohibited zone; and accordingly during that period (which was, of course, the relevant period) there was a cesser of insurance.'

Point 2: the club were in breach of their letter of undertaking to the bank. The club had failed to inform the bank 'promptly' that the vessel had become uninsured pursuant to undertaking 3 of their letter of undertaking.

An automatic discharge of liability for breach of warranty under s 33(3) is a discharge for the purposes of undertaking 3. The wording of the undertaking, taken in the context its purpose, also determines the time that the club's liability is discharged. Lord Goff cited a comment made by Hobhouse J:

'Once a vessel entered into a prohibited area she was, in ordinary business terminology, and in truth, uninsured, and so the club had ceased to insure her within the meaning of undertaking 3.'

Whether it was found by s33(3) or by reference to ordinary business terminology, it was clear that the club's obligation to notify the bank of cessation of cover arose at the time they became aware that the vessel was in a prohibited zone and uninsured. They gave notification but it was after the loss had occurred. Should the requirement to notify 'promptly' be construed as allowing the club a reasonable time before giving notice to consider whether a breach had occurred without want of diligence on the part of the shipowners so as to enable them to rely on the proviso to rule 25 of the policy? Lord Goff rejected this idea. It was clearly meant to be taken as an obligation to give notice to the bank in as short a time as was reasonable after relevant information had been received, irrespective of other matters that the club or GFG might need to consider. The undertaking was intended to protect the bank's interests in the insurance as assignees and Lord Goff pointed out that:

'To postpone the time for giving notice ...

could expose the bank to a prolonged risk of the ship being uninsured without the bank's knowledge of that fact at a time when it could be of crucial importance to the bank to have that knowledge.'

Point 3: the failure by the club to comply with its obligations led to the bank making an advance which was inadequately secured and which it would not otherwise have made, and the bank's loss was accordingly caused by the breach of the club's letter of undertaking.

Lord Goff took the view, in agreement with the reasoning and conclusions of Hobhouse J, that the bank would have adopted a different course of action if they had received notice from the club that The Good Luck was uninsured by reason either of being in a prohibited area or in an additional premium area without additional cover. This was, or should have been, within the contemplation of the club. It was a strong probability that the bank's consideration of any value to be attached to her hull or its insurances would have been put on one side until the situation had been clarified. The existing mortgage would not have been discharged, the security values and advances figures of the refinancing would have been reduced accordingly, and the mortgagees' interest insurance would have been preserved.

The bank's loss was not too remote. Their failure to query the insurance position on the vessel might be have been improvident, but it was not the cause of the loss nor did not amount to a novus actus interveniens breaking the chain of causation between the club's breach and the bank's loss. Lord Goff:

'... if the bank suffered loss by reason of failure in the course of refinancing arrangements to take advantage of an opportunity to reduce or restrict its lending to the shipowners to take account of the cesser of a particular vessel's insurance cover of which the club, in breach of its letter of undertaking, failed to inform the bank, such loss would be within the contemplation of the parties at the time when the letter of undertaking was given as a serious possibility or real danger. No special knowledge was needed by the club to bring this possible loss within the contemplation of the parties; the possibility of such a loss was, in my opinion, well within the contemplation of the club as a result of its general knowledge, derived from the ordinary experience of its directors and managers, of the nature of ship financing.'

Comment

This is a milestone case on the issue of the nature of a promissory warranty and the legal effects of its breach. It settles a number of uncertainties in the law that hitherto pertained. A promissory warranty is defined by s33 (1) of the Marine Insurance Act 1906 as 'a warranty by which the assured undertakes that some particular thing shall or shall not be done, or that some condition shall be fulfilled, or whereby he affirms or negatives the existence of a particular state of facts'. The common practice in marine insurance of using the term 'warranty' as signifying a condition precedent referred to by Lord Goff of Chieveley is reflected in the s33(3) definition of warranty as 'a condition which must be exactly complied with, whether it be material to the risk or not' and the provision that, subject to any express provision in the policy, the insurer is discharged from liability as from the date of the breach of warranty. The decision in the instant case adds to that the notion that the insurer's discharge from liability is automatic and is not dependent upon any decision by the insurer to treat the contract or the insurance as at an end.

Hobhouse J drew a distinction between pre-contractual and post-contractual disclosure which he viewed as being distinct and separate duties ([1988] 1 Lloyd's Rep 514 at 545–46). Once the contract is made there is no duty to disclose matters relevant to the making of the contract but there is a continuing duty of utmost good faith in respect of any later stages of the contract for which disclosure should be made such as, in the instant case, the fixing of the rate of additional premiums. The Court of Appeal ([1989] 3 All ER 628) agreed with the judge's findings in respect of the continuing

duty of utmost good faith (see especially May LJ at p263). See also *Black King Shipping Corporation* v *Massie, The Litsion Pride* [1985] 1 Lloyd's Rep 437 (below) and *Container Transport International Inc* v *Oceanus Mutual Underwriting Association (Bermuda) Ltd* [1984] 1 Lloyd's Rep 476 (below).

Berger and Light Diffusers Pty Ltd v *Pollock* [1973] 2 Lloyd's Rep 442 High Court (Kerr J)

• *A non-disclosure is material if it would have affected not only a reasonable insurer, but the insurer in question*

Facts

The plaintiffs were owners of four large steel injection moulds which they used to manufacture plastic diffusers for fluorescent lighting. The moulds were made in Hong Kong and after various tests found to be unsuitable for use in their present state.

The plaintiffs shipped the moulds from Australia to England where the fault could be corrected. Shipment took place in October 1966. The bill of lading issued for the goods stated that they were 'insufficiently packed', 'unprotected' and second-hand.

The moulds arrived in England in December and were found to be rusty as a pipe had broken in the hold of the ship, and the moulds had been immersed in water. The plaintiffs claimed indemnity from their insurers, having obtained open cover under which the value of the moulds was declared at £20,000. The defendant insurers repudiated liability on the grounds of non-disclosure of material facts, namely:

1. the history of the moulds;
2. the fact that they had been over-valued;
3. the fact that the bills of lading were claused.

Held

Judgment for the plaintiffs. The defendant had

not proved that the non-disclosure of the clausing of the bill of lading, or of history of the moulds, or of the over-valuation, were material.

Kerr J:

'... It must always be borne in mind that in the absence of fraud an excessive over-valuation is not in itself a ground for repudiating a contract of insurance. Over-valuation is only one illustration of the general principle that insurers are entitled to avoid policies on the ground of non-disclosure of material circumstances. It must therefore always be shown that the over-valuation was such that if it had been disclosed it would have entitled the insurer to avoid the policy, because it would have affected his judgement as a prudent insurer in fixing the premium or determining whether or not to take the risk. This is not established by the mere fact that the court subsequently, with knowledge of all the facts and the assistance of expert opinion, arrives at a much smaller value ...

The court's task in deciding whether or not the defendant insurer can avoid the policy for non-disclosure must be to determine, as a question of fact, whether by applying the standard of judgment of a prudent insurer, the insurer in question would have been influenced in fixing the premium or determining whether to take the risk if he had been informed of the undisclosed circumstances before entering into the contract. Otherwise, one could in theory reach the absurd position where the court might be satisfied that the insurer in question would in fact not have been so influenced, but that other insurers would have been. It would then be a very odd result if the defendant underwriter could nevertheless avoid the policy. I do not think that this is the correct interpretation of section 18 (Marine Insurance Act 1906) despite the generality of the language used in subsection 2. The effect of the non-disclosure may, of course, be so clear that the court will require no evidence or, only little evidence, to decide in favour of the insurer. In doubtful cases, on the other hand, the court may require evidence from the insurers themselves before being able to hold that the right to avoid the policy has been established.'

Comment

With regard to the issue of overvaluation of cargo, this case should be compared with *Ionides* v *Pender* (1874) LR 9 QB 531 where there was gross overvaluation of cargo. In such a case non-disclosure of the true value may be a ground for avoidance of the insurance contract by the underwriter.

Black King Shipping Corporation v *Massie, The Litsion Pride* [1985] 1 Lloyd's Rep 437 High Court (Hirst J)

• *Utmost good faith applies before and after conclusion of the contract*

Facts

The Litsion Pride and her cargo of sugar were insured for a voyage from Europe to the Persian Gulf. The insurance covered War Risks. The policy expressly provided that in the event that the vessel sailed into the territorial waters of certain countries, the assured must inform the underwriters of the fact as soon as practicable and would be held covered on the payment of additional premiums.

The vessel entered a war zone on 2 August. The plaintiffs wrote a letter purportedly on that date, stating this fact. It was received by the brokers on 12 August, three days after the vessel was attacked and sank with her cargo.

The underwriters denied liability on the basis that:

1. notification to them under the held covered clause was a condition precedent to liability for loss;
2. the owners had acted fraudulently or at least they were in breach of utmost good faith.

Held

Judgment for the underwriters.

Under a normal 'held covered' clause reasonable notice of the circumstances in question is a condition precedent to liability on the part of the insurer. However, this clause contained the words: 'the absence of prior advice shall not affect the cover'.

This seemed to suggest that even if the underwriters were not given prompt information, they would remain liable and that the giving of such information was not a condition precedent. If underwriters wished the notification f information to create a condition precedent they must express this in clear words.

All the facts seemed to support the suggestion that it was the intention of the assured to ship in and out of the area and avoid paying additional premium. Even if they were not fraudulent they were at least in breach of the duty of utmost good faith which required the communication of all material facts, eg the likely time of arrive in the war zone, the duration of the stay etc.

The underwriters contended that they need not show fraud in order to succeed, but only that there had been non-disclosure of a material fact whatever the motive of the assured. This would amount to a breach of the duty of utmost good faith. This was imposed by s17 of the Marine Insurance Act 1906, and it applied before and after the contract of insurance had been concluded between the parties. They said that the duty to disclose in ss18 and 19 is merely an aspect of the overriding duty of good faith in s17. In this respect they relied on *Container Transport International Inc* v *Oceanus Mutual Underwriting* [1984] 1 Lloyd's Rep 476, which stated that even if circumstances are not material under ss18 or 19 they would still need to be fully disclosed under s17 (Parker LJ at p512). The assured on the other hand stated that whilst s17 does apply both before and after the contract is concluded, once the contract is concluded the only duty which is required of the assured is not to act fraudulently towards the underwriter with regard to the terms of the contract and warranties therein and in making a claim. However, there is no duty to make disclosure

once the contract is concluded. Hirst J held that the duty of utmost good faith applied as regards making claims under that policy. It was an implied term of the policy.

Thus if during the course of the journey the assured comes into possession of relevant information he/she must communicate it to the insurer and particularly where it conflicts with information which he/she has already given although this is a duty which requires that there should not be culpable non disclosure or misrepresentation.

If there is a fraud is it necessary for the underwriter to show materiality? Hirst J said that the test of materiality in relation to fraudulent statements was satisfied if the fraudulent statement would in influence the decision of a prudent underwriter to accept, reject or compromise the claim.

When s17 talks about avoidance of the contract it means avoidance ab initio and this is true even where the non-disclosure is post contractual.

All the defences which can be raised against the assured can be raised against his assignee and can therefore be raised against a mortgagee.

Comment

This case is important by reason of various aspects of the assured's duty of utmost good faith in arranging for marine insurance under the Marine Insurance Act 1906. This duty is a continuing one when, in the course of the journey, the assured becomes aware of relevant information.

This case extended the duty of disclosure to circumstances beyond the conclusion of the contract. The case has made it clear that the duty of utmost good faith is both overriding and continuing. In addition, Hirst J referred to the duty not to make fraudulent claims as a facet of the duty to observe utmost good faith and this has found approval in later cases: see especially *Bank of Nova Scotia* v *Hellenic Mutual War Risk Association (Bermuda) Ltd, The Good Luck* [1991] 3 All ER 1 (above).

Colonia Versicherung AG v Amoco Oil Co [1997] 1 Lloyd's Rep 261 Court of Appeal (Hirst, Gibson and Pill LJJ)

• *Deed of assignment – doctrine of subrogation – right to treat payment as extinguishing assured's loss*

Facts

The defendants (Amoco) sold a cargo of naphtha on fob terms to Astra Oil Co who on-sold it, again on fob terms, to AOT Ltd who, in turn, on-sold it but on cif terms to ICI. The insurance was 'according to Institute Cargo Clauses (All Risks) including contamination ... shoretank to shoretank' and was placed with Colonia by AOT.

When the naphtha arrived at the ICI plant at Teeside, UK, it was contaminated. It was later revealed, and not disputed, that the contamination occurred, due to Amoco's negligence, in the shorelines between the Amoco shoretank and the carrying vessel. ICI submitted a claim under the marine insurance policy and also claimed against Amoco. However, ICI's losses were settled by Amoco who then claimed under the insurance as assignee and/or as a co-assured under the policy. The insurers Colonia refused to pay.

Held

Judgment for Colonia.

The intention of the payment by Amoco to ICI was to be gleaned from the wording of the settlement agreement (contained in two deeds, the second of which was headed 'Deed of Assignment'), which was the compromise of the dispute between the companies arising out of this shipment and was clearly a commercial transaction. Such a payment would undoubtedly have assisted Amoco's trading relations with ICI and, in such circumstances, the payment could not be considered a gift. Rather, it could be seen as a payment by a third party to the insurance contract (Amoco) to the assured (ICI) and, as such, had the effect of extinguishing, or at least reducing, ICI's

loss arising out of the contamination of the naphtha.

Under the doctrine of subrogation, an insurer is entitled to take into consideration money which has been paid to the assured ex gratia to diminish his loss unless intended by the donor to benefit the assured to the exclusion of the insurer. On the facts, there was no intention on the part of Amoco in making payment to benefit ICI to the exclusion of Colonia. In fact, the wording of the assignment included a qualification 'except to the extent of the insurance underwriter's subrogation rights'.

Hirst LJ interpreted this qualification as including Colonia's rights as against ICI to treat Amoco's payment as extinguishing ICI's, the assured's, loss. Furthermore, as the Deed of Assignment provided that 'no warranty' is given express or implied that Amoco will be able to pursue all or any claims (against Colonia), it was clear that even the parties themselves accepted that Amoco might not be entitled to claim against Colonia. As such, Amoco, in return for the payment to ICI, received not an outright assignment of ICI's rights against Colonia, but one with reservations which clearly indicated that Colonia's rights were to be preserved.

Counsel for Amoco had argued in the alternative that the contractual arrangements between Amoco, Astra and AOT indicated that Amoco were to be a co-assured. However, on the evidence, it was clear that the terms of the policy which was arranged by AOT was only ever intended to cover that company's interest as cif seller. There was no intention to cover AOT's interests before the time that company purchased the cargo. Furthermore, the contract on fob terms between Astra and AOT stated expressly that marine insurance was to be arranged by the buyer (AOT) for his own account.

ICI became an assured under the policy by virtue of being a cif buyer, but there never was any intention for Amoco to benefit under the policy. The insurance covered loss of or damage to goods in transit – it was not a liability insurance. As such, if the insurers had indemnified Amoco, who were in effect the negligent party who caused the loss in the first place, against whom would they have exercised their subrogation rights?

Compania Maritima San Basilio SA v Oceanus Mutual Underwriting Association (Bermuda) Ltd, The Eurysthenes [1976] 3 All ER 243 Court of Appeal (Lord Denning MR, Roskill and Geoffrey Lane LJJ)

• *Time policy is 'definite' under s25(1) Marine Insurance Act 1906 even though extensions are permitted – insurer's liability excluded under s39(5) Marine Insurance Act 1906 where ship sent to sea in unseaworthy state with privity of the assured*

Facts

The Eurysthenes was stranded whilst carrying cargo from the USA to the Philippines in April 1974. Much of the cargo was lost or damaged. The cargo owners claimed against the plaintiff shipowners in respect of their loss, alleging that the ship had been sent to sea in an unseaworthy state since there had not been a proper complement of certified deck officers nor proper charts and there was a defective echo-sounder and an inoperative boiler. The plaintiffs sought an indemnity against these claims from the defendant P & I Club (the club). The risks covered did appear to cover the casualty in that rule 3 included cover for liability for damage to or loss of cargo arising 'out of unseaworthiness or unfitness of the entered ship'. There were however a number of exceptions and limitations of the club's liability in rules 3 and 4 and, in particular, rule 4(9) conferred on the club a discretion to reject, or to deduct from, a claim if the club were of the opinion that the member had 'not taken such steps to protect his interest as he would have done if the ship had not been entered in' the club. On the basis of this dis-

cretion the club refused the shipowners' claim for an indemnity and the shipowners brought an action against the club.

The club contended that the ship was sent to sea in an unseaworthy condition and that she was so sent 'with the privity of the assured' (the shipowners) so that the club was not liable to indemnify the shipowners under s39(5) of the Marine Insurance Act 1906:

> 'In a time policy there is no implied warranty that the ship shall be seaworthy at any stage of the adventure, but where, with the privity of the assured, the ship is sent to sea in an unseaworthy state, the insurer is not liable for any loss attributable to unseaworthiness.'

The shipowners contended that s39(5) did not apply to the contract since it was not for a 'definite period of time' and, therefore, was not a 'time policy' within s25(1)b of the 1906 Act, and, that in any event, s39(5) was impliedly excluded since all the exceptions to the club's liability were contained in rules 3 and 4. They claimed in the alternative that if s39(5) were applicable, it did not apply to mere negligence in sending the ship to sea in an unseaworthy state but instead acted to exclude the shipowners' right to an indemnity only if the shipowners had personally been guilty of wilful misconduct in sending the ship to sea in that state.

These preliminary issues were heard by Donaldson J who dismissed the action holding that it did constitute a defence to the club to prove that the ship was sent to sea in an unseaworthy state with the privity of the shipowners within s39(5) Marine Insutance Act 1906 and that it was not for the club to prove 'privity' on the basis of proof of negligence on the part of the shipowners personally but on the basis of knowledge on the part of the shipowners personally of the facts constituting unseaworthiness or some deliberate or reckless conduct on the part of the shipowners personally.

The shipowners appealed.

Held

Appeal allowed in part.

The contract of insurance was a 'time policy' for a specified period, ie 17 to 20 February 1972, and was therefore for a 'definite period of time' within s25(1). The fact that it would be renewed or continued automatically at the end of that period was immaterial; the policy was for a specified period of time.

The policy was therefore subject to s39(5) unless that provision was impliedly excluded by the club's rules.

Lord Denning MR:

'Is s39(5) of the 1906 Act impliedly excluded by the rules? It was suggested that s39(5) did not apply in this case because the rules of the association made the club liable to indemnify the shipowner even though he was privy to the unseaworthiness. Now I quite agree that r 3(17) does contain a promise by the club to indemnify a member against liability for damage to cargo 'arising out of any breach by the Member ... or out of unseaworthiness or unfitness of the entered ship'. And r 4(7) and (8) does contain express provisions excluding the liability of the club in the circumstances there specified. But these rules do not cover all the ground. They still leave room for s39(5) to operate. I think it does still operate so as to disentitle the assured from recovering if he is privy to the ship being sent to sea in an unseaworthy state.'

Roskill LJ:

'I am ... clearly of the view that a policy for a period of time and not for a voyage does not cease to be a time policy as defined merely because that period of time may thereafter be extended or abridged pursuant to one of the policy's contractual provisions. The duration of the policy is defined by its own terms and is thus for a 'definite period of time'. In my view, the word 'definite' was added to emphasise the difference between a period of time measured by time and a period of time measured by the duration of a voyage. ...'

The shipowners acted with 'privity' within s39(5) if they had knowledge personally of the facts constituting the unseaworthiness and knowledge that those facts rendered the ship unseaworthy. However, mere negligence in not knowing the facts or realising their implication would not be sufficient to make the shipowners 'privy' to the unseaworthiness. Their knowledge had to be either positive or knowledge which could have been acquired if the shipowners had not refrained from enquiry when they were suspicious of the truth.

Lord Denning MR:

'... when the old common lawyers spoke of a man being 'privy' to something being done, or of an act being done "with his privity", they meant that he knew of it beforehand and concurred in it being done. If it was a wrongful act done by his servant, then he was liable for it if it was done "by his command or privity", that is with his express authority or with his knowledge and concurrence. "Privity" did not mean that there was any wilful misconduct by him, but only that he knew of the act beforehand and concurred in it being done. Moreover, "privity" did not mean that he himself personally did the act, but only that someone else did it and that he knowingly concurred in it. Hence, in the later Merchant Shipping Acts, the owner was entitled to limit his liability if the act was done without his "actual fault or privity". Without his "actual fault" meant without any actual fault by the owner personally. Without his 'privity' meant without his knowledge or concurrence.

Such is, I think, the meaning we should attach to the word "privity" in s 39(5). If the ship is sent to sea in an unseaworthy state, with the knowledge and concurrence of the assured personally, the insurer is not liable for any loss attributable to unseaworthiness that is to unseaworthiness of which he knew and in which he concurred. To disentitle the shipowner, he must, I think, have knowledge not only of the facts constituting the unseaworthiness, but also knowledge that those facts rendered the ship unseaworthy, that is not reasonably fit to encounter the ordinary perils of the sea. And when I speak of knowledge, I mean not only positive knowledge, but also the sort of knowledge expressed in the phrase "turning a blind eye". If a man, suspicious of the truth, turns a blind eye to it, and refrains from enquiry – so that he should not know it for certain – then he is to be regarded as knowing the truth. This "turning a blind eye" is far more blameworthy than mere negligence. Negligence in not knowing the truth is not equivalent to knowledge of it.

The knowledge must also be the knowledge of the shipowner personally, or his alter ego, or, in the case of a company, its head men or whoever may be considered their alter ego. It may be inferred from evidence that a reasonably prudent owner in his place would have known the facts and have realised that the ship was not reasonably fit to be sent to sea. But, if the shipowner satisfies the court that he did not know the facts or did not realise that they rendered the ship unseaworthy, then he ought not to be held privy to it, even though he was negligent in not knowing.'

Roskill LJ:

'I therefore seek to resolve the present problem, namely ascertaining the meaning of the word "privity" in s39(5), by looking at, and only at, the 1906 Act. One asks why, if "privity" means the same as "wilful misconduct", the same language was not used both in s39(5) and in s55(2)(a). One also asks why, if "privity" means the same as "actual fault or privity", the latter phrase was not used in s39(5). Section 39(5) by its opening words plainly excludes in the case of a time policy any implied warranty of seaworthiness at any stage of the adventure. In other words, if there is a total or partial loss of the subject-matter insured under a time policy brought about by unseaworthiness, there is no breach of warranty by the assured, using the word "warranty" in its technical sense, and underwriters pay. But the subsection goes on to free underwriters from liability in the case of a loss by unseaworthiness under a time policy if, notwithstanding the absence of any warranty of unseaworthiness, the assured has been privy

to sending the ship to sea in an unseaworthy state. The subsection does not talk of negligence; it does not mention fault, whether personal or otherwise. But s55(2)(a), which excepts liability for losses by the wilful misconduct of the assured, expressly provides that the underwriter is liable for losses by perils insured against, even though such losses would not have happened but for misconduct or the negligence of the master or crew.

In the context of the 1906 Act as a whole, I think it is clear that "privity" in s39(5) is not the same as "wilful misconduct". Nor is it the same as negligence or fault, whether personal or otherwise. The subsection says that the underwriter is excused if the ship is sent to sea in an unseaworthy state with the privity of the assured. That must mean that he is privy to the unseaworthiness and not merely that he has knowledge of facts which may ultimately be proved to amount to unseaworthiness. In other words, if the ship is sent to sea in an unseaworthy state with his knowledge and concurrence and that unseaworthiness is causative of the loss, the time policy does not pay. There must be causative unseaworthiness of which he knew and in which he concurred. Counsel for the shipowners at one point of his argument used the phrase "conscious realisation of the implication of the facts making the ship unseaworthy". I would accept that phrase as correctly conveying the underlying intention of this subsection, though I have rejected his wider argument that privity must be equated with wilful misconduct.

But, like Lord Denning MR, I would emphasise that knowledge does not only mean positive knowledge, but includes that type of knowledge which is expressed in the phrase "turning a blind eye". If the facts amounting to unseaworthiness are there staring the assured in the face so that he must, had he thought of it, have realised their implication on the seaworthiness of his ship, he cannot escape from being held privy to that unseaworthiness by blindly or blandly ignoring those facts or by refraining from asking relevant questions regarding them in the hope that by his lack of enquiry he will not know for certain that which any enquiry must have made plain beyond possibility of doubt.

This point is well illustrated by the example of an insufficient crew which was put to counsel for the club by Geoffrey Lane LJ during the argument. If a shipowner honestly believes as a prudent owner that a dozen men will suffice to man his ship and sends her to sea with that number on board, but subsequently a court holds that the ship was unseaworthy because she should have had a larger crew, he is not privy to that unseaworthiness merely because he knew the fact that she only had that dozen men on board. But if he knows as a prudent shipowner that a dozen men were required and he deliberately sends her to sea with only ten, thereby making her unseaworthy, he is privy to that unseaworthiness because he knew that she should have had a dozen men and yet with that knowledge he sent her to sea with only ten. ...

I turn to consider counsel for the club's contrary argument that "privity" and "actual fault or privity" mean the same thing. Prima facie they do not. "Actual fault" means what it says – actual personal fault of the shipowner. Privity is directed to a different subject-matter, not to acts or matters which the assured either personally did or omitted to do, but to acts or matters which were done with his knowledge or concurrence. If authority be required for the distinction between actual fault and privity, it is to be found in *Asiatic Petroleum Co Ltd* v *Lennard's Carrying Co Ltd* in the judgments of Buckley LJ and of Hamilton LJ ([1914] 1 KB at 432, 436). ...

I see no justification for construing "privity" as if it means the same thing as "actual fault", so that any personal act of omission or commission by the shipowner, including any personal negligence by him, would be "privity" within s39(5), so as to enable underwriters on a time policy to escape liability if the resultant unseaworthiness were causative of the loss. I agree with counsel for the shipowners that so to hold would in practice go far to destroy the affir-

mative cover afforded by r3(17), against loss or damage to cargo caused by unseaworthiness or unfitness of the ship. '

Container Transport International Inc v Oceanus Mutual Underwriting Association (Bermuda) Ltd [1984] 1 Lloyd's Rep 476 Court of Appeal (Stephenson, Kerr and Parker LJJ)

• *Marine Insurance Act 1906, ss18 and 19 – utmost good faith and materiality of disclosure – misrepresentation and non-disclosure of material facts not been waived by underwriters – insurance cover not affirmed*

Facts

From 1974 to 76 the plaintiffs obtained insurance with a whole series of underwriters in respect of possible damage to containers hired out for ocean transport. Each of the underwriters who had given the insurance cover had refused its renewal upon its expiry on the ground that they were not happy with the calculation of the claims under the policy. Eventually, the plaintiffs obtained insurance cover from the defendants.

The defendants sought to avoid the policy in 1978 on the grounds of misrepresentation in that the plaintiffs had put forward a misleading and inaccurate past claims' record, and non-disclosure, based on failure to tell them of other underwriters' refusals to renew the policy.

Held

Appeal allowed, judgment for the plaintiffs.

Kerr LJ:

'The duty of disclosure as defined ... by s18 and s19, is one aspect of the overriding duty of utmost good faith mentioned in s17. The actual insurer is thereby entitled to the disclosure to him of every fact which would influence the judgment of a prudent insurer in fixing the premium or determining whether he will take the risk ... The word "influence" means that the disclosure is one which would have had an impact on the formation of his opinion and on his decision making process in relation to the matters covered by s18(2).'

The Court then considered the circumstances in which the insurer can be said to have waived the non-disclosure of the information in question.

'The principle is that if a certain fact is material for the purposes of ss18(2) and 20(2) so that a failure to draw the underwriter's attention to it, distorts the fairness of the broker's presentation of the risk, then it is not sufficient that this fact could have been extracted by the underwriter from material to which he had access or which was cursorily shown to him. On the other hand, if the disclosed facts gave a fair presentation of the risk, then the underwriter must inquire if he wishes to have more information. …

The doctrine of waiver cannot be applied to undisclosed facts which are unusual or special so that their non-disclosure distorts the presentation of the risk. In such areas the underwriter is not put on inquiry about the existence of any such facts.'

The Court held that there had been both misrepresentation and non-disclosure of material facts which had not been waived by the underwriters, nor had they affirmed the insurance cover.

Comment

The Court here applied a narrow meaning to the principle of waiver by underwriters as to the disclosure obligations of the assured under a policy of marine insurance.

Eide UK Ltd and Another v *Lowndes Lambert Group Ltd and Another* [1998] 1 All ER 946 Court of Appeal (Phillips, Waller and Chadwick LJJ)

• *The right of lien of a broker under*

s53(2) Marine Insurance Act 1906 does not apply to composite insurance

Facts

Brokers arranged two hull and machinery policies on behalf of Colne Standby Ltd, operators of a fleet of vessels. One policy was with Lloyd's and the other with members of the Institute of London Underwriters. Eide UK Ltd owned the vessel called The Sun Tender which was demise chartered to Colne Stanby Ltd. The Sun Tender was mortgaged to the bank.

The charterparty included a clause providing for insurance cover to be arranged by the charterers to protect the interests of the owners, the charterers and any mortgagees. Colne Stanby, the owners, and the bank were co-assureds under the insurance policies.

The Sun Tender was damaged and needed repairs carried out. Claims were made under the policies. The insurance claims were paid out and the brokers paid the proceeds into a mixed bank account.

The brokers contended that they had a general lien over the policies in respect of money owed by Colne Stanby to the brokers relating to other policies. The brokers also contended that the lien entitled them to apply the whole of the insurance proceeds in reduction of the amount owed by Colne Standby. The brokers based their claim on s53 of the Marine Insurance Act 1906.

Held

A broker who has a lien over a policy of marine insurance is normally entitled to apply the proceeds in discharge of the debt owed. However, when dealing with a composite insurance, s53(2) of the Marine Insurance Act 1906 is not applicable. It is a general principle of the law of agency that no-one can create a lien beyond his own interest (per Phillips LJ at p956).

Comment

A composite insurance arises where there are a number of persons interested in the subject matter but one person takes the insurance out on behalf of all of them. Each person has a right to sue in respect of his/her own interest.

General Accident Fire and Life Insurance v Tanter, The Zephyr
[1984] 1 Lloyd's Rep 58 Queen's Bench Division (Commercial Court) (Hobhouse J)

• *Function of the slip is to record the insurance contract – Marine Insurance Act 1906, ss 21 and 22*

Facts
This was an intricate case in which the statement of the facts intertwines matters relating to the slip for marine insurance and that for reinsurance. One complication was that the reinsurance was placed by the broker before the placement of the original insurance. One of the main issues that the Court considered was the function of the slip in a contract of insurance.

Held
The slip was the record of the contract between the assured and the underwriter, not merely evidence of an oral contract, and it is not open to either party to contend that part of the contract between the assured and the underwriter was to be found elsewhere.

Hobhouse J:

> 'Thus if something is agreed between underwriter and broker as part of the contract between underwriter and assured, it must be written in the slip ... the contract is in the slip. What the broker says may of course be a representation or disclosure and affect the validity of the contract. But any agreement with the broker not incorporated in the slip will not be part of the contract.'

Comment
Section 21 of the Marine Insurance Act 1906 states that the marine insurance contract is concluded when the proposal of the assured is accepted by the underwriter irrespective of the fact that the policy would not have been issued. The proposal is accepted when the slip is signed. Although the slip is the record of the contract between the assured and the underwriter it is not admissible in evidence unless it is embodied in the policy: s22 Marine Insurance Act 1906.

General Re-Insurance Corporation v Forsakringsaktiebolaget Fennia Patria [1982] 2 WLR 528 High Court (Staughton J)

• *The assured may cancel the contract before 100 per cent subscription by underwriters.*

Facts
The defendants insured a quantity of paper valued at Finnmarks 27 million and which was stored in warehouses in Antwerp. The defendants then reinsured their risk under two separate contracts, the first being a contract of reinsurance for the whole of the risk up to the sum of Finnmarks 20 million and the second being for risk of damage or loss by fire or flood for Finnmarks 15 million subject to an excess of Finnmarks 15 million. This was entered into with 28 insurance companies. The defendants subsequently instructed their brokers to amend cover raising the excess from Finnmarks 15 million to Finnmarks 25 million retrospectively to 1 January.

Unknown to the defendants, the paper had been destroyed by fire and when they heard of this they cancelled their request for amendment of the slip. However, by the time the first and second plaintiffs learnt of the fire they had initialled the slip, making themselves liable beyond the higher excess. The question to be determined was whether the plaintiffs were entitled to rely on the amendment slip or whether Fennia were entitled as of right to cancel it.

Held

When the underwriter initials the broker's slip this is an act of acceptance which creates an immediate and binding contract between the parties.

Staughton J:

'I must choose between the view ... that the act of initialling the slip is an offer by the underwriters that none would be so bold as to revoke or, that it is an acceptance which there and then creates a contract binding upon both parties ... I hold it to be an acceptance.'

The assured was entitled to cancel the contract at any time before the risk had been 100 per cent subscribed. Staughton J stated:

'The right to cancel ... is binding both on the underwriter and the assured by reason of the custom and practice of the London Assurance market ... (and) the need to give business efficacy to the contract.'

Where subsequent underwriters inserted terms or amended terms which had been accepted by earlier underwriters, then the earlier underwriters had the option of adopting those amendments or rejecting them, in which case the assured could cancel the whole slip. Thus, when the defendants requested the slip to be amended to provide cover subject to an excess of 25 million, even though that amendment was to operate retrospectively, the defendants were entitled to cancel it before it had been subscribed to by all the original underwriters.

Hamilton, Fraser & Co v Pandorf

(1887) 12 App Cas 518 House of Lords (Lords Halsbury LC, Watson, Bramwell, Fitzgerald, Herschell and McNaughten)

• *Gnawing of rats is a peril of the sea*

Facts

A cargo of rice was shipped from Aykab to Bremerhaven. The charterparty exempted the carrier from loss or damage caused by Act of God, Queen's enemies, restraints of princes, fire and every other danger and accident of the sea etc. The bill of lading contained some of these exemptions. During the voyage rats gnawed a hole in a pipe. Sea water escaped from the pipe and damaged the cargo.

The question to be determined was:

'... whether in a seaworthy ship the gnawing by rats of some part of the ship so as to cause sea water to come in and cause damage, is a danger and accident of the sea' (Lord Halsbury LC).

Held

The damage by the rats was a peril of the sea and accordingly the carriers were not liable.

Lord Halsbury LC:

'I think the idea of something fortuitous and unexpected is involved in both words "peril" or "accident". I think in this case that it was a danger, accident or peril, in the contemplation of both parties, that the sea might get in and spoil the rice. I cannot think it was less such a peril or accident because the hole through which the sea came was made by vermin from within the vessel, and not by a sword fish from without – the sea water did get in.'

Comment

This case illustrates that 'peril of the sea' is wide enough to include vermin within the vessel, but when looking at other cases in this area, eg *Sassoon* v *Yorkshire Insurance Co* (1923) 16 Ll LR 129 where it was held that the rotten hull of a ship was responsible for seawater entering the hold, it is difficult to state when something will come within a 'peril'. What is clear is that a peril of the sea does not cover the ordinary action of the wind and waves but would cover unforeseen action by things peculiar to the sea, eg severe storms: *The Stranna* [1938] 1 All ER 458.

Inglis, John Gillanders v William Ravenhill Stock (1885) 10 App Cas 263 House of Lords (Earl of Selborne, LC, Lords Blackburn, Watson and Fitzgerald)

• *Passing of risk upon shipment under fob contract*

Facts

D contracted to sell to B 200 tonnes of sugar, on fob terms, payment to be in London in exchange for the bill of lading. The price was a variable one based on the percentage saccharine content of the sugar, within upper and lower limits of acceptability. B resold to the present respondent the same quantity at a higher price, but otherwise on the same terms. D also sold to the respondents 200 tonnes of sugar, on the same terms. With regard to these contracts 390 tonnes were shipped on a vessel at Hamburg for Bristol.

The respondent was insured under floating policies upon 'any kind of goods and merchandises' between Hamburg and Bristol. The ship was lost during the voyage from Hamburg to Bristol.

After receiving news of the loss of the vessel, D allocated 200 tonnes of sugar to B's account and 190 tonnes to the contract with the respondents.

Held

As the sales were 'fob Hamburg', the sugar was at the respondents' risk after shipment and they had an insurable interest in the sugar. The appellant underwriters were liable under the policy.

Comment

This is an early case that turns on the concepts and effects of appropriation and the passing of risk. The risk and property usually pass together as between buyer and seller, but in this case they were separated with risk of loss passing prior to any passing of property. Risk having passed to the respondents on shipment,

the underwriters were liable under the insurance policy.

International Container Service Inc v British Traders Insurance Co Ltd [1984] 1 Lloyd's Rep 154 Court of Appeal (Eveleigh, Griffiths and Dillon LJJ)

• *Sue and labour clause – assured only to show that acted reasonably in all the circumstances*

Facts

The plaintiffs were the owners of containers that were leased to various shippers. The containers were insured under an All Risks policy incorporating the Institute Containers Clauses and containing a clause that obliged the carrier to take measures which may be reasonable for the purposes of averting or minimising loss and to ensure the preservation of rights against third parties. This was the sue and labour clause (found in s78 of the Marine Insurance Act 1906 and cl 16 of the ICC). The plaintiffs leased a large number of containers to Oyama Shipping Ltd. Oyama did not take out their own insurance and became bankrupt three years later. It was therefore impossible to preserve rights against Oyama's non-existent insurers and therefore the plaintiffs incurred expense to recover the containers.

They then made a claim under the policy for the costs incurred, ie $56,026, and the lost and damaged containers. The defendants refused to pay the $56,026 incurred in recovery costs which they said had only been incurred to recover the containers from the bankrupt lessees, and did not come about as a result of a peril insured against.

Held

The sue and labour clause required the assured to take 'such measures as may be reasonable for the purpose of averting or minimising loss'. This means that he only has to show he acted reasonably. He does not have to show that if he had not acted then loss would 'very probably' have occurred.

It would be unreasonable to demand such a high degree of proof from the assured who is in the position that if he does not act he may find he can recover nothing under the policy, having failed to act.

The only obligation is for the assured to show that he acted in circumstances where a reasonable man, who is intent on preserving his property and does not want to incur a loss of that property, would also have acted. It is not necessary for him to act *as an assured making a claim*.

If he can show that he has acted, reasonably in all the circumstances then he can recover all expenses incurred as a result, even if those expenses are extraordinary, providing that a prudent assured would also have incurred this.

The true test to be applied is whether, given that the insurers might have to bear a loss, the assured acted reasonably to avoid that loss.

In this case, if the assured had not taken steps to recover the containers then anything might have happened to them.

The sue and labour clause ceased to apply once the insured goods were again in the custody and control of the assured and free from damage or the threat thereof. In this case that meant at the time when they reached the plaintiffs' depot, and all expenses incurred prior to that time would come under the clause.

Comment

Clause 16 of the Institute Cargo Clauses A, B and C require the assured to take such steps as may be reasonable to minimise loss. The assured can recover the expenses for so doing. Also see post: *Royal Boskalis Westminster NV and Others* v *Mountin and Others* [1999] QB 674 (below).

Kyzuna Investments Ltd v *Ocean Marine Mutual Insurance Association (Europe)* [2000] 1 Lloyd's Rep 505 Queen's Bench Division (Commercial Court) (Thomas J)

• *Difference between valued and unvalued marine insurance policies*

Facts

Prior to granting insurance cover on a yacht acquired by the claimants in March 1996 for £50,000, the defendants, through their managing agents, had insisted that a valuation and survey be carried out. The policy was issued upon attachment to the proposal form of the survey and valuation expressed as 'sum insured' for £106,500.

Thereafter, whilst on a voyage from Portugal to Spain, a fire broke out on the yacht and, despite efforts by members of the crew to put it out, the yacht sank. Following unsuccessful claims under the policy, the claimants brought proceedings for £100,000 as the agreed value of the yacht on the basis that it had been lost by the peril of fire.

Apart from the issues of misrepresentation also raised, the preliminary issue to be tried here was whether the policy was a valued or unvalued policy. If it was a valued policy the amount the insurers would have to pay upon an actual or constructive total loss was the value agreed to in the policy. However, if it was an unvalued policy the value stated was the maximum that could be recovered and the actual amount recoverable would be the actual value of the yacht just before the loss.

Held

This policy was an unvalued policy under which the assured was limited, up to the policy limits, to the amount actually lost by reason of loss of the yacht.

Although the difference may seem to be only semantic, the different expressions of 'valued at' commonly used for valued policies and of 'sum insured' commonly used for unvalued policies are indicative of the parties' intentions. The use of the expression of 'sum insured' here was suggestive that an unvalued policy was intended.

A valued policy is defined by s27(2) Marine Insurance Act 1906 as 'a policy which specifies the agreed value of the subject-matter insured'. If the precise words 'valued at' are not employed, the intention of the parties must be clear that there is a specified agreed value, proposed by the assured and accepted by the underwriter.

Comment
This case is a very helpful guide to the difference between valued and unvalued policies in marine insurance.

Pan Atlantic Insurance Co Ltd and Another v Pine Top Insurance Co Ltd [1995] 1 AC 501; [1994] 2 Lloyd's Rep 427 House of Lords (Lords Templeman, Goff of Chieveley, Mustill, Slynn of Hadley and Lloyd of Berwick)

• *Test for avoiding insurance contract under s18 Marine Insurance Act 1906*

Facts
The plaintiffs were the reassured and the defendants were the reinsurers under a contract for reinsurance. The contract in question related to losses for the calendar year 1982. It was a renewal of other contracts by which the defendants were reinsurers for the years 1980 and 1981, other reinsurers having been contracted with for previous years.

The reinsurance contract provided that the business covered was the liability of the reinsurer under

'... all policies and/or contracts and/or binders of insurance and/or reinsurance ... allocated to their so called casualty account ...'

The plaintiffs claimed for payment or damages for non-payment of paid losses and a declaration that they were entitled to have letters of credit opened with regard to outstanding losses due to them. The case was one which turned on non-disclosure and misrepresentation under the Marine Insurance Act 1906, involving the years 1977 to 79 when another reinsurer was involved and 1980 and 1981 as to dealings with the present reinsurer. As it developed, the claims record for 1987 amounted to US $468,168 and not US $235,768. As expressed by Lord Templeman (at p430):

'No juggling with figures can obscure the clear indication, found by the judge, that the true 1981 figures were more alarming than the disclosed figures and would have caused the prudent insurer in 1982 to reject the risk or increase the premium: the insurer is therefore entitled to avoid the policy.'

Held
The 'decisive influence' test is not the appropriate one in determining whether the insurer can avoid the contract. The *CTI* case, *Container Transport International Inc v Oceanus Mutual Underwriting Association (Bermuda) Ltd* [1984] 1 Lloyd's Rep 476 (above), which approved this test ten years previously, should be overruled in part. Indeed, here, in the judgment of Lord Mustill at pp438–40, the holding and effect of the *CTI* case is criticised for at least five reasons.

The 'actual inducement test' which requires that a particular insurer has been actually induced by reason of non-disclosure or a misrepresentation is the more appropriate test. This raises the threshold for allowing the insurer to avoid the contract.

Comment
This case which exercised their Lordships for 39 pages in the reports is a major and recent one in the law of marine insurance. Its holding requires that the insurer succeed in a double-barrelled test to avoid the contract. First, the statement or lack thereof must pass the mate-

riality test, and, second, it must have actually induced this insurer to enter into this contract of insurance on the terms agreed.

Royal Boskalis Westminster NV and Others v *Mountin and Others* [1999] QB 674 Court of Appeal (Stuart-Smith, Pill and Phillips LJJ)

• *If a waiver is effective and enforceable, a loss arising from a waived claim can in principle be recovered under the sue and labour clause in the marine insurance contract*

Facts
A dredging fleet owned by the plaintiffs was insured against war risks by the defendants under an insurance contract which contained a sue and labour clause and was governed by the Marine Insurance Act 1906. Dredging work was undertaken at an Iraqi port and the dredging contract provided for arbitration in Paris.

Following the invasion of Kuwait by Iraq, the United Nations imposed sanctions against Iraq and a law was then passed in Iraq under which assets of companies of countries which had complied with the sanctions were to be seized. The plaintiffs signed an agreement with the Iraq authorities under which the plaintiffs paid money into bank accounts in Switzerland and Austria and waived all further claims under the dredging contract. The plaintiffs sought to recover the loss from the waived claims under the sue and labour clause in the insurance contract.

Held
The loss arising from the waived claims could in principle be recovered under the sue and labour clause but in order to recover the loss it was necessary to show that the arbitrators would give effect to the waiver. The waiver would be unenforceable in English law since the agreements had been made under duress and, on the assumption that French law on this point would be the same as English law, the waiver of claims would, therefore, be unenforceable in the arbitration in Paris. As the plaintiffs had not proved that they had suffered any effective loss to form the basis of a sue and labour charge, their claim must fail.

Comment
The sue and labour clause is found in the old Lloyd's SG Policy and is now replaced by the Institute Cargo Clause 16, the 'Duty of the Assured Clause', which allows the assured to recover any expenses reasonably incurred in pursuance of his duty to minimise loss.

10 Marine Insurance (2): Institute Cargo Clauses, Loss and Indemnity

Asfar & Co v *Blundell & Another*
[1896] 1 QB 123 Court of Appeal
(Lord Esher MR, Lopes and Kay LJJ)

• *There is actual total loss when the goods shipped have become for business purposes something else*

Facts
A cargo of dates was shipped from the Persian Gulf to London, freight being payable on delivery. When the cargo arrived at its destination some of it had become impregnated with sewage and was unfit for human consumption, although the dates were still of some use for distillation purposes.

Held
Freight was not payable by the shipper as the goods were no longer merchantable as dates.

Lord Esher MR:

'... it is contended that although these dates were under water for two days and when brought up were simply a mass of pulpy matter impregnated with sewage and in a state of fermentation, there had been no change in their nature and they were still dates. There is a perfectly well known test which has for many years been applied to cases such as the present – that the test is whether, as a matter of business, the nature of the thing has been altered. The nature of a thing is not necessarily altered because the thing itself has been damaged; wheat or rice may be damaged, but may still remain the thing dealt with as wheat or rice in business. But if the nature of the thing is altered and it becomes for business purposes something else, so that it is not dealt with by business

people as the thing which it originally was, the question for determination is whether the thing insured ... has become a total loss. If it so changed in its nature by the perils of the sea as to become an unmerchantable thing which no buyer would buy, and no honest seller would sell, then there is a total loss.'

Thus, there had been a total loss of the subject matter of the insurance.

Comment
Apart from this case illustrating that if the nature of goods has changed so much that they have become unmerchantable they will be seen as an actual total loss (s57 Marine Insurance Act 1906), it also is an authority for stating that if the goods have become a total loss the carrier cannot claim the freight. On this point, the case should be compared with *Dakin* v *Oxley* (1864) 10 LT 268.

British & Foreign Marine Insurance v *Gaunt* [1921] 2 AC 41 House of Lords (Lord Birkenhead LC, Lords Atkinson and Sumner, Viscounts Core and Finlay)

• *'All risk' policies cover fortuitous accidents or casualties*

Facts
The respondent plaintiffs were the assignees of marine insurance policies in respect of wool shipped fob Punta Arenas, Chile, to the respondent's mills at Bradford.

The policies provided 'all risks' cover in the following terms:

'Including all risk of craft, fire, coasters, hulks, transhipment and inland carriage by land and /or water, and all risks from the sheep's back and for station while awaiting shipment and/or forwarding and until safely delivered ... with liberties as per bill of lading.'

The wool was found to be water damaged on arrival at Bradford and this damage had occurred during the transit to the port of departure. It transpired that, before being loaded into an ocean going vessel at Punta Arenas, the wool had been carried by waterway in southern Chile on the decks of local steamers without the insurers being informed. The insurers therefore rejected the claim made by the respondent on his policy of insurance.

Held

Judgment for the assured.

The expression 'all risks' was considered.

Lord Birkenhead LC:

'In construing these policies it is important to bear in mind that they cover "all risk". These words cannot of course be held to cover damage however caused, for such damage as is inevitable from ordinary wear and tear and inevitable depreciation, is not within these policies ... Damage if it is to be covered by policies such as these must be due to some fortuitous circumstance or casualty.'

Lord Sumner:

'There are of course limits to all risks. There are risks and risks insured against. Accordingly, the expression does not cover inherent vice or mere wear and tear ... It covers a risk not a certainty; it is something which happens to the subject matter from without, or the natural behaviour of that subject matter being what it is, in the circumstances under which it is carried. Nor is it a loss which the assured brings about by his own chance, for then, he has not merely exposed the goods to the chance of injury, he has injured them himself ...'

The burden of proof rests with the claimant who must establish his case but, with an 'all risks' policy the burden of proof placed upon a claimant is less rigorous. The claimant is not required to show how the loss occurred. It is enough to be able to show that the loss has in fact occurred and that it was a casualty not a certainty and this leaves the onus to prove otherwise with the insurer. Lord Birkenhead LC:

'We are of course, to give effect to the rule that the plaintiff must establish his case, that he must show that the loss comes within the terms of his policies; but where all risks are covered by the policy and not merely risks of a specified class or classes, the plaintiff discharges his special onus when he has proved that the loss was caused by some event covered by the general expression, and that he is not bound to go further and prove the exact nature of the accident or casualty which, in fact, occasioned his loss.'

Lord Sumner commented on the 'quasi-universality' of the description 'all risks' and that, as such, it should not affect the onus of proof one way as with, for example, the need for a claimant averring a loss by fire to prove that the loss is by fire and is not caused by something else. His Lordship said:

'When he avers loss by some risk coming within "all risks", as used in this policy, he need only give evidence reasonably showing that the loss was due to a casualty, not to a certainty or to inherent vice or to wear and tear. That is easily done. I do not think he has to go further and pick out one of a multitude of risks covered, so as to show exactly how this loss was caused.'

Transportation in this way by local steamers was 'common usage' in the trade and Viscount Finlay gave careful consideration to words as to 'usage' in relation to deck cargo:

' ... I think these words would be satisfied by proof of a usage in a particular trade, or generally, to carry on deck goods of a particular kind. The underwriter is bound to know of the existence of such usages, and the description of particular goods as of the class to which such usage applies gives him the information that the goods will or may be carried on deck. If there is such a usage, there is no reason for requiring a statement that the goods which fall within it, are, in fact, to be carried on deck, as the mere description of the goods gives the necessary information.'

Canada Rice Mills v Union Marine & General Insurance Co [1941] AC 55 Privy Council (Viscount Maugham, Lords Russell of Kilowen, Wright and Porter)

• *The accidental incursion of sea water into a vessel will be a peril of the sea where entry is in a manner and at a part of the vessel where sea water is not expected to enter in the ordinary course of things*

Facts

A shipment of rice sent by the appellants to their rice mills in British Columbia was covered by a marine insurance policy which protected against loss or damage as a result of, inter alia, perils of the sea. Due to bad weather, it had become necessary to close cowl ventilators and hatches from time to time during the voyage and on arrival at Vancouver, the port of discharge, the rice was found to been damaged by excessive heat in the hold.

The appellants claimed that as the adverse weather was a peril of the sea, then the closing of the ventilators was also as a direct result of a peril of the sea and, accordingly, the loss fell within their insurance against perils of the sea.

The underwriters rejected the claim on the basis that the damage to the rice was caused by inherent vice. The appellants brought an appeal against the decision of the Court of Appeal of British Columbia which had set aside the jury's finding that the rice was damaged by a peril of the seas.

Held

Judgment was given for the appellants on the basis that where there was damage to a cargo not by sea water as such but by an act of seamanship reasonably and necessarily taken to prevent the incursion of the water, then loss was due to a peril of the sea. Accordingly, since the damage to the rice had resulted from the closing of the ventilation hatches which, in turn, had been closed to prevent an incursion of sea water, the loss was brought about because of a peril of the sea.

Lord Wright, in considering whether loss was caused by a 'peril of the sea' as covered by the policy, said:

'... the purpose of the policy is to secure an indemnity against accidents which may happen, not against events which must happen (*Hamilton v Pandorf* (1887) 12 App Cas 518). ...

Where there is an accidental incursion of sea water into a vessel at a part of the vessel, and in a manner, where sea water is not expected to enter in the ordinary course of things, and there is consequent damage to the thing insured, there is prima facie a loss by the perils of the sea. The accident may consist in some negligent act, such as improper opening of a valve, or a hole made in a pipe by mischance, or it may be that seawater is admitted by stress of weather or some like cause bringing the sea over openings ordinarily not exposed to the sea, or even without stress of weather, by the vessel heeling over owing to some accident, or by the breaking of hatches or other coverings. These are merely a few amongst many possible instances in which there may be a fortuitous incursion of sea water. It is the fortuitous entry of the sea water which is the peril of the sea in such cases.'

His Lordship went on to identify the cowl ventilators as being openings through which water is not expected to enter and said:

'If they were not closed at the proper time to prevent sea water coming into the hold, and sea water does accidentally come in and do damage, that is just as much an accident of navigation ... as the improper opening of a valve or other sea connection. The rush of sea water which, but for the covering of the ventilators, would have come into them and down to the cargo was in this case due to a storm which was sufficiently out of the ordinary to send seas or spray over the orifices of the ventilators.'

On the matter of whether damage caused by an action taken to prevent incursion of water is recoverable as a loss by perils of the sea Lord Wright said:

'There remains the second question, whether the damage which was caused not by the incursion of sea water, but by action taken to prevent the incursion, is recoverable as a loss by perils of the sea. It is curious that, so far as their Lordships know, there is no express decision on this point under a policy of marine insurance. But, in their Lordships' judgment, the question should be answered in the affirmative, as they think the jury did. The answer may be based on the view that where the weather conditions so require, the closing of the ventilators is not to be regarded as a separate or independent cause, interposed between the peril of the sea and the damage, but as being such a mere matter of routine seamanship necessitated by the peril that the damage can be regarded as the direct result of the peril.
...
In cases of fire insurance, it has been said that loss caused from an apparently necessary and bona fide attempt to put out the fire, by spoiling goods by water, and in other ways, is within the policy, per Kelly CB in *Stanley* v *Western Insurance Co* (1868) LR 3 Ex 71. Their Lordships agree with this expression of opinion, and accordingly, are prepared to hold that the damage to the rice, which the jury have found to be due to action necessary and reasonably taken to prevent the peril of the sea affecting the goods, is a loss due to the peril of the sea and is recoverable as such.'

In considering whether the peril of the sea was the proximate cause of loss, thus allowing the assured to recover under his policy, Lord Wright continued:

'It is now established that causa proxima in insurance law does not necessarily mean the last cause in time, but what is "in substance" the cause, to be determined by common sense principles ... [thus] in *Samuel* v *Dumas* [1924] AC 431 ... where a ship insured by the mortgagee was lost by being scuttled by the deliberate act or procurement of the mortgagor, it was not in insurance law, to be deemed a loss by perils of the sea. The proximate cause was the intentional and fraudulent act which let in the sea water and sank the vessel ... the damage to the rice ... is a loss (proximately caused by a) peril of the sea and is recoverable as such.'

Comment

The case establishes that any loss or damage caused by actions taken to prevent a loss caused by an insured peril is recoverable as a loss caused by that insured peril. It is necessary to establish an existing state of affairs producing danger and an imminent peril. In *The Knight of St Michael* [1898] P 30 the shipowner claimed on a policy of insurance for loss of freight after part of a cargo of coal had had to be discharged at a port of call. The cargo of coal had started to heat and the court ruled that although none of the cargo was lost as a result of the fire itself, it was lost due to the necessary preventive action of the master and it was reasonably certain that, if the voyage had continued with all the cargo, spontaneous combustion would have taken place and the ship and cargo would have been destroyed by fire.

In considering whether it made any difference that no fire had actually broken out, Gorrell Barnes in that case said:

'There was an imminent danger of fire, and an existing condition of things producing this danger, and if this cannot, strictly speaking, be termed a loss by fire, it is, in my opinion, a loss ejusdem generis, and covered by the general words 'all other losses and misfortunes, etc.'

In *Symington and Co* v *Union Insurance Society of Canton Ltd* (1928) 34 Com Cas 23 (CA) a cargo lying on a wharf was wetted to help stop a nearby fire from spreading and Scrutton J took the view that

'... there being an existing fire and an imminent peril, the damage caused by water either used to extinguish the fire or prevent it from spreading was a proximate consequence of fire which could be recovered under the general words ... being ejusdem generis with fire.'

Noten (T M) BV v Harding [1990] 2 Lloyd's Rep 283 Court of Appeal (Glidewell and Bingham LJJ, Sir David Croon-Johnson)

• *Inherent vice*

Facts
A consignment of leather gloves were found to be damaged by mould and mildew. The gloves had been carried on a warehouse to warehouse basis and at some time between leaving the warehouse and being later packed into their container for carriage, they had absorbed moisture. The insurance did not expressly provide cover for inherent vice.

Held
The Court of Appeal reversed the fact finding of the trial judge and held that the loss was caused by inherent vice or nature of the subject matter. As there was no express cover in the insurance for inherent vice, the loss was excluded and the insurers were not liable.

It was the hygroscopic tendency of leather, ie its tendency to absorb moisture from the air, that had caused the defect. This was the natural behaviour of leather if placed in a humid atmosphere and, therefore, 'an inherent vice or the nature of the subject matter'.

Bingham LJ:

'The goods deteriorated as a result of their natural behaviour in the ordinary course of the contemplated voyage, without the intervention of any fortuitous external accident or casualty. The damage was caused because the goods were shipped wet ...'

The origin of the moisture was directly traceable to the gloves; it had been present in the gloves when packed. The gloves had not been affected by other cargo or by any other external source during the transit and Bingham LJ added:

'I regard it as immaterial that the moisture travelled round the containers before doing the damage complained of.'

Rhesa Shipping Co SA v Herbert David Edmunds, The Popi M [1985] 2 Lloyd's Rep 1 House of Lords (Lords Brandon of Oakbrook, Templeman, Fraser of Tullybelton, Diplock and Roskill)

• *Proof of seaworthiness is not vital to proving loss by a peril insured against*

Facts
The hull and machinery of The Popi M was insured by the plaintiffs against perils of the sea and loss directly caused by the negligence of the master or crew, providing it did not result from want of due diligence by the plaintiffs.

The vessel sank off the coast of Algeria and in good weather when the shell plating in the vicinity of the engine room sprang apart and allowed a large volume of water to enter the vessel. The plaintiffs claimed under the policy for loss caused by peril of the sea or by negligence of the crew. The defendants denied liability claiming that the vessel was unseaworthy or that the crew had failed to show due diligence.

Held
The House of Lords overturned the decisions of both the lower courts on the basis that they had not been justified in inferring that the loss had been due to a peril of the seas. The reason for the loss of The Popi M remained in doubt and the plaintiffs had failed to discharge the burden of proof.

Lord Brandon:

'The first matter is that the burden of

proving, on the balance of probabilities, that the ship was lost by perils of the sea is, and remains throughout, on the shipowners. Although it is open to underwriters to suggest and seek to prove some other cause of loss, against which the ship was not insured, there is no obligation on them to prove, even on a balance of probabilities, the truth of their alternative cause.

The second matter is that it is always open to a court, even after the kind of prolonged inquiry with a mass of expert evidence which took place in this case, to conclude, at the end of the day, that the proximate cause of the ship's loss, even on a balance of probabilities, remains in doubt, with the consequence that the shipowners have failed to discharge the burden of proof which lay upon them.'

Lord Brandon was at pains to point out that a common sense approach must be applied.

'... the legal concept of proof of a case on a balance of probabilities must be applied with common sense. It requires a judge of first instance, before he finds that a particular event occurred, to be satisfied on the evidence that it is more likely to have occurred than not. If such a judge concludes, on a whole series of cogent grounds, that the concurrence of an event is extremely improbable, a finding by him that it is nevertheless more likely to have occurred than not, does not accord with common sense. This is especially so when it is open to the judge to say simply that the evidence leaves him in no doubt whether the event occurred or not, and that the party on whom the burden of proving that the event occurred lies has therefore failed to discharge such burden.'

Comment

The case has clarified beyond doubt that the standard of proof required upon the plaintiff to prove that the loss was caused by a peril of the seas is the balance of probabilities. It is also authority for the proposition that the degree of proof required to establish whether an occurrence is probable or not is a matter requiring a commonsense approach. It is inter-esting to note that where both or all accounts of the loss are equally probable or improbable, the court is not obliged to make a choice and may instead take the view that the evidence leaves the matter in too much doubt to be resolved and that the party with the burden of proving that the event occurred has failed to discharge that burden.

Where the loss is by peril of the seas, the burden of proof remains throughout on the shipowners. There is no obligation on the insurers to suggest and seek to prove some other cause of loss, against which the ship is not insured. However, it open for them to do so and should the insurers so choose, there is no obligation on them to prove, even on a balance of probabilities, the truth of their alternative case (per Lord Brandon at p2).

Sassoon and Co v *Yorkshire Insurance Co* (1923) 16 Ll LR 129
Court of Appeal (Atkin, Bankes and Scrutton LJJ)

• *Inherent vice*

Facts

Following considerable delay on the voyage, a cargo of cigarettes was found to be badly mildewed on arrival.

A clause in the insurance gave cover against 'mould and mildew'. The plaintiffs argued that the damage was caused by mould and mildew so was covered by the express term in the insurance. The defendants denied liability, pleading that the goods were damaged by inherent vice and not by any peril insured against.

Held

Mould and mildew can grow as a result of either an internal or an external cause and the defendants were unable to prove that the growth of either in this case was due to the inherent nature of the goods. Accordingly, the Court found that the loss was as a result of some fortuitous circumstance and not as the result of inherent vice.

On the issue of what must be proved to establish inherent vice Scrutton LJ said:

' ... if it could be shown that this mould or mildew resulted entirely from the condition of the goods when shipped and must have resulted from that condition when shipped as an ordinary incident of the voyage then the underwriters would not be liable ...'

Atkin LJ agreed with the trial judge, Roche J, that a distinction has to be drawn between

'... mould and mildew which are the result of inherent vice and or the nature of the subject matter of the insurance, and mould and mildew which are produced by some fortuitous external cause ...'

The intentions of the parties in expressly inserting the clause was considered. Did it intend to act as a cover for inherent vice and thereby displace the prima facie rule that the insurer will not be liable for loss caused by inherent vice? Scrutton LJ thought that it did not. He regarded the clause as being a provision for insurance cover against 'mould or mildew' fortuitously caused:

'... where you are insuring against a specific peril and have to show some damage caused by that specific peril, subject to that reservation that if the peril results from the condition of the thing itself, the underwriter is relieved.'

Atkin LJ said, obiter:

'In this particular case ... there is something to be said for the view that the intention of the parties here was to cover mould or mildew arising from any cause whatsoever; that is one of the matters that was in the mind of the assured.'

Proof of the intentions of the parties do not necessarily lie with why they have inserted the clause. The reasons for the growth of mould and mildew are several and complex and vary according to the commodity on which they grow. That an assured may wish to provide for such cover without knowledge of how mould or mildew might grow on his

goods or, indeed, whether it will at all, mattered not. It was what the words of the clause said that established whether the loss was insured against. Lord Atkin expressed this as follows:

'It seems to me conceivable if apt words are used that an assured might cover a loss occasioned by mould which he does not know enough about ...'

Smith Hogg & Co Ltd v *Black Sea and Baltic General Insurance Co Ltd* [1940] AC 997 House of Lords (Viscount Maugham, Lords Atkin, Wright, Romer and Porter)

• *Assured may only rely on the exception of peril of the sea if it is the 'real and effective cause' of the loss*

Facts
The appellants' ship was chartered to carry timber from Soroka to Garston. The charterparty provided that the shipowner should not be liable for loss or damage resulting from unseaworthiness unless caused by want of due diligence on the part of the shipowner to make the vessel seaworthy, and also that the shipowner should not be responsible for loss or damage arising from (amongst other things) act, neglect or default of the master in the navigation or management of the ship or from perils, dangers and accidents of the sea.

While loading timber on deck at Soroka the vessel listed five degrees to port and sailed with that list. During the voyage she put in at Stornoway to refuel by taking on coal and during this process the vessel again listed but so heavily that she fell on her beam ends. In order to save her from sinking, she was beached, with the result that a good deal of the cargo was lost and some of it was damaged. The shipowners claimed general average contribution from those interested in the cargo. The respondents resisted the claim on the ground that the owners had not exercised due diligence in accordance with the charter to make the vessel seaworthy and that the average act was occasioned by the unseaworthiness. The shipowners alleged that the accident was the fault of the master in taking on bunkers without discharging or reducing the deck cargo.

It was found as a fact that the ship was unseaworthy upon leaving Soroka, but the experts agreed that the ship could have been bunkered at Stornoway in such a manner as to have brought her back to the upright and to have allowed her to proceed safely to Garston and deliver her cargo.

Held

The owners could not recover general average loss. The cause of the loss was the unstable and unseaworthy condition of the vessel, which was due to a failure on the part of the owners and master to exercise due diligence.

Lord Wright took the view that the vessel was 'unseaworthy on any definition of the term' and, on the matter of whether the lack of seaworthiness was due to lack of diligence on the part of the shipowner, drew a distinction between 'latent defects' and 'overt acts':

'... it seems clear that the deck cargo rendered the vessel unstable and too tender for the voyage. ... she was liable to fall, as she did in fact, on her beam ends, and become a derelict. She was clearly unfit to carry and deliver the cargo safely, and her condition endangered the lives of the crew. She was unseaworthy on any definition of the term.
...

There is no clear finding that the master was negligent, but, whether he was negligent or not, what he did could have done no harm if The Lilburn had not been unseaworthy. The unseaworthiness, constituted as it was by loading an excessive deck cargo, was obviously only consistent with want of due diligence on the part of the shipowner to make her seaworthy. Hence the qualified exception of unseaworthiness does not protect the shipowner. In effect, such an exception can excuse only against latent defects. The overloading was the result of overt acts.'

In consideration of the shipowners' argument that the act, neglect or default of the master was the real cause, so as to come within the exception, Lord Wright said:

'I can draw no distinction between cases where the negligent conduct of the master is a cause and those where any other cause, such as perils of the seas or fire, is a co-operating cause. A negligent act is as much a co-operating cause, if it is a cause at all, as an act which is not negligent. The question is the same in either case – namely, would the disaster not have happened if the ship had fulfilled the obligation of seaworthiness, even though the disaster could not have happened if there had not also been the specific peril or action?'

Lord Porter expressed a similar view:

'The master merely acted in the usual way, and, indeed, exercised what he thought was exceptional care in diverting the coal shipped towards the port bunker. In a seaworthy ship, his action would have been a safe one. It was the instability of the ship which caused the disaster. In such circumstances, it is unnecessary to decide what would be the result if the loss were attributable partly to the coaling and partly to the unseaworthiness, or to determine whether the fact that the unseaworthiness was a substantial cause, even though some other matter relied upon were a substantial cause also, would be enough to make the owners liable for failure to use due care to make the vessel seaworthy.'

Lord Porter was also 'clearly of opinion that the ship was unseaworthy, and that her unseaworthiness was due to the failure of the owners to take proper steps' and noted:

'... where a timber-carrying vessel sails with a list, due to the fact that her cargo carried is heavier on one side than on the other, I cannot take the view that [that] ship ... is, therefore, so unstable that the placing of a comparatively small additional weight either to port or starboard [which] causes her to list suddenly and violently from one side to the other, is in a seaworthy state.'

In consideration of the appellants argument that they were protected by the exception of perils of the sea, and that, even though the ship was unseaworthy, the unseaworthiness did not cause the loss, Lord Porter said:

'I think that the loss was incontestably due to the inability of the ship to take in bunkers by a method which would have been both safe and usual in the case of a seaworthy ship. It was not the coaling which was at fault, nor the method adopted. It was the fact that that coaling took place and that that method was adopted in a tender ship. If a vessel is to proceed on her voyage, bunkers must be shipped, and, though in one sense the change of balance caused by taking in bunkers was responsible for the accident to The Lilburn, it was not the dominant cause, even if it be necessary to show what the dominant cause was.'

Comment

Branson J, who tried the case in the Commercial Court, decided in favour of the appellants, but his decision was reversed by the Court of Appeal ([1939] 2 All ER 855). Whilst both courts decided that the steamship was unseaworthy on sailing, and that the appellants had not exercised due diligence to make her seaworthy, the Court of Appeal took the view that the cause of the disaster was the unstable and unseaworthy condition of the vessel, which was due to a failure to exercise due diligence (and it is this decision that was affirmed by the House of Lords), whereas Branson J held that the unseaworthiness did not cause the loss because the vessel could have been bunkered at Stornoway in such a manner as to bring her back to upright and enable her to proceed and deliver her cargo at Garston. This raised an important question of mercantile law in that Branson J found that the necessary nexus between the unseaworthiness and the disaster was absent and held that the accident took place, not by reason of the unseaworthiness of the ship, but by reason of the acts of the master, which were wrong in the circumstances, and entitled the appellants to succeed by reason of the exception in the charterparty.

Counsel for the appellants strenuously contended that the master's action, whether or not negligent, was a novus actus interveniens, which broke the nexus or chain of causation, and reduced the unseaworthiness from a causa causans to a causa sine qua non and on this, Lord Wright commented:

'I cannot help deprecating the use of so-called Latin phrases in this way. They only distract the mind from the true problem, which is to apply the principles of English law to the realities of the case. Causa causans is supposed to mean a cause which causes, while causa sine qua non means, I suppose, a cause which does not, in the sense material to the particular case, cause, but is merely an incident which precedes in the history or narrative of events, but as a cause is not in at the death, and hence is irrelevant. ...

There is always a combination of co-operating causes, out of which the law, employing its empirical or commonness view of causation, will select the one or more which it finds material for its special purpose of deciding the particular case. ...

I think that the contract may be expressed to be that the shipowner will be liable for any loss in which those other causes covered by exceptions co-operate if unseaworthiness is a cause, or, if it is preferred, a real, or effective or actual cause.'

Soya GmbH Mainz Kommanditgesellschaft v *White*
[1983] 1 Lloyd's Rep 122 House of Lords (Lords Diplock, Keith of Kinkel, Scarman, Roskill and Templeman); [1982] 1 Lloyd's Rep 136 Court of Appeal (Waller, Donaldson and O'Connor LJJ)

• *Inherent vice can be covered by general words which on their true construction have that meaning*

Facts

The plaintiffs purchased three shipments of soya beans cif Indonesia. All three shipments were insured with the defendant, a Lloyd's underwriter, under an open cover. The cover on the first shipment was amended to include soya beans but gave no HSSC cover (heat, sweat and spontaneous combustion). When the cargo arrived it was found to be heat damaged. The plaintiffs arranged for an HSSC clause to be added to the cover for the next two shipments. These cargoes also arrived in a heat-damaged and deteriorated condition.

The plaintiffs claimed on their policy of insurance and the insurers denied liability on the ground, inter alia, that the proximate cause of damage was inherent vice in that the soya beans were shipped in such a condition that they were unable to withstand the ordinary incidents of the voyage, and, accordingly, there was a good defence under s55(2)(c) Marine Insurance Act 1906.

Held

On the issue of inherent vice, the main issues were (i) whether the loss was caused by inherent vice and, (ii) if it was, whether that loss was covered by the HSSC cover added to the policy. The House found that loss was caused by inherent vice and that the HSSC cover did displace the prima facie rule that an insurer will not be liable 'for inherent vice or nature of the subject matter insured' laid down in s55(2)(c). Accordingly, the insurers were liable for the loss.

The first issue involved determination of what constitutes an inherent vice.

Lord Diplock defined the term 'inherent vice' as used in s55(2)(c) in the following manner:

'This phrase (generally shortened to "inherent vice") where it is used in s55(2)(c) refers to a peril by which a loss is proximately caused; it is not descriptive of the loss itself. It means the risk of deterioration of the goods shipped as a result of their natural behaviour in the ordinary course of the contemplated voyage without the intervention of any fortuitous external accident or casualty.'

Since the term 'inherent vice' describes the risk and not the loss itself, the description for a loss must be found elsewhere. Lord Diplock considered the descriptions for 'heat', 'sweat', and 'spontaneous combustion' when used for HSSC cover:

' "Heat", if it stood alone as a descriptive peril, would be equally apt to describe both the heating of the insured cargo from an external source and its becoming hot as a result of some internal chemical, biological or bacterial process taking place in the cargo itself. But "heat" does not stand alone; it appears in conjunction with two other perils insured against, "sweat" and "spontaneous combustion". "Sweat" means the exudation of moisture from within the goods which comprise the cargo to their exterior, as a result of something which happens inside the goods; while "spontaneous combustion" can refer only to a chemical reaction which takes place inside the goods themselves and results in their becoming incandescent or bursting into flames. Referring as they do to something which can only take place inside the goods themselves, these two expressions in their ordinary and natural meaning appear to me to be clearly intended to be descriptive of particular kinds of inherent vice; and "heat" appearing in immediate conjunction with them is apt to include heating of the cargo as a result of some internal action taking place inside the cargo itself.'

Sweat can thus be viewed as a second stage, possibly followed by spontaneous combustion. It is heat that starts the process and so becomes a key determinant of whether there is an inherently caused vice as opposed to one triggered by an external source. If the vice or nature of the cargo is such that it will inevitably deteriorate or destroy or damage itself in the course of the carriage, the loss is not recoverable because it is not a fortuitous loss; it is a certainty. Soya beans have moisture levels that give them a tendency to heat and sweat features. They will deteriorate even in the course of a normal voyage and the House accepted that they will certainly start to heat at a moisture level of more than 14 per cent. The House was also willing to accept that heating will not start at a level of 12 per cent or lower. The soya beans in question fell between these levels. They therefore suffered a risk of heating which may, or may not, cause them to deteriorate during the course of an ordinary voyage. The House arrived at the conclusion that the loss was caused by inherent vice. There had been no event in the course of the transit that would establish loss caused by a casualty and there was no evidence of another external cause.

Whilst the loss had been found to be caused by inherent vice, there remained the issue of whether it was a risk insured against in the policy. The provision in s55(2)(c) commences with the words 'Unless the policy otherwise provides'. Lord Diplock thought that the standard HSSC policy does 'otherwise provide':

' ... the standard HSSC policy does "otherwise provide" so as to displace the prima facie rule of construction laid down in s55(2)(c) that the insurer is not liable for "inherent vice or nature of the subject matter insured". It does so to the extent that such inherent vice consists of a tendency to become hot, to sweat, or to combust spontaneously. To hold otherwise would, in my opinion, be contrary to commercial common sense.'

But did this policy have that effect? The question of whether particular kinds of inherent vice are covered is one of the construction of the policy. The words used in this particular policy referred to something which could only take place inside the goods and, given their ordinary and natural meaning, these words appeared to be descriptive of particular kinds of inherent vice.

In the Court of Appeal in this case Waller and Donaldson LJJ expressed the following views on whether the words of the policy were sufficiently clear.

Waller LJ:

'In my opinion, the words of this policy are clear, it was an insurance against risks which were inherent in the cargo, ie inherent vice. In my opinion the damage caused to these cargoes of soya beans was due to heating caused by conditions within the beans themselves and some other unknown circumstances. This was a peril against which the buyers had specifically covered themselves in the policy.'

Donaldson LJ:

'That where an insurer was to be made liable for loss or damage proximately caused by inherent vice, it was not necessary that the words "inherent vice" were themselves adopted in defining his liability for inherent vice if on their true construction such a meaning could be given to those words. ...

[This] is an insurance which clearly covers ... inherent vice, namely, spontaneous combustion, which both parties must be taken to have regarded as a risk ... heat and sweat, which are but stages on the way to spontaneous combustion ... should be construed in a like manner as including heat and sweat caused by inherent vice, provided always that the heat and sweat are risks and not known certainties.'

Both their Lordships gave consideration to whether insurance coverage for losses of known certainty was possible. Donaldson LJ:

'Any abnormal or exceptional damage sustained under an enumerated risks policy will be recoverable only if the assured is able to refer to a specific peril as the proximate cause of loss. In an all risks policy, he need only give evidence to show that, by reason of the exceptional character of the damage, the loss must have arisen fortuitously.'

He also commented:

'That is not to say that known certain losses cannot be the subject matter of a contract of indemnity; merely that very clear words will be required since it is a highly improbable contract for someone to make in the course of his business as an insurance underwriter.'

Waller LJ:

'If inherent vice means something that will

certainly happen, it is not a risk but a certainty. It is therefore not something against which insurance can be taken. If, however, it is a cause of damage which may or may not happen because of conditions within the substance itself, then it will be excluded unless the risk is specifically covered.'

Comment

An inevitable loss, a certainty, would not be recoverable under any marine insurance policy, not even one on 'all risks'. Where the policy is an 'all risks' policy, for example, on Institute Cargo Clauses A, the policy will 'otherwise provide' within the terms of s55(2)(c) but in practice this makes little difference since the General Exclusions clause (cl 4) contains almost the same exclusions as are found in s55(2)(c). In any event, 'all risks' does not automatically mean every happening. See *British & Foreign Marine Insurance v Gaunt* [1921] 2 AC 41.

In the Court of Appeal, Waller LJ found the damage to have be 'due to heating caused by conditions within the beans themselves and some other unknown circumstances' (see above). If it can be established that loss is due to both an internal and an external cause, the court may apportion loss as in *Birds Cigarette Manufacturing Co Ltd v Rouse and Others* (1924) 19 Ll LR 301 (KBD), where badly mildewed cigarettes were either soaked by sea water or wet with fresh water that seemed to be as a result of evaporation from within. Bailhache J found the loss for the latter to be caused by inherent vice which was excluded and so not recoverable but, since the sea-water damaged cigarettes were a loss caused by an external cause for which a claim stood, he allowed apportionment of loss for the amount by which the presence of sea water in the cargo had accelerated their destruction by mildew.

Williams v *Atlantic Assurance*
[1933] 1 KB 81 Court of Appeal
(Scrutton, Greer and Slesser LJJ)

• *Prime cost equals invoice price or market value at or near the time of shipment or the time when the goods were first at risk*

Facts

Goods owned and shipped by Valsamis were shipped aboard the vessel Parthian for a voyage from Alexandria to Liverpool but were lost when the ship, which caught fire in Oran harbour, Algeria, in suspicious circumstances, was sunk by the port authorities in order to extinguish the blaze.

The goods were insured under an open policy and were said to be worth £8,000 but there was no agreement on value. One of the issues before the court was what, in an unvalued policy on goods, was the 'prime cost' of those goods.

Held

The Court of Appeal considered the meaning of the words 'prime cost' as found in s16(3) of the Marine Insurance Act 1906 which states:

'In insurance on goods and merchandise, the insurable value is the prime cost of the property insured, plus the expenses of and incidental to shipping and the charges of insurance upon the whole.'

The court ruled that the 'prime cost' of the goods was the invoice or market value at or near the time of shipment or the time when the goods were first at risk. On this measure, the actual value of the goods in this case was established as being no more than £250.

Scrutton LJ:

'Prime cost would ordinarily mean the first cost of manufacturing and would, on the cardinal principle of insurance indemnity, refer to the state of the goods at or about the time of their first being at risk, the time of commencing the venture. The underwriters would not pay on an open policy on goods for the loss of a profit or rise in the market price which was expected to be made or to occur in the future; nor would the assured recover for a loss which had already been made at the time of starting the adventure because the market price had fallen heavily since the assured bought or manufactured the goods.'

A cardinal principle of insurance indemnity is that the assured may not recover for greater loss than he suffers and this was pertinent to the reasoning of their Lordships.

Greer LJ:

'I think the words "prime cost" in that section mean the prime cost to the assured at or about the time of shipment, or at any rate at some time when the prime cost can be reasonably deemed to represent their value to the owner at the date of shipment ...

I am disposed to think that the values as stated in the invoices should, in the absence of evidence justifying a finding of fraud, be taken to be the value at the time when Valsamis acquired the goods towards the end of 1919, or the early part of 1920.'

Slesser LJ:

'The misrepresentation that the goods were worth £8,000, when in fact they were worth, as I find, at any rate not more than £250, is an over-valuation so gross that it is calculated to influence, and must in fact have influenced, the underwriter in taking the risk.'

Comment

The only real concern raised in this case was whether 'prime cost' is equated to invoice price. Scrutton LJ noted that:

'The prime cost of the goods is generally evidenced by the invoice price [which] is by far the most convenient standard'

However, he did give consideration to what the measure of value would be if the assured was not the manufacturer or had bought some time before commencement of the adventure and concluded that the prime cost in such circumstances is the 'market value at the place and commencement of risk'. This alternative method of establishing 'prime cost' is useful where, for example, the original cost or invoice price does not represent the true value of the goods and this issue was dealt with by Kerr J in *Berger and Light Diffusers Pty Ltd v Pollock* [1973] 2 Lloyd's Rep 442.

11 Conflict of Laws and Procedure

*Amin Rasheed Shipping Corp v
Kuwait Insurance Co, The Al Wahab*
[1984] 1 AC 50; [1983] 2 All ER 884
House of Lords (Lords Diplock,
Wilberforce, Roskill, Brandon of
Oakbrook and Brightman)

• *English law to be inferred as proper law
from use of Lloyd's marine insurance
policy – leave to serve writ out of jurisdiction: RSC O.11 rr1(1)(f)(iii) and 4(2)*

Facts

The defendants were a Kuwaiti insurance
company who insured The Al Wahab, a vessel
owned by the plaintiffs, a Liberian-registered
company resident in Dubai. The insurers had
branches in the Gulf, including Dubai, but no
office or representative in England. The policy
was issued in Kuwait but was a renewal of a
policy first issued by an English company
through English brokers and English reinsurance brokers. Although it provided for claims
to be paid in Kuwait, the currency specified
was expressed in sterling. It was in the English
language only and was based on the Lloyd's
SG form as set out in Sch 1 to the Marine
Insurance Act 1906 with adaptation for use as
a time, instead of a voyage, policy and with
attachment without amendment of Institute
War and Strikes Clauses Hulls.

It was alleged that The Al Wahab had been
attempting to smuggle oil and she was seized
by the Saudi Arabian authorities. The plaintiffs claimed under the policy for constructive
total loss of the vessel. The defendants
rejected the claim and the plaintiffs applied for
leave to serve out of the jurisdiction under

RSC O.11 r1(1)(f)(iii)(a) which empowered
the court to give leave to serve proceedings
out of the jurisdiction if the action was
brought to recover damages for breach of a
contract which was 'by its terms, or by implication, governed by English law'.

The actions brought gave rise to a considerable diversity of judicial reasoning.
Bingham J set aside leave to issue a writ out of
the jurisdiction granted by Robert Goff J on
the ground that the proper law of the contract
was Kuwaiti law, not English law. The Court
of Appeal dismissed an appeal by the plaintiffs. The plaintiffs appealed to the House of
Lords.

Held

Appeal dismissed.

Lord Diplock identified two obstacles that
the assured had to overcome in order to pursue
its claim against the insurers in the English
court which he called 'the jurisdiction point'
and the 'discretion point'.

The jurisdiction point

In order to obtain leave to serve a writ on the
insurers out of the jurisdiction the case had to
be brought within RSC O.11 r1(1).

The test relevant to the jurisdiction point
in the instant case under O.11 r1(1)(f)(iii) was
that the policy was 'by implication, governed
by English law'. This required consideration
of the system of law with which the contract
had its closest and most real connection and
was to be determined from the terms of the
contract and the relevant surrounding circumstances. In the present case, little assistance
could be derived from a consideration of the
place where the contract was made or performed but it was clear that the parties had

intended the contract to be governed by English law.

Diplock LJ:

'The applicable English conflict rules are those for determining what is the "proper law" of a contract, ie the law that governs the interpretation and the validity of the contract and the mode of performance and the consequences of breaches of the contract: *Compagnie d'Armement Maritime SA* v *Compagnie Tunisienne de Navigation SA* [1970] 3 All ER 71 at 91; [1971] AC 572 at 603. To identify a particular system of law as being that in accordance with which the parties to it intended a contract to be interpreted, identifies that system of law as the "proper law" of the contract. The reason for this is plain; the purpose of entering into a contract being to create legal rights and obligations between the parties to it, interpretation of the contract involves determining what are the legal rights and obligations to which the words used in it give rise. This is not possible except by reference to the system of law by which the legal consequences that follow from the use of those words is to be ascertained. ...

English conflict rules accord to the parties to a contract a wide liberty to choose the law by which their contract is to be governed. So the first step in the determination of the jurisdiction point is to examine the policy in order to see whether the parties have, by its express terms or by necessary implication from the language used, evinced a common intention as to the system of law by reference to which their mutual rights and obligations under it are to be ascertained. ...'

Lord Diplock agreed with the definition of the 'proper law' of the contract given by Lord Simonds's in *Bonython* v *Commonwealth of Australia* [1951] AC 201, ie 'the system of law by reference to which the contract was made or that with which the transaction has its closest and most real connection' and said:

'If it is apparent from the terms of the contract itself that the parties intended it to be interpreted by reference to a particular system of law, their intention will prevail and the latter question as to the system of law with which, in the view of the court, the transaction to which the contract relates would, but for such intention of the parties, have had the closest and most real connection, does not arise.'

Under English conflict rules the 'proper law' of a contract is the substantive law of the country which the parties have chosen as the law under which their rights are to be determined just as if the matter was being litigated in the courts of that country. It therefore excludes the doctrine of renvoi. Lord Diplock clarified this in the following terms:

'For example, if a contract made in England were expressed to be governed by French law, the English court would apply French substantive law to it notwithstanding that a French court applying its own conflict rules might accept a renvoi to English law as the lex loci contractus if the matter were litigated before it. Conversely, assuming that under English conflict rules English law is the proper law of the contract, the fact that the courts of a country which under English conflict rules would be regarded as having jurisdiction over a dispute arising under the contract (in casu Kuwait) would under its own conflict rules have recourse to English law as determinative of the rights and obligations of the parties, would not make the proper law of the contract any the less English law because it was the law that a Kuwaiti court also would apply.'

In the present cases all the relevant surrounding circumstances pointed to English law as the proper law of the contract. The crucial surrounding circumstance was that, at the time the policy was entered into, Kuwaiti law had no indigenous law of marine insurance. A code of marine insurance law with significant differences to the English law of marine insurance was later adopted but without retrospective effect so did not apply to the present policy taken out before that law was introduced. Whilst the courts in Kuwait would have no difficulty in applying English law as the 'proper law' of the contract, they would not be able to interpret various clauses in the policy without recourse to the Marine Insurance Act 1906 and to judicial interpretation of its provisions. Accordingly, the court had jurisdiction to grant leave for the writ to be served out of the jurisdiction.

Diplock LJ:

'My Lords, contracts are incapable of existing in a legal vacuum. They are mere pieces of paper devoid of all legal effect unless they were made by reference to some system of private law which defines the obligations assumed by the parties to the contract by their use of particular forms of words and prescribes the remedies enforceable in a court of justice for failure to perform any of those obligations; and this must be so however widespread geographically the use of a contract employing a particular form of words to express the obligations assumed by the parties may be. To speak of English law and practice providing a useful source of persuasive authority on the construction of the policy wherever it may be used begs the whole question: why is recourse to English law needed at all? The necessity to do so is common ground between the experts on Kuwaiti law on either side; it is because in the absence of an indigenous law of marine insurance in Kuwait English law was the only system of private law by reference to which it was possible for a Kuwaiti court to give a sensible and precise meaning to the language that the parties had chosen to use in the policy. As the authorities that I have cited earlier show, under English conflict rules, which are those your Lordships must apply in determining the jurisdiction point, that makes English law the proper law of the contract.'

The discretion point

The assured must satisfy the requirements of O.11 r4(2) which provides that no leave shall be granted unless it sufficiently appears to the court that 'the case is a proper one for service out of the jurisdiction under this Order'.

English jurisdiction was being sought to be forced on an unwilling defendant. English courts should remember whenever asked to give leave to grant service that the jurisdiction conferred on the court by RSC O.11 r.1(1)(f)(iii) was an 'exorbitant jurisdiction'. English courts would not recognise such a power in a foreign court unless it had a treaty which required recognition, therefore:

'Comity thus dictates that the judicial discretion to grant leave under this paragraph of O.11 r1(1) should be exercised with circumspection in cases where there exists an alternative forum, viz the courts of the foreign country where the proposed defendant does carry on business, and whose jurisdiction would be recognised under English conflict rules. Such a forum in the instant case was afforded by the courts of Kuwait.'

Kuwait was also a convenient forum because it was competent to decide the factual question of whether there had been a constructive total loss. Diplock LJ:

'Bingham J was of opinion that the factual question could be determined as well in Kuwait as in England, possibly better, and with no clear overall balance of convenience. His own view that the proper exercise of his discretion would be to refuse leave to serve the writ out of the jurisdiction, even if the proper law of the policy were English law, was influenced largely by the fact that the jurisdiction sought to be invoked by the assured is an exorbitant jurisdiction, and that he had "been given no reason to doubt that a Kuwaiti judge would set himself thoroughly and justly to determine the truth in this case". To this I myself would add that a Kuwaiti judge would be likely to have greater familiarity even than the Commercial Court in England with the sort of thing that goes on in purely local trading in the Arabian Gulf, to which the vessel was by express warranty confined.'

In such circumstances the court would normally exercise its discretion under O.11 r4(2) by refusing to grant a plaintiff leave to serve the proceedings out of the jurisdiction unless he satisfied the court that: (a) justice could not be obtained if proceedings were taken in the alternative legal system; or (b) could only be obtained with excessive cost, delay or inconvenience. The plaintiffs had failed to satisfy the judge that there were sufficient grounds to compel the defendants to submit to the jurisdiction of the English courts.

Comment
See also *Compagnie d'Armement Maritime SA* v *Compagnie Tunisienne de Navigation SA* [1971] AC 572 (below) and *Brittania Steamship Insurance Association* v *Ausonia Assicurazioni* [1984] 2 Lloyd's Rep 98 (CA).

Benarty, The [1985] QB 325 Court of Appeal (Ackner, Dunn and Dillon LJJ)

• *Hague-Visby Rules art III r8 cannot be ousted by a choice of jurisdiction that implies a choice of law*

Facts
The appellants were Indonesian shipowners, operating a service between Europe and Indonesia and charterers of the vessel in question. The cargo owners were the respondents, being both shippers and consignees of the goods and the bills of lading. The cargo was shipped on board at various European ports, including London, and damaged in transit. Section 1(2) of the Carriage of Goods by Sea Act 1971 states that the Hague-Visby Rules shall have the force of law and the parties therefore have no choice regarding their application. In support of this art III r8 renders void any clause covenant or agreement to that end. The charterers issued to the shippers, bills of lading stating that the Hague Rules should apply, that the proper law of the contract was Indonesian and, the Indonesian courts had jurisdiction over disputes. Indonesian law, in particular art 474 of the Indonesian Commercial Code, limited the carrier's liability to a level below that prescribed by the Rules.

The question which fell to be determined was whether the choice of law jurisdiction would be upheld or invalidated by reason of art III r8. The carrier claimed that it had the right to pick such a limiting statute despite art III r8 since art VIII preserved the right to rely on any statute. Sheen J had previously held that this meant any English statute, it did not therefore extend to a provision of the Indonesian Commercial Code.

Held
A choice of jurisdiction which implies a choice of law may offend art III r8 if the reason for that choice is to avoid the Hague-Visby Rules altogether. In this case, the parties had given affidavit evidence to the effect hat they were not seeking to utilise any point of Indonesian law that would be more favourable to them than the Rules. They were, however, seeking to rely on the provision of the Indonesian Code which provided them with a tonnage limitation. This, they were permitted to do. Article III r8 only prevented limitation upon the duties and obligations in the Rules. There was not, however, any tonnage limitation in the Rules. It fell outside the Rules and, the right to rely on it was preserved by art VIII which applied not only to English statutes. Therefore, the jurisdiction clause was not ex facie void and ineffective since it was not a provision by which the carrier had attempted to avoid the rules altogether nor, any individual provision. In fact, the reverse was true. The carrier was attempting to rely on a limiting statute, the subject matter of which was not covered by the Rules at all and therefore it was a perfectly valid choice.

Comment
In *The Morviken* [1983] 1 Lloyd's Rep 1 the House of Lords held that the Hague-Visby Rules were to be treated as if they were part of directly enacted statute law and there is no scope for the parties to oust the operation of the Rules. The Carriage of Goods by Sea Act 1971 which brings the Rules into English law is an 'overriding statute'.

Cathiship SA v Allanasons Ltd, The Catherine Helen [1998] 3 All ER 714; [1998] 2 Lloyd's Rep 511 Queen's Bench Division (Commercial Court) (Mr Geoffrey Brice QC, sitting as a Deputy High Court Judge)

• *Claim under an amended Centrocon arbitration clause. Extension of time under s12 Arbitration Act 1996*

Facts

In October 1995 The Catherine Helen was voyage chartered by the plaintiff shipowners to the defendant charterers on an amended Gencon form for the carriage of bagged rice. Shipment of the rice was in December 1995 at Bombay, India, and was acknowledged by a bill of lading on the Congenbill form. The cargo was discharged at Dakar, Senegal, between 25 March and 13 April 1996.

The plaintiffs' sought to claim against the charterers for an indemnity in respect of cargo claims on the grounds that there is an implied indemnity when the master is required by the charterers to sign or permit to be signed bills of lading which impose on the owners greater liability than that which they have assumed under the charterparty. The plaintiffs contended that box 15 of the bill of lading contained terms more onerous than cls 5(b) and 9 of the charterparty. Clause 9 required the master or agents to sign bills of lading at such rate of freight as presented without prejudice to the charterparty.

Clause 23 of the charterparty contained an amended Centrocon arbitration clause (amended from a period of three months to a period of one year), the relevant part of which read: 'Any claim must be made in writing and claimants' arbitrator appointed within one year of final discharging and where this provision is not complied with the claim shall be deemed waived and absolutely barred.'

In May 1996 the plaintiffs appointed an arbitrator 'in respect of all and any disputes

under the charterparty' and in June 1996 they made a claim against the charterers for demurrage and additional berthing and shifting expenses at Dakar. The parties exchanged submissions as to these claims and the arbitrators were asked to adjudicate upon them on documents alone. (*Note:* this claim did not incorporate a claim for an indemnity since these claims are a separate cause of action and the owners later maintained that the indemnity claim was still reserved.)

Shortly before and shortly after completion of discharge of the cargo at Dakar in April 1996, the cargo owners' P & I Club had given letters of guarantee in respect of cargo claims. The plaintiffs first knew of these claims (which were later reduced) in October 1996 which is when they informed the arbitrators of a possible cargo claim and that an indemnity might be sought. No claim was made arising from the security given by the owners' insurers and the arbitrators took the view that their jurisdiction was restricted to claims in existence. They accordingly proceeded to an award on the monetary claims.

In this action the plaintiffs applied to the court by originating summons for a declaration that, as required by cl 23 of their amended Gencon form of charterparty,

1. they made a claim in writing against the defendant charterers for an indemnity in respect of the plaintiffs' liability to the owners (or insurers) of the cargo of rice; and

2. that they had appointed an arbitrator within a period of one year of final discharge of cargo so that their claim was not time barred.

They alternatively applied under s12 of the Arbitration Act 1996 for an extension of time for commencing arbitration proceedings for such an indemnity against the charterers. (The provision in the now repealed s27 of the Arbitration Act 1950 which was more liberal and the case illustrates that the operation of the Centrocon clause requires careful analysis in the light of the provisions of s12.)

Held

The plaintiffs' application failed. Their claim for an implied indemnity was not made as required by their amended arbitration clause and they had failed to appoint an arbitrator in time. The extension of time was refused.

There was no 'claim' made by the plaintiffs in respect of the implied indemnity claim. Intimating a possible claim in the future is wholly different to making a claim under the Centrocon arbitration clause.

Geoffrey Brice QC commented:

'The concept of making a claim is quite simple. The claimant simply notifies in writing the party against whom he claims "I claim [the appropriate relief] from you" (or words to the same effect). Thus if the claimant claims demurrage he states that fact. In my view a statement "I may at some time in the future claim [eg demurrage]" is not a claim but merely an intimation of a possible claim in the future. The purpose of giving notice of a claim in – the case of an arbitration clause similar to the Centrocon clause was explained by Lord Wright in *A/S Rendal* v *Arcos Limited, The Rendal* (1937) 58 Ll LR 287 at p292 where he dealt with the arbitration clause applicable to that case as follows –

"That clause requires 'notice of claim'. That in my opinion does not mean a precisely formulated claim with full details, but it must be such a notice as will enable the party to whom it is given to take steps to meet the claim by preparing and obtaining appropriate evidence for that purpose."

Although that case was concerned with "notice of claim", I believe the passage cited applies equally to the making of a claim under the Centrocon clause. One therefore has to consider the nature of the claim in writing addressed on behalf of the owners to the charterers in the present case so far as a claim for an indemnity is concerned and whether it met the requirements of Lord Wright set out above. Mr Nolan referred me to the observations of Lord Denning MR in *Nea Agrex SA* v *Baltic Shipping Co Ltd*

[1976] 2 Lloyd's Rep 47, 49, 52 where he held –

"In a commercial dispute, a letter requesting arbitration should not be construed too strictly. The writer should not be impaled on a time bar because he writes in polite and courteous terms, or because he needs open the possibility of settlement by agreemen ... When such a letter follows upon a genuine claim promptly made, it should be interpreted as a request for arbitration ..."

On the facts of that case there had been a clear claim (page 49) followed by a request to nominate an arbitrator if settlement could not be reached. What occurred there seems to contrast with what occurred in the present case: in any event one is concerned with the particular facts of each case and the particular arbitration clause.'

On the facts, the plaintiffs had merely indicated that a claim might be made, not made a claim. To comply with the arbitration clause the shipowner has to make it clear, once the amount of the liability is known, that he is claiming to be indemnified under the charterparty in respect of claims successfully made against him by cargo owners. In respect of present disputes there was no difficulty with making such a claim:

'In the case of a subsisting claim for a monetary sum (whether in debt or damages) there should be no difficulty in one party making a clear and unequivocal claim in writing even if the precise sums are not known or ascertainable as at the date of the making of the claim. No particular form of words is required for making such a claim provided it is clear that a claim is being made ...'

Geoffrey Brice QC was of the opinion that the same applies to contingent disputes. Although the cargo owners' claim was not progressed during the 12-month limitation period, the plaintiffs' claim could be made even though the formal cause of action might not be enforceable until after the expiry of the limitation period. They knew that there was a claim against which they might have to claim an indemnity under the charterparty against the charterers and had ample time to put in that claim:

> '... the ship owners knew that a claim had been made against them by the cargo owners because they had been required to put up security for a cargo claim 1 day before cargo discharge had been completed (although that security was replaced a few days later by other security). Although the claim appears not to have been formulated in precise terms no party ordinarily puts up security unless there is a claim, however imprecise, against him. Thus the ship owners were or ought to have been aware that they might at some time have to claim an indemnity under the charterparty against the charterers. Given the 12 months period allowed by clause 23 the ship owners had ample time to consider whether they could comply with the terms of clause 23 during the contractual limitation period.'

Geoffrey Brice QC commented on the purposes of the Centrocon clause:

> 'It is useful when interpreting the Centrocon clause to have regard to what has been said to be its purposes. In *Sparta Navigation Co* v *Transocean America Inc, The Stephanos* [1989] 1 Lloyd's Rep 506 at p509 Saville J (as he then was) explained the purposes underlying the Centrocon clause as follows –
>
>> "... it is designed not only to require all disputes arising under the contract to be referred to arbitration, but also to bar all claims arising under the contract save claims arising before the end of the stipulated period, in respect of which the claimant has made a written claim and appointed his arbitrator. On this construction, whether or not the claimant has a valid or sustainable claim (ie a cause of action) during the stipulated period and whether or not he knew or ought to have known during that period that he had or might have a claim of any nature are quite immaterial considerations. The commercial sense of such a construction is to my mind obvious – at the end of the stipulated

period the parties will know where they stand in the sense of knowing what claims (if any) are outstanding against each other; and the difficulties and uncertainties often inherent in trying to deal with claims only long after the event would be largely, if not wholly, averted".'

The plaintiffs had not appointed an arbitrator in respect of the indemnity claim as required under the charterparty clause. The appointment defined his jurisdiction at the same time as creating it and could not be taken as giving him jurisdiction over something which did not at that time exist. When he was appointed there was no dispute relating to the indemnity. Although it is open to the parties to increase consensually the jurisdiction of an arbitrator or arbitral tribunal, that did not occur here.

Since the arbitrator was not appointed as required under the charterparty clause it was necessary to look at s12(3) and (4) of the Arbitration Act 1996 which provides:

> '(3) The court shall make an order only if satisfied –
> (a) that the circumstances are such as were outside the reasonable contemplation of the parties when they agreed the provision in question, and that it would be just to extend the time, or
> (b) that the conduct of one party makes it unjust to hold the other party to the strict terms of the provision in question.
> (4) The court may extend the time for such period and on such terms as it thinks fit, and may do so whether or not the time previously fixed (by agreement or by a previous order) has expired.'

The court must look at all the relevant circumstances and consider what the parties could have reasonably contemplated at the time of making the arbitration agreement. A mistake as to making a claim and appointing an arbitrator could have been contemplated by the parties when concluding the charterparty. The consequences of the fact that the owners turned out to be wrong in their interpretation of the arbitration clause and failed to comply with the time limit, therefore, was not something outside the reasonable contemplation of the parties under s12(3)(a) of the 1996 Act.

Geoffrey Brice QC viewed the Centrocon arbitration clause to be well established and quite straightforward in its operation and consequences and said:

'... in a common commercial transaction such as a Gencon charterparty and operations under or in respect of it the parties would reasonably have in contemplation the type of events which experience has demonstrated are prone if not certain to occur. One may be cargo claims against owners where owners wish to be indemnified under the ordinary principles of English law by the charterers. In my judgment this must be taken to the within the reasonable contemplation of owners and charterers. Similarly their reasonable contemplation will include the making of a claim and the appointment of an arbitrator under the Centrocon arbitration clause and the consequences which must follow if the time limit imposed by clause 23 is not observed.'

The question whether it would be just to extend time did not arise. Geoffrey Brice QC referred to the fact that s12 is markedly more restrictive than its predecessor s27 of the 1950 Act and, together with s9 of the 1996 Act, the discretion of the courts when dealing with arbitration agreements is considerably reduced. He pointed out that:

'... the whole climate of extending time in arbitral proceedings has changed strikingly.'

He was of the opinion that as a matter of ordinary English, s12 limits the discretion of the courts so that it is not open to the court to extend time just because the court concludes that it would be just to do so:

'... one must conclude that such extensions nowadays will probably be very much the exception rather than the rule. Further, it must be borne in mind that s12 applies to all forms of arbitration and not simply to maritime arbitration and certainly not just to the Centrocon arbitration clause.'

In any case, there was nothing in the conduct of the charterers which would make it unjust to hold the owners to the strict terms of the arbitration clause.

Comment

On the issue of whether the plaintiffs could be said to have made a claim, Geoffrey Brice QC noted that it was not for the court to seek to put matters right by finding some extension of the parties intentions by reference to their correspondence. He said:

'I would comment generally that this is not a case where the owners were inhibited in their choice of language by some lack of comprehension of the English language: all the relevant letters written on their behalf in the correspondence were written by experienced English solicitors. Although perhaps one has a natural instinct to try to put matters right by seeing if it is possible to stretch the language used, the court is concerned in a case such as this to interpret the actual words used and any unjustifiable extension of the meaning of plain words in favour of the owners would work an injustice to the charterers.'

In *Sparta Navigation Co* v *Transocean America Inc, The Stephanos* [1989] 1 Lloyd's Rep 506 the voyage charterparty incorporated a Centrocon arbitration clause but with the normal three-month limitation period. Discharge was completed in May 1986 and at the beginning of July the cargo receivers asserted (or re-asserted) cargo damage. They commenced legal proceedings against the shipowners in March 1987 and in the April the shipowners' P and I insurers caused a writ to be issued by the shipowners and a notice to be served (and an arbitrator appointed) claiming an indemnity against the charterers. This was about 11 months after completion of discharge and about eight months outside the three-month time limit and the charterers asserted that the claim was by then time-barred. The shipowners in response asserted that the claim was not time-barred, contending that the Centrocon arbitration clause did not bar a claim which only arose out of the stipulated limitation period. They alternatively claimed relief under s27 of the Arbitration Act 1950. Saville J rejected their claim in respect of their being no time bar and held that the claim was time-barred, but he did grant the s27 relief, ie an extension of time. Following the decision in *The Catherine Helen* it is clear that such relief is no longer available under the more rigorous s12 of the Arbitration Act 1996.

4 *Compagnie d'Armement Maritime SA* v *Compagnie Tunisienne de Navigation SA* [1971] AC 572 House of Lords (Viscount Dilhorne, Lords Reid, Morris of Borth-y-Gest, Wilberforce and Diplock)

* *Tests for determining the proper law of a contract*

Facts
In 1967 the plaintiffs, a Tunisian company, and French shipowners negotiated a contract through brokers in Paris for the carriage of crude oil from one Tunisian port to another. The main issue to be decided was that of what law applied to the contract.

In the judgments of the House of Lords and below, the following factors were considered as being relevant:

1. The contract was concluded in Paris.
2. The standard form for a voyage charter was in the English form.
3. Clause 13 thereof provided that 'this contract shall be governed by the laws of the flag of the vessel carrying the goods'.
4. Clause 18 of the printed form provided that disputes were to be settled by arbitrators in London.
5. An additional typed cl 28 provided that 'shipments to be effected in Tonnage owned, controlled or chartered' by the French shipowners of 16,000/25,000 tons at owners' option.
6. Payment was to be made by French francs in Paris.

Held
The proper law of the contract was French law. The general rule is that where there is no express choice, the proper law of the contract is that of the place or system with which it is most closely associated.

Comment
In this case, the House of Lords clearly disassociated itself from the previously held view that a choice of location for the carrying out of an arbitration (which would be carried out under the procedural or curial law of that place) is conclusive of the proper law of the contract unless it provides expressly to the contrary. Here the contacts with French law (not France) clearly suggested that French law was the proper law of the contract.

The House of Lords made clear the difference between curial law and proper law and stated that the curial law is only one factor in determining the proper law of the contract.

5 *Dubai Electricity* v *Islamic Republic of Iran Shipping Lines, The Iran Vojdan* [1984] 2 Lloyd's Rep 380 High Court (Bingham J)

* *Choice of law clause invalid where 'floating proper law' envisaged*

Facts
The plaintiffs were owners and shippers of a number of steel drums, shipped on the defendants' vessel, The Iran Vojdan, for carriage from Hamburg, Germany, to Dubai in 1980. The bill of lading provided that all disputes were to be governed either by Iranian law in which case the courts of Teheran were to have exclusive jurisdiction, or by German law, in which case the courts of Hamburg were to have exclusive jurisdiction, or English law, in which case the English courts had exclusive jurisdiction.

The choice between these three was to be with the carrier in the event of proceedings being started other than in one of these three, and the Hague Rules of that particular country would apply.

The steel drums were found to be damaged when they were discharged at Dubai and in 1983 the plaintiffs issued a writ against the carriers. The defendants applied for a stay of proceedings on the ground that the Hamburg courts had exclusive jurisdiction and they said the proper law was Iranian. The plaintiffs said the proper law was German.

Held

The stay would not be granted.

The choice of law/jurisdiction clause in the bill of lading was invalid because it envisaged that the proper law should change and would depend directly on the court having jurisdiction. It was impossible to separate the clause and treat the jurisdiction element independently of the choice of law. It would be artificial to give effect to the jurisdiction element whilst ignoring the choice of law when the two are intimately connected with each other. Therefore, since the clause envisaged 'a floating proper law' as a result the whole clause must fail. This was to be treated as a case in which there is no exclusive jurisdiction clause and therefore, the question of a stay was to be considered on normal principles.

The factors seemed evenly balanced but the defendants had not shown that the matter could be dealt with in another forum at substantially less cost and inconvenience than England. It was appropriate for the plaintiffs to bring an action in England because they administered their European business from England.

The fact that the vessel flew an Iranian flag was more influential than it normally is but the system of law with which the contract had its closest and most real connection was German law.

If the defendants had shown another more suitable forum, it would then have been necessary to consider whether to stay the English action and this would require consideration of whether the plaintiffs would be deprived of some legitimate juridical or personal advantage if they were compelled to litigate in that forum. Bingham J was not favourably disposed to the argument that under English law the plaintiffs would have had a substantial advantage in the form of a package limitation provision which they would not have had in Hamburg.

If the jurisdiction clause had not failed and instead been held to be valid, then the stay would have been given because the defendants would have had a prima facie right to a stay and the plaintiffs would not have succeeded in defeating that right by their arguments for proceedings in England.

Forum Craftsman, The [1985] 1 Lloyd's Rep 291 Court of Appeal (Ackner and Browne-Wilkinson LJJ, Sir John Megaw)

• *The place a tort occurred may be displaced as the natural forum*

Facts

The defendants, a Panamanian incorporated company managed by a ship-managing company based in Greece, were owners of The Forum Craftsman which flew a Greek flag. The vessel was chartered to the tortfeasors who were also Greek. The tort however occurred in Yokohama, Japan, when the goods were damaged shortly after being loaded fob on board the vessel for shipment to buyers in Angola. The plaintiff buyers alleged that the damage was caused through the negligence of the shipowners, their servants or agents. The charterparty contained a clause requiring all disputes to be referred to arbitration in London. The bill of lading gave exclusive jurisdiction to the Tokyo District Court and stated that Japanese law should govern any such disputes.

The plaintiffs issued a writ in London and the defendants applied for a stay on the basis that the parties had agreed to the jurisdiction of the Japanese courts and that Japan was the convenient and proper forum to determine the dispute.

This was an appeal from the decision of Sheen J who was of the view that neither Japan nor England was the natural forum because the most substantial and real connection had been in Greece. The shipowners contended that importance should have been attached to the place where the tort occurred and that there are many authorities to suggest that the courts of the country where the substance of the tort is committed is the natural and proper forum.

Held

The Court refused to grant the stay.

It was not the shippers who sought to rely on the exclusive jurisdiction clause in the bill of lading but the shipowners who were not party to the document. Their burden of proof therefore was to establish that under the proper law which governs that bill of lading, they had the right to rely on the jurisdiction clause. Under Japanese law, if an action in tort is brought by the buyers, the shipowners cannot rely on the bill of lading to which they are not parties. Japanese law was the proper law. The shipowners owners therefore had not discharged their burden of proof.

In order to succeed in their claim of forum non conveniens, the shipowners had to satisfy the two limbs of the test set down by Lord Diplock in *MacShannon* v *Rockware Glass* [1978] AC 795:

'(a) the defendant must satisfy the court that there is another forum to whose jurisdiction he is amenable in which justice can be done at substantially less cost and inconvenience between the parties;
(b) the stay must not deprive the plaintiff of some legitimate personal or juridical advantage which would be available to him if he invoked the jurisdiction of the English court.'

The Court of Appeal accepted that the jurisdiction in which the tort is committed is prima facie the natural forum, but that rule is capable of being displaced where the damage occurred on a vessel which, although still at her moorings, was about to leave Japanese territorial waters for another country and would have left but for the accident.

The defendants had failed to show that justice could be done in Tokyo at substantially less cost and inconvenience than London and it was also relevant to have regard to the fact that expense had already been incurred in London in relation to the proceedings.

7 *Halki Shipping Corporation* v *Sopex Oils Ltd, The Halki* [1998] 2 All ER 23 Court of Appeal (Hirst, Henry and Swinton Thomas LJJ)

• *RSC O.14 where claim arises under a contract which contains an arbitration clause*

Facts

The plaintiff shipowners, Halki Shipping Corporation, chartered their motor tanker, 'Halki', to the defendants, Sopex Oils, under a tanker voyage charterparty for the carriage of palm oil and coconut oil from various ports in the Far East to various ports in Europe.

The plaintiffs alleged that the defendants had failed to load and discharge the vessel within the lay time provided by the charterparty and claimed liquidated damages for demurrage. The defendants did not admit liability and relied on an arbitration clause in the charterparty which provided:

'... Any dispute arising from or in connection with this charterparty shall be referred to arbitration in London. ...'

The plaintiffs issued a specially endorsed writ claiming demurrage on the grounds that the dispute did not come within the arbitration clause because the defendants did not have a defence to the claim that the amount of demurrage was due: RSC O.14. The defendants countered by seeking an order staying the action under s9 of the Arbitration Act 1996. Clarke J granted the stay of action. The arbitration clause must be looked at in its context.

There was a dispute relating to demurrage and it did not make commercial sense to hold that arbitration should only apply where there was an arguable defence.

The plaintiffs appealed. Two questions were before the court:

1. did the action brought by the plaintiffs come within the meaning of 'dispute' to be referred to arbitration; and
2. if the dispute did come within the arbitration clause, was the agreement null and void, inoperative or incapable of being performed?

Held (Hirst LJ dissenting)
Appeal dismissed.

Summary judgment under O.14 was available if there was no genuine dispute. In the present case there was a dispute even if there was no arguable defence. The defendants had refused to pay a sum which was claimed or had denied that it was owing and this was a dispute between the parties, to be referred to arbitration under the charterparty.

Under s9(4) of the Arbitration Act 1996 the court shall grant a stay 'unless satisfied that the arbitration agreement is null and void, inoperative, or incapable of being performed.' The arbitration agreement in question was not null and void and it was capable of being performed. The stay of proceedings would, therefore be upheld.

The court looked at the history of the Arbitration Act 1996. Section 9(4) of 1996 Act replaced s1(1) of the 1975 Act which had provided:

'... and the court unless satisfied that the arbitration agreement is null and void, inoperative or incapable of being performed or that there is not in fact any dispute between the parties with regard to the matter agreed to be referred [to arbitration], shall make an order staying the proceedings.'

The change brought about in the law by the 1996 Act means that if the court is satisfied that there is a dispute, which it was in this case, then it must grant a stay unless the arbi-

tration agreement was found to be null and void, etc. which it was not.

The words 'or that there is not in fact any dispute between the parties' found in the 1975 Act and its predecessors had been the source of the court's jurisdiction to grant summary judgment. Their omission in the 1996 Act was intended to exclude the O.14 jurisdiction. The cases heard under the 1975 Act and relied on by the plaintiff dealt with particular interpretations of s1 of the 1975 Act. Authorities such as *Nova (Jersey) Knit Ltd* v *Kammgarn Spinnerei GmbH* [1977] 1 WLR 713; [1977] 1 Lloyd's Rep 463 were founded on those interpretations. Clarke J had been right to follow the authority of *Ellerine Bros Pty Ltd* v *Klinger* [1982] 1 WLR 1375 and *Hayter* v *Nelson* [1990] 2 Lloyd's Rep 265. Hirst LJ dissented from this view and preferred the view that *Nova (Jersey) Knit* v *Kammgarn Spinnerei GmbH* was still binding authority to the effect that 'dispute' did not include a defence which had no real substance, ie was not 'a genuine or real dispute'. He was also of the opinion that the enactment of s9 without the 1975 qualification had not effected an abolition of the existing O.14 practice. He thought its effect was to exclude the O.14 jurisdiction if there was a dispute.

Swinton Thomas LJ:

'The case for the appellants, put very shortly, is that before there can be a dispute capable of being referred to the Arbitrator there must be an arguable case for disputing the claim, and if the defence put forward is unsustainable then there is no dispute or put another way, no "real" or "genuine" dispute. It is said that the plaintiff's claim is indisputable. It is of importance, to my mind, that the clause in the agreement makes no reference to a real or genuine dispute, or any reference to whether or not the claim is indisputable, but refers only to "any dispute". The respondents submit that if the defendants to a claim refuse to pay then there is in any ordinary language a dispute and that word includes any claim which is not admitted. They stress, rightly in my view, that the parties themselves have agreed that matters in issue between should be referred to arbitration as opposed to being adjudicated upon by the courts. ...

In my judgment if a party has refused to pay a sum which is claimed or has denied that it is owing then in the ordinary use of the English language there is a dispute between the parties. ... [But] the Court no longer has to consider whether there is in fact any dispute between the parties but only where there is a dispute with the arbitration clause of the agreement, and the cases which turn on that distinction are now irrelevant.'

Henry LJ:

'If I had to decide this matter untroubled by previous authority construing both the statutory framework governing international arbitrations prior to and since the 1996 Arbitration Act and/or the construction of individual arbitration agreements, I would unhesitatingly conclude that there was a dispute as to the entirety of the sum claimed, and that the proceedings should be stayed and referred to arbitration.

My reasoning would be that, by their arbitration clause referring all disputes to arbitration, the parties were, without qualification, agreeing on a form of dispute resolution alternative to that provided by the courts. And, as arbitration procedures make their own provision for the possibility of obtaining prompt interim awards for the minimum sum plainly due, I would not be immediately impressed by a submission that I should construe "dispute" with so artificial a narrowness as to be restricted to such disputes (as to liability or quantum) as are found by the Court to merit the grant of leave to defend – after a contested hearing for summary judgment under O.14, which often takes hours and sometimes takes days ....

To put it another way, when the parties have chosen arbitration for their dispute resolution, I would not (if unconstrained by statute or authority) interpret their choice as being restricted to referring only those disputes that cannot be resolved by the courts' summary judgment procedures. ...

What the words "there is not in fact any dispute" meant in the 1930 amendment is now history, and no longer a relevant question to be asked. In my judgment Mr Justice Clarke was right to follow the line of authority from *The M Eregli* [1981] 3 All ER 344 to *Ellerine Bros (Pty) Limited* v *Klinger* [1982] 1 WLR 1375 which focused on the meaning of dispute in the arbitration agreement.'

§ Hiscox v *Outhwaite* [1992] 1 AC 562 House of Lords (Lord Mackay of Clashfern LC, Lords Keith of Kinkel, Brandon of Oakbrook, Ackner and Oliver of Aylmerton)

• *An arbitration award is made in the place of signature*

Facts
An arbitration clause in a contract for the sale provided for disputes to go to arbitration in London and that English law was the applicable law. When a dispute went to arbitration, the arbitration proceedings were held in stages and the award was finally signed in Paris. A question arose as to whether the award could be appealed in the English courts.

Held
An arbitration award is perfected in the place where it is signed, irrespective of where the arbitration took place. As the award was signed in a country that was a party to the New York Arbitration Convention it was enforceable under the Arbitration Act 19975. The English courts could therefore hear the appeal.

Comment
This case has now been superseded by the Arbitration Act 1996 which provides that the seat of the award is what governs where the award is made. If the seat is in a country that is party to the New York Arbitration Convention the award may be enforced or appealed in the English courts.

Mauritius Oil Refineries v *Stolt Neilson* [1997] 1 Lloyd's Rep 273 Queen's Bench Division (Rix J)

• *A significant factor in determining the presumed intention of the parties was that they had chosen English law and English arbitration*

Facts

The claimants chartered the respondents' vessel under a charterparty that expressly provided for London arbitration and English law. However, it also contained a USA Clause Paramount which stated the bill of lading and/or the contract of affreightment to be subject to the USA Carriage of Goods by Sea Act 1936 and to have effect subject to the effect of that Act, which was deemed incorporated. The Act reproduces art III r6 of the Hague Rules but s3(6) of the Act provides that:

> 'In any event the carrier and the ship shall be discharged from all liability in respect of loss or damage unless suit is brought within one year after delivery of the goods or the date when the goods should have been delivered.'

A dispute arose as to demurrage which became subject to much correspondence and delay. The claimants eventually sought to have the dispute decided in arbitration. The respondents claimed that the claimants were time-barred under the one-year time limit contained in s3(6) on the grounds that, by the incorporation of art III r6, 'suit' was to be construed according to English law and be taken as including an arbitration. The claimants argued that by virtue of the USA Clause Paramount in the bill of lading, the interpretation to be taken was that of American law which does not bring arbitration within the meaning of 'suit', and that their claim therefore was not time barred.

Held

The claimants' application was dismissed.

Where a foreign statute, which in turn incorporates an international convention such as the Hague Rules, is incorporated into an English law contract, the English law will have its own body of case law interpreting that international convention. There is therefore, less need for an English court to have regard to the case law interpreting the foreign statute to which the contract refers.

The parties were not deemed to have to have adopted the American law construction of the Hague Rules in preference to the English construction only by virtue of having incorporated the version of them given with the USA Carriage of Goods by Sea Act 1936. A more significant factor in determining the presumed intention of the parties was that they had chosen English law and English arbitration. The parties should be deemed as having chosen to incorporate into the contract the English law interpretation of the Hague Rules.

Rix J also considered whether the claimants would suffer undue hardship by refusal of extension of time or whether the respondents would suffer serious prejudice. He opined that it was 'a claim of uncertain merit but no great size, where the claimants have been seriously at fault' and was of the opinion that the claimants would not suffer undue hardship by the refusal to extend time for appointment of their arbitrator. The respondents, on the other hand, had not contributed to the delay in the bringing of the claim which amounted to a delay in total of three years since time expired in respect of the claim, and would now be seriously prejudiced in seeking to meet the burden of proof with inadequate documentation.

Rix J:

> 'If an English law charterparty incorporates an USA Clause Paramount, does a question of construction under the Hague Rules as so incorporated fall to be decided according to English law as the proper law or United States law as the law to which English law will refer?
>
> In my judgment it may often be of the utmost relevance to the construction of an

English law contract to consider what the position is under some foreign law to which the contract makes reference. ...

Where, however, a foreign statute is incorporated as a source of an international convention such as the Hague Rules, it is perhaps less likely that an English court would need to be informed of the foreign law decisions upon that foreign statute: for English law would have numerous decisions of its own upon identical wording. Even so, the wording of a foreign statute might incorporate such Rules in slightly different terms, and then foreign law decisions of the relevant jurisdiction may again be relevant to expound the significance of such changes. And foreign law decisions on the rules will in general be relevant on a point on which there is no English decision: see *The River Gurara* [1996] 2 Lloyd's Rep 53 ...

[It was submitted] that the parties' choice of US COGSA, rather than any other version of the Rules, is important and that proper effect can only be given to that choice by adopting US law decisions on the wording of the Act even in preference to English decisions on the Rules and the English Carriage of Goods by Sea Act. That, however, is to give too much emphasis to the choice of clause paramount. The choice may reflect differences in the underlying wording of the Rules. It may reflect the requirements of the law in force at the port of shipment (although not in the present case). In any event, where international legislation of this kind is concerned, it is hard to think that, in the absence of different substantive provisions, there is intended to be any critical significance to the particular version of the Rules which have been incorporated.

In the present case the unusual feature is that English and US law have thrown up conflicting decisions on the meaning of art III r6. Whatever might have been the position if the US decision had stood alone, it can hardly be said, in the light of The Merak, that the parties, in choosing English law and the incorporation of US COGSA, must have intended to give precedence to the US decision in *Son* v *De Fosse*. But the

matter can be put more positively than that. The parties have deliberately chosen not only English law, but also London arbitration. Therefore, under the parties' contract, any dispute must be arbitrated in London, and this is an agreement which the parties must be viewed as knowing would be mandatorily enforced under the terms of the New York Convention. If one asks, therefore, whether the parties must have intended that failure to arbitrate within the year was a bar within section 3(6) or not, it seems to me that there can be only one possible answer: such a failure was intended to bar the claim, and the approach of *The Merak* [1964] 2 Lloyd's Rep 527 was to prevail. Otherwise the parties' agreement to arbitrate would have been ill-sorted with the parties' agreement upon a one year time bar.

At the beginning of this judgment I asked whether a question of construction under an English law charter which incorporated an USA Clause Paramount fell to be decided according to English law as the proper law or US law as the law to which English law will refer. In the course of considering that question I believe that it has been shown to offer a false choice, or at any rate to disguise the possible difficulties of such a combination. Of course ultimately the question of construction must be answered as a matter of the proper law of the contract. But along the path of finding that answer, it may well be that English law may have to refer to the foreign law, to assist it in discovering the parties' presumed intentions. Indeed, in some cases the English law answer may be profoundly affected by the guidance which the foreign law provides (as in *Stafford Allen*). Where, however, the English and foreign law differ as to the meaning to be given to the identical wording of an international rule enacted in both England and the foreign country, it is hard to think that there are any circumstances in which the foreign law's view could prevail over that of the proper law. But the ultimate question will still remain: What, in accordance with the proper law, must be taken to be the presumed intention of the parties? ...

In the circumstances there has been a total

delay of over three years since time expired, in respect of a claim of uncertain merit but no great size, where the claimants have been seriously at fault, and where the respondents have not contributed to the delay but would suffer serious prejudice in seeking to meet the burden of proof with inadequate documentation. In my judgment the charterers would not suffer undue hardship if I declined to extend time for the appointment of their arbitrator.

In conclusion, therefore, this application fails on both its limbs.'

Morviken, The [1983] 1 Lloyd's Rep 1 House of Lords (Lords Diplock, Keith of Kinkel, Roskill, Brandon of Oakbrook and Brightman)

• *The Hague-Visby Rules operate as an overriding statute in English law*

Facts

In March 1978 an English company (the cargo owners) shipped a road-finishing machine on board a vessel belonging to Dutch carriers for carriage from Scotland to Bonaire in the Netherlands Antilles. The machine was transhipped at Amsterdam onto a Norwegian vessel for carriage to Bonaire. During discharge at Bonaire the machine was severely damaged the cost of which was estimated at £22,000.

Under the Hague-Visby Rules, as set out in the schedule to the Carriage of Goods by Sea Act 1971, the carrier's liability for loss or damage to the goods was limited to some £11,500. The bill of lading however, provided

1. that the proper law of the contract was to be Dutch law (where the original form of the Hague Rules applied);
2. that the Court of Amsterdam was to have exclusive jurisdiction; and
3. that the liability of the carrier under the bill of lading was to be limited to £250 per package.

The cargo owners brought an action in

England against the carriers claiming damages. The cargo owners claimed to be entitled by virtue of art X of the Hague-Visby Rules to bring their action in England because the bill of lading was issued in and the carriage was from a port in a 'contracting state', ie the UK. By art III r8 of the Hague-Visby Rules it was provided that

'Any clause in a bill of lading lessening the liability of the carrier ... shall be null land void and of no effect.'

The carrier applied to the English court for, and were granted, a stay of the action on the ground that the cargo owners were bound by the exclusive jurisdiction clause in the bill of lading and the action should accordingly proceed in The Netherlands. The cargo owners appealed contending that the contract was governed by the Hague-Visby Rules and not by Dutch law.

The Court of Appeal allowed the appeal, removing the stay and allowing the English action to proceed, inter alia, on the following grounds:

1. By s1(2) of the 1971 Act the courts of the UK were required to give 'the force of law' to the Hague-Visby Rules as set out in the schedule to that Act, with the result that those Rules applied, inter alia, to any bill of lading which was issued in the UK and any provision in such a bill of lading which was inconsistent with or derogated from the effect of those rules was, by virtue of art III r8 of those Rules, null and void and of no effect.

2. The provision which sought to limit the carriers' liability to a sum less than that provided for in the Hague-Visby Rules and that which sought to give exclusive jurisdiction to the Dutch Court were null and void and of no effect.

On appeal by the defendants to the House of Lords.

Held

Appeal dismissed, inter alia, on the following grounds:

The Hague-Visby Rules were to have the force of law in the United Kingdom, they were to be treated as if they were part of directly enacted statute law.

The bill of lading in question fell within both paragraphs (a) and (b) of art X and it also came within s1(3) of the Carriage of Goods by Sea Act 1971.

The choice of forms clause did not in itself offend against art III r8; it was subject to a condition subsequent and it came into operation only upon the occurrence of a future event that might or might not occur.

Having regard to the nature of the dispute, the bill of lading in question should be treated as if it did not contain a choice of forum clause, and the plaintiffs were, therefore, at liberty to avail themselves of the right of access to the Admiralty Court.

Comment
See *The Benarty* [19985] QB 325 (above).

Spiliada Maritime Corp v *Cansulex Ltd, The Spiliada* [1986] 3 All ER 843 House of Lords (Lords Keith, Templeman, Griffiths, Mackay and Goff of Chieveley)

* *Forum with which action has most real and substantial connection*

Facts
The appellants, a Liberian corporation, were the owners of The Spiliada, a vessel which flew the Liberian flag and was managed partly in Greece and partly in England. In 1980 they voyage chartered The Spiliada to a third party, Minerals and Metals Trading Corp of India Ltd (MMTC). The charterparty contained a London arbitration clause. The vessel was used for the carriage of bulk sulphur loaded by Cansulex, the respondents, a Canadian (British Columbia) firm of exporters, who were the fob sellers of the sulphur to MMTC. The shipped bill of lading named Cansulex as the shippers and, by cl 21, provided that the

bill of lading 'no matter where issued, shall be construed and governed by English law, and as if the vessel sailed under the British Flag'.

The sulphur was carried from Vancouver, British Columbia, and discharged at ports in India. The shipowners alleged that sulphur that was wet when loaded had caused severe corrosion to the holds of the vessel and claimed damages from Cansulex under the contract of carriage contained in or evidenced by the bills of lading. They obtained leave ex parte to issue and serve a writ on Cansulex outside the jurisdiction under RSC O.11 r1(1)(f)(iii) on the ground that the action was brought to recover damages in respect of the breach of a contract which was by its terms governed by English law. Cansulex issued a summons under RSC O.12 r8 asking that the ex parte order be discharged on the ground, inter alia, that the case had not been shown to be 'a proper one for service out of the jurisdiction' under RSC O.11 r4(2).

At the time the ex parte leave was granted, the respondents were also involved in a second action involving Cansulex. This again was for damages for corrosion damage allegedly caused by the loading of wet sulphur at Vancouver on board The Cambridgeshire, a vessel owned by an English company, and brought against the charterers of the vessel, Cansulex as shippers and two other shippers. The respondents had obtained leave to serve proceedings on Cansulex outside the jurisdiction on the same ground as in the present case. Cansulex had applied for that order to be set aside and the application was heard by Staughton J who dismissed it, holding that there was a good arguable case that the Canadian companies were parties to a contract governed by English law, and that the case was a proper one for service out of the jurisdiction. There was no appeal from that decision and the trial proceedings, again before Staughton J, had started by the time of the hearing of Cansulex's application for set aside in The Spiliada action. This application also came before Staughton J who dismissed the application holding that it was a proper case for service out of the jurisdiction on the grounds: (a) that a detailed knowledge of the facts and issues had already been acquired by the lawyers (who were the same for Cansulex in both actions) in the course of the Cambridgeshire action and therefore it was in the interests of efficiency, expedition and economy that the appellants' action proceed in England rather than British Columbia; and (b) that if the action proceeded in England the parties would probably settle on the basis of the outcome of the Cambridgeshire action.

Cansulex appealed against Staughton J's refusal to discharge the leave contending, inter alia, that since the relevant limitation period for bringing an action had expired in British Columbia but not in England they would be deprived of a legitimate juridical advantage if they were forced to bring their action in British Columbia. This factor had not been considered before Staughton J and the Court of Appeal held that although it was a further factor, it was a neutral factor and that it was impossible to conclude that the factors considered by the judge, when taken together, showed that the English court was distinctly more suitable for the ends of justice. Accordingly, the Court of Appeal allowed the appeal and set aside the writ. The shipowners appealed.

Held
Appeal allowed.

In considering the many factors brought to the attention of the court, the fundamental principle was the choice of a forum in which the case could be tried more suitably for the interests of all the parties and for the ends of justice. The question of whether there was another forum which was more appropriate was to be determined by finding that forum with which the action had the most real and substantial connection. The burden of proof in an action to grant a stay was on the defendant who was required to show not only that England was not the natural or appropriate forum for the trial but also that there was

another available forum which was clearly or distinctly more appropriate than the English forum. Factors to be taken into consideration by the court included: convenience or expense, availability of witnesses, the law governing the relevant transaction, and the places where the parties resided or carried on business.

The fundamental principle governing the choice of forum in an application to stay a grant was equally to be applied to the grant of leave to serve proceedings out of the jurisdiction under RSC O.11 r1(1) subject to the burden being on the plaintiff who was required to show not merely that England was the appropriate forum for the trial of the action but that it was clearly the appropriate forum, and to the court being required to consider both the residence or place of business of the defendant and the relevant ground invoked by the plaintiff when deciding whether to exercise the discretion to grant leave. However, the plaintiff was not confined to showing that justice could not be obtained in an alternative forum or if so, only at excessive cost, delay or inconvenience. The nature of the dispute, the legal and practical issues involved, availability of witnesses and their evidence and expense, and local knowledge were also matters that the plaintiff could rely on in discharging the burden lying on him.

The court would normally grant a stay where it concluded that there was another forum which was prima facie more appropriate, and would normally refuse a stay where it concluded that there was no other available forum which was more appropriate than the English court.

As a general rule, if the court was satisfied that substantial justice would be done to all the parties in the available appropriate forum, the court was not to be deterred in granting a stay, or refusing leave under RSC O.11 r1(1) to serve proceedings out of the jurisdiction, only by reason that it might deprive the plaintiff of a legitimate personal or juridical advantage available to him under the English jurisdiction.

Lord Templeman:

'If Staughton J had good reason to try The Cambridgeshire, it is difficult to see that he had bad reason for trying The Spiliada.

The factors which the court is entitled to take into account in considering whether one forum is more appropriate are legion. The authorities do not, perhaps cannot, give any clear guidance as to how these factors are to be weighed in any particular case. Any dispute over the appropriate forum is complicated by the fact that each party is seeking an advantage and may be influenced by considerations which are not apparent to the judge or considerations which are not relevant for his purpose. In the present case, for example, it is reasonably clear that the respondents, Cansulex Ltd, prefer the outcome of the Roseline proceedings in Canada to the outcome of the Cambridgeshire proceedings in England and prefer the limitation period in British Columbia to the limitation period in England. The appellants, Spiliada Maritime Corp (the shipowners), and their insurers hold other views. There may be other matters which naturally and inevitably help to produce in a good many cases conflicting evidence and optimistic and gloomy assessments of expense, delay and inconvenience. Domicile and residence and place of incident are not always decisive.

In the result, it seems to me that the solution of disputes about the relative merits of trial in England and trial abroad is pre-eminently a matter for the trial judge. Commercial court judges are very experienced in these matters. In nearly every case evidence is on affidavit by witnesses of acknowledged probity. ...

An appeal should be rare and the appellate court should be slow to interfere. I agree with my noble and learned friend Lord Goff that there were no grounds for interference in the present case and that the appeal should be allowed.'

Lord Goff of Chieveley:

'In my opinion, having regard to the authorities (including in particular the Scottish authorities), the law can at present be summarised as follows.

(a) The basic principle is that a stay will only be granted on the ground of forum non conveniens where the court is satisfied that there is some other available forum, having competent jurisdiction, which is the appropriate forum for the trial of the action, ie in which the case may be tried more suitably for the interests of all the parties and the ends of justice.

(b) ... in general the burden of proof rests on the defendant to persuade the court to exercise its discretion to grant a stay ... It is, however, of importance to remember that each party will seek to establish the existence of certain matters which will assist him in persuading the court to exercise its discretion in his favour, and that in respect of any such matter the evidential burden will rest on the party who asserts its existence. Furthermore, if the court is satisfied that there is another available forum which is prima facie the appropriate forum for the trial of the action, the burden will then shift to the plaintiff to show that there are special circumstances by reason of which justice requires that the trial should nevertheless take place in this country (see para (f) below).

(c) ... In my opinion, the burden resting on the defendant is not just to show that England is not the natural or appropriate forum for the trial, but to establish that there is another available forum which is clearly or distinctly more appropriate than the English forum. In this way, proper regard is paid to the fact that jurisdiction has been founded in England as of right ... and there is the further advantage that on a subject where comity is of importance it appears that there will be a broad consensus among major common law jurisdictions. ...

(d) Since the question is whether there exists some other forum which is clearly more appropriate for the trial of the action, the court will look first to see what factors there are which point in the direction of another forum. ... I respectfully consider that it may be more desirable, now that the English and Scottish principles are regarded as being the same, to adopt the expression used by Lord Keith in *The Abidin Daver* [1984] 1 All ER 470 at 479; [1984] AC 398 at 415 when he referred to the "natural forum" as being "that with which the action has the most real and substantial connection". So it is for connecting factors in this sense that the court must first look; and these will include not only factors affecting convenience or expense (such as availability of witnesses), but also other factors such as the law governing the relevant transaction ... and the places where the parties respectively reside or carry on business.

(e) If the court concludes at that stage that there is no other available forum which is clearly more appropriate for the trial of the action, it will ordinarily refuse a stay ...

(f) If, however, the court concludes at that stage that there is some other available forum which prima facie is clearly more appropriate for the trial of the action, it will ordinarily grant a stay unless there are circumstances by reason of which justice requires that a stay should nevertheless not be granted. In this inquiry, the court will consider all the circumstances of the case, including circumstances which go beyond those taken into account when considering connecting factors with other jurisdictions. One such factor can be the fact, if established objectively by cogent evidence, that the plaintiff will not obtain justice in the foreign jurisdiction: see *The Abidin Daver* [1984] 1 All ER 470 at 476; [1984] AC 398 at 411 per Lord Diplock, a passage which now makes plain that, on this inquiry, the burden of proof shifts to the plaintiff.'

As concerns how the principle is applied in cases where the court exercises its discretionary power under RSC O.11, Lord Goff considered in detail the apparent difference of view to be found in the speeches of Lords Diplock and Wilberforce in the *Amin Rasheed* case [1983] 2 All ER 884 (see above) and agreed with the reasoning of Ackner LJ in *Ilyssia Cia Naviera SA* v *Bamaodah* [1985] 1 Lloyd's Rep 107, who found that there is no conflict between Lord Diplock's statement and that of Lord Wilberforce who had said

that the court 'must take into account the nature of the dispute, the legal and practical issues involved, such questions as local knowledge, availability of witnesses and their evidence and expense.' Lord Goff of Chieveley concluded that the principle expressed by Lord Kinnear in *Sim* v *Robinow* (1892) 19 R (Ct of Sess) 665 at 668, viz to identify the forum in which the case can be suitably tried for the interests of all the parties and for the ends of justice, was the correct one and that it was desirable to identify the distinctions between the groups of cases which he found to be a threefold distinction:

'The first is that, as Lord Wilberforce indicated, in the O.11 cases the burden of proof rests on the plaintiff, whereas in the forum non conveniens cases that burden rests on the defendant. A second, and more fundamental, point of distinction (from which the first point of distinction in fact flows) is that in the O.11 cases the plaintiff is seeking to persuade the court to exercise its discretionary power to permit service on the defendant outside the jurisdiction. Statutory authority has specified the particular circumstances in which that power may be exercised, but leaves it to the court to decide whether to exercise its discretionary power in a particular case, while providing that leave shall not be granted "unless it shall be made sufficiently to appear to the Court that the case is a proper one for service out of the jurisdiction" (see RSC O.11, r4(2)).

Third, it is at this point that special regard must be had for the fact stressed by Lord Diplock in the *Amin Rasheed* case [1983] 2 All ER 884 at 891; [1984] AC 50 at 65 that the jurisdiction exercised under O.11 may be "exorbitant". This has long been the law. In *Société Générale de Paris* v *Dreyfus Bros* (1885) 29 Ch D 239 at 242–243 Pearson J said:

"... it becomes a very serious question ... whether this Court ought to put a foreigner, who owes no allegiance here, to the inconvenience and annoyance of being brought to contest his rights in this country, and I for one say, most distinctly, that I think this Court ought to be exceedingly careful before it allows a writ to be served out of the jurisdiction."

That statement was subsequently approved on many occasions ... The effect is, not merely that the burden of proof rests on the plaintiff to persuade the court that England is the appropriate forum for the trial of the action, but that he has to show that this is clearly so. In other words, the burden is, quite simply, the obverse of that applicable where a stay is sought of proceedings started in this country as of right.

Even so, a word of caution is necessary. I myself feel that the word 'exorbitant' is, as used in the present context, an old-fashioned word which perhaps carries unfortunate overtones; it means no more than that the exercise of the jurisdiction is extraordinary in the sense explained by Lord Diplock in the *Amin Rasheed* case. ... Furthermore, in O.11 cases, the defendant's place of residence may be no more than a tax haven to which no great importance should be attached. It is also significant to observe that the circumstances specified in O.11, r1(1), as those in which the court may exercise its discretion to grant leave to serve proceedings on the defendant outside the jurisdiction, are of great variety, ranging from cases where, one would have thought, the discretion would normally be exercised in favour of granting leave (eg where the relief sought is an injunction ordering the defendant to do or refrain from doing something within the jurisdiction) to cases where the grant of leave is far more problematical. In addition, the importance to be attached to any particular ground invoked by the plaintiff may vary from case to case. For example, the fact that English law is the putative proper law of the contract maybe of very great importance ... or it may be of little importance as seen in the context of the whole case. In these circumstances, it is, in my judgment, necessary to include both the residence or place of business of the defendant and the relevant ground invoked by the plaintiff as factors to be considered by the court when deciding whether to exercise its discretion to grant leave; but, in so doing, the court should give to such factors the weight which, in all the circumstances of the case, it considers to be appropriate.'

Traugutt, The [1985] 1 Lloyd's Rep 76 High Court (Sheen J)

- *Refusal to stay English proceedings*

Facts
The plaintiffs were the owners of a cargo of butteroil carried from Antwerp to Bombay on the defendants' vessel in 1979. The bill of lading contained a jurisdiction clause which provided that all disputes must be decided in Poland under Polish law. It also stated that Belgian Maritime law was to apply to a cargo shipped from a Belgian port.

Following a fire, both the ship and the cargo became a total loss. The plaintiffs began proceedings in 1981 and at the same time proceedings were started in Antwerp for the same damage but by another party, not by the plaintiffs.

The defendants applied for a stay of the English proceedings. They claimed that the proper law of the contract was Belgian and that therefore proceedings should continue in Antwerp which was the proper forum.

Held
Stay refused.

The defendants claim that England was forum non conveniens failed. A mere balance of convenience is not of itself sufficient reason for a stay. The two conditions that must be met if a stay is to be granted were those laid down by Lord Diplock in *MacShannon* v *Rockware Glass* [1978] AC 795:

'(a) the defendant must satisfy the court that there is another forum to whose jurisdiction he is amenable in which justice can be done at substantially less cost and inconvenience between the parties;

(b) the stay must not deprive the plaintiff of some legitimate personal or juridical advantage which would be available to him if he invoked the jurisdiction of the English court.'

The defendants themselves considered that the dispute could be decided in Poland, under Belgian law. In that case any question of law could equally be decided in England. Whilst there seemed to be some difference between Belgian and English law as to what was meant by 'actual fault or privity' in that Belgian law seemed to give the phrase a wider meaning, the fact that the assistance of the Belgian court would have to be sought did not mean that the defendants had shown that justice could be done in Antwerp at substantially less cost and inconvenience. On the issue of convenience of the witnesses it was in fact more convenient to have the action in London.

Sheen J rejected the plaintiffs' contention that if the action were stayed they would be deprived of a legitimate juridical advantage, namely the process of discovery which takes place in England. He was not willing to make a value judgment on the relative merits of the processes of justice since each system had its own advantages and disadvantages.

Law Update 2003 edition – due March 2003

An annual review of the most recent developments in specific legal subject areas, useful for law students at degree and professional levels, others with law elements in their courses and also practitioners seeking a quick update.

Published around March every year, the Law Update summarises the major legal developments during the course of the previous year. In conjunction with Old Bailey Press textbooks it gives the student a significant advantage when revising for examinations.

Contents

Administrative Law • Civil and Criminal Procedure • Commercial Law • Company Law • Conflict of Laws • Constitutional Law • Contract Law • Conveyancing • Criminal Law • Criminology • English and European Legal Systems • Equity and Trusts • European Union Law • Evidence • Family Law • Jurisprudence • Land Law • Law of International Trade • Public International Law • Revenue Law • Succession • Tort

For further information on contents or to place an order, please contact:

Mail Order
Old Bailey Press
at Holborn College
Woolwich Road
Charlton
London
SE7 8LN

Telephone No: 020 7381 7407
Fax No: 020 7386 0952
Website: www.oldbaileypress.co.uk

ISBN 1 85836 477 9
Soft cover 246 x 175 mm
450 pages approx
£10.95
Due March 2003

Unannotated Cracknell's Statutes for use in Examinations

New Editions of Cracknell's Statutes

£11.95 due 2002

Cracknell's Statutes provide a comprehensive series of essential statutory provisions for each subject. Amendments are consolidated, avoiding the need to cross-refer to amending legislation. Unannotated, they are suitable for use in examinations, and provide the precise wording of vital Acts of Parliament for the diligent student.

Commercial Law ISBN: 1 85836 472 8	**European Community Legislation** ISBN: 1 85836 470 1
Conflict of Laws ISBN: 1 85836 473 6	**Family Law** ISBN: 1 85836 471 X
Criminal Law ISBN: 1 85836 474 4	**Public International Law** ISBN: 1 85836 476 0
Employment Law ISBN: 1 85836 475 2	

For further information on contents or to place an order, please contact:

Mail Order
Old Bailey Press
at Holborn College
Woolwich Road
Charlton
London
SE7 8LN

Telephone No: 020 7381 7407
Fax No: 020 7386 0952
Website: www.oldbaileypress.co.uk

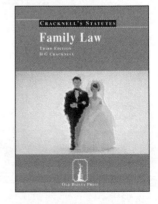

UNIVERSITY OF GLAMORGAN
PRIFYSGOL MORGANNWG

Faculty of Humanities and Social Sciences

Assignment Cover Sheet

DRAFT

Award:

Module Code:	LC4H039	Module Tutors:	Roland Fletcher
Module Title:	International Trade Law		
Submission Date:	Thursday 16th June Assignments to be submitted by **4:00pm** **via Turnitin and two hard copies in D Block**	Return Date:	You work will be returned within **20 working days** of the date of submission.

Suggested Solutions to Past Examination Questions 2000–2001

The Suggested Solutions series provides examples of full answers to the questions regularly set by examiners. Each suggested solution has been broken down into three stages: general comment, skeleton solution and suggested solution. The examination questions included within the text are taken from past examination papers set by the London University. The full opinion answers will undoubtedly assist you with your research and further your understanding and appreciation of the subject in question.

Only £6.95 Due December 2002

Constitutional Law
ISBN: 1 85836 478 7

Criminal Law
ISBN: 1 85836 479 5

English Legal System
ISBN: 1 85836 482 5

Elements of the Law of Contract
ISBN: 1 85836 480 9

Jurisprudence and Legal Theory
ISBN: 1 85836 484 1

Land Law
ISBN: 1 85836 481 7

Law of Tort
ISBN: 1 85836 483 3

For further information on contents or to place an order, please contact:

Mail Order
Old Bailey Press
at Holborn College
Woolwich Road
Charlton
London
SE7 8LN

Telephone No: 020 7381 7407
Fax No: 020 7386 0952
Website: www.oldbaileypress.co.uk

Learning Resources
Centre

Old Bailey Press

The Old Bailey Press integrated student law library is tailor-made to help you at every stage of your studies from the preliminaries of each subject through to the final examination. The series of Textbooks, Revision WorkBooks, 150 Leading Cases and Cracknell's Statutes are interrelated to provide you with a comprehensive set of study materials.

You can buy Old Bailey Press books from your University Bookshop, your local Bookshop, direct using this form, or you can order a free catalogue of our titles from the address shown overleaf.

The following subjects each have a Textbook, 150 Leading Cases/Casebook, Revision WorkBook and Cracknell's Statutes unless otherwise stated.

Administrative Law
Commercial Law
Company Law
Conflict of Laws
Constitutional Law
Conveyancing (Textbook and 150 Leading Cases)
Criminal Law
Criminology (Textbook and Sourcebook)
Employment Law (Textbook and Cracknell's Statutes)
English and European Legal Systems
Equity and Trusts
Evidence
Family Law
Jurisprudence: The Philosophy of Law (Textbook, Sourcebook and
    Revision WorkBook)
Land: The Law of Real Property
Law of International Trade
Law of the European Union
Legal Skills and System
    (Textbook)
Obligations: Contract Law
Obligations: The Law of Tort
Public International Law
Revenue Law (Textbook,
    Revision WorkBook and
    Cracknell's Statutes)
Succession

Mail order prices:	
Textbook	£14.95
150 Leading Cases	£11.95
Revision WorkBook	£9.95
Cracknell's Statutes	£11.95
Suggested Solutions 1998–1999	£6.95
Suggested Solutions 1999–2000	£6.95
Suggested Solutions 2000–2001	£6.95
Law Update 2002	£9.95
Law Update 2003	£10.95

Please note details and prices are subject to alteration.

To complete your order, please fill in the form below:

Module	Books required	Quantity	Price	Cost
	Postage			
	TOTAL			

For Europe, add 15% postage and packing (£20 maximum).

For the rest of the world, add 40% for airmail.

ORDERING

By telephone to Mail Order at 020 7381 7407, with your credit card to hand.

By fax to 020 7386 0952 (giving your credit card details).

Website: www.oldbaileypress.co.uk

By post to: Mail Order, Old Bailey Press at Holborn College, Woolwich Road, Charlton, London, SE7 8LN.

When ordering by post, please enclose full payment by cheque or banker's draft, or complete the credit card details below. You may also order a free catalogue of our complete range of titles from this address.

We aim to despatch your books within 3 working days of receiving your order.

Name

Address

Postcode   Telephone

Total value of order, including postage: £

I enclose a cheque/banker's draft for the above sum, or

charge my   ☐ Access/Mastercard   ☐ Visa   ☐ American Express

Card number

☐☐☐☐ ☐☐☐☐ ☐☐☐☐ ☐☐☐☐

Expiry date   ☐☐☐☐

Signature: ....Date: ....